ESSAYS ON MEDIEVAL GERMAN LITERATURE
AND ICONOGRAPHY

ANGLICA GERMANICA SERIES 2

Editors: LEONARD FORSTER, S. S. PRAWER, AND
A. T. HATTO

Other books in the series

ESSAYS ON MEDIEVAL GERMAN LITERATURE AND ICONOGRAPHY

F. P. PICKERING

Emeritus Professor of German
University of Reading

CAMBRIDGE UNIVERSITY PRESS

CAMBRIDGE

LONDON   NEW YORK   NEW ROCHELLE

MELBOURNE   SYDNEY

CAMBRIDGE UNIVERSITY PRESS
Cambridge, New York, Melbourne, Madrid, Cape Town, Singapore,
São Paulo, Delhi, Dubai, Tokyo, Mexico City

Cambridge University Press
The Edinburgh Building, Cambridge CB2 8RU, UK

Published in the United States of America by Cambridge University Press, New York

www.cambridge.org
Information on this title: www.cambridge.org/9780521159340

First published 1980
First paperback edition 2010

A catalogue record for this publication is available from the British Library

Library of Congress Cataloguing in Publication Data
Pickering, Frederick Pickering, 1909-
Essays on medieval German literature and iconography.
(Anglica Germanica: Series 2)
Includes bibliographical references.
'Publications of F. P. Pickering': p.
1. German literature - Middle High German, 1050-1500 -
History and criticism - Addresses, essays, lectures.
2. Symbolism in literature - Addresses, essays, lectures.
3. Art, Medieval- Themes, motives - Addresses, essays,
lectures. I. Title. II. Series.
PTI77.P5 830'.9 78-7381 5

ISBN 978-0-521-22627-1 Hardback
ISBN 978-0-521-15934-0 Paperback

CONTENTS

PREFACE

My colleagues in German studies kindly invited me some time ago to prepare and introduce a selection of my shorter writings, and asked Arthur T. Hatto to assist me editorially. I wish to thank them for their confidence, and him for sound counsel. The decision to translate three essays originally written in German was, however, my own. I hope thereby, without discourtesy, to have increased the inter-disciplinary appeal of my final selection.

It seemed from the outset sensible to consider only work published in and since 1953, the year of my appointment to the new Chair of German at Reading, which I occupied until my retirement in 1974. I did not go empty-handed to Reading, however, and the essay of 1953 (now translated) which opens the selection is firmly associated in my mind with the preceding period – my years in Manchester and Sheffield, and with friends and colleagues there. The essay was the outcome of background reading for my edition in 1952 of a late-medieval German Passion tract, *Christi Leiden in einer Vision geschaut*. It served as a delayed introduction to that text, but has wider implications for the study of Christian iconography.

After my move to Reading I began almost immediately to take my bearings in the Warburg Institute of the University of London, where I was made most welcome. There Dame Fortune, my candidate for further (but different) iconographical enquiries, took an unexpectedly firm hand. She led me not only to a study of her image in Antiquity and in the Middle Ages, but also back to texts: to familiar passages in our German authors (medieval and modern), which I began to understand somewhat differently, and perhaps just as frequently into new areas, particularly medieval historiography, see below. Reviewing these somewhat erratic developments, and the writings to which they gave rise over the years, I feel concern under two heads. First, there is the inconvenient dispersal of my shorter writings in a variety of journals, miscellanies and conference proceedings. I am unsure how many of them are known, even accessible. Secondly, there is the question of their present status in relation to my two longer studies: *Literatur und darstellende Kunst im Mittelalter*, 1966 (revised and translated as *Literature and Art in the Middle Ages*, 1970), and *Augustinus oder Boethius?* (etc.) in its two parts, 1967 and 1976. Which articles are superseded by the books, and which are still useful appendages to them? I am now able to give better guidance on these questions than the reader will find in various forewords and footnotes written in the past (see the introductory note to each of the essays), but in the remainder of this preface I will refer in more general terms to the interrelation of my articles and books.

Most of my work since 1953 has centered on two main ideas, or rather insights. These I tested over the years in the light of whatever evidence, literary or pictorial, I encountered or had put before me by others. One concerns the ultimately patristic and scholarly origins of what is customarily seen as the 'realism' of late medieval Christian art and devotional literature, mainly Passion tracts and plays. The idea itself is already worked out in many of its aspects in the article of 1953, already mentioned. It is then amplified with closer reference to chronologies in *Literatur und darstellende Kunst* (1966), and for the first time pictorially illustrated in *Literature and Art* (1970). An essay of 1971 on Rupert of Deutz (see pp. 31–45), to whom I attribute a share of responsibility for the familiar 'gruesomeness' of late Gothic art, will probably be my last contribution in print on the subject. I was happy to leave any further active pursuit of realistic treatments of the Passion of Christ to an able young American scholar, James Marrow (now Professor of Art History at Yale), who has meantime chronicled it in phenomenal detail down to its final resolution in the tracts and the devotional art of the Low Countries.*

As for the second idea, I can no longer recall precisely in

* *Passion Iconography in Northern European Art of the Late Middle Ages and Early Renaissance* (etc.), Kortrijk (Belgium), 1979.

what areas I was reading – probably several, our German prescribed texts certainly among them – when I began to focus attention on the figure of Fortune in Boethius's *De Consolatione Philosophiae*. Suffice it to say that my first, primarily icono-graphical interest in Fortune at her Wheel (see above) was soon absorbed in a more comprehensive concern with fortune and history proper. That is of course the subject of my second study, *Augustinus oder Boethius?*, which, with some interruptions, was in progress from 1962 to 1975. I have two observations to make at this point. To my surprise, I must admit, a section of my essay 'On coming to terms with Curtius' (here pp. 177–90) shows me already committed by 1958 to the thesis of 'two economies of history'. My second observation is that by now reprinting that essay and a number of others, I reveal how often I have repeated myself, both in preambles and in the mustering of evidence. My excuse must be that there are precedents for seeking to persuade by the device of repetition with variation.

There is a final twist to my story (as I myself tell it). I refer to an item among my publications (p. 226) representing what is at first sight the most wayward of my departures from the normal progress of a Professor of German, namely my edition in 1971 of the Anglo-Norman text of the *Holkham Bible Picture Book* – I am of course not the only 'Germanist' to have taken an interest in that remarkable product of a London work-shop, the date of which is about 1320–30. The first copy of W. O. Hassall's facsimile edition which I saw, belonged in fact to the late Kenneth C. King. Characteristically he bought it in the year of publication, 1954. To my cost I did not buy mine until 1967, by which time, however, I knew that, come what may, I was going to edit the text in some form, so that I could write more fully about both the text and the pictures (I had already used a couple of passages and reproduced two pictures). I wanted to introduce and to annotate the text in the light of my knowledge of Christian narrative tradition (*inter alia* its 'realism'), to describe afresh some of the pictures with closer reference to the accompanying text, and, above all, to make better sense of the three introductory pictures (out of over two hundred). First in the edition, and subsequently in *Augustinus oder Boethius?*, Part II, pp. 180–2, I endeavoured to show that the compilers of the Holkham book prefaced their narration and illustration of *sacred* history with a short pictorial declaration that their undertaking was a commercial venture under the aegis of Dame Fortune and Divine Providence. In my parlance this amounts to a Boethian preface to an Augustinian work. For the rest – namely the Anglo-Norman! – I add merely that it was my privilege, at age sixty-plus, to be T. B. W. Reid's tutorial student. I am not conscious of serious waywardness.

The final arrangement of my selection of twelve essays is not in the two groups which the foregoing remarks may have suggested, but under three roughly descriptive headings. Of these it may fairly be said that I have so far given little indication of the third. Under it I recall my efforts to keep our university study of German on acceptable lines. There was to have been a third essay in the group ('Erwägungen zum Studium des deutschen Mittelalters', see *Publications*, p. 227). I was, however, reluctant to translate it, and as the only essay in German it would have seemed out of place.

Two technical points remain. For book-title abbreviations (*L. & A.*, *A.o.B.* 1/11), please see *Publications*, p. 226; those for journals and text-series should be familiar. As to typographical and other conventions, it proved, despite my efforts, impossible to achieve uniformity in all matters throughout the volume. For help in these matters and others I am grateful to the Cambridge University Press, and to Professor Peter Ganz of Oxford who read proofs with me.

Finally, permission to reprint (or submit in English translation) the essays now assembled in this volume was generously given by the following publishers and editors of journals and miscellanies: Basil Blackwell Oxford (three articles from *German Life and Letters*), The Director of the Institute of Germanic Studies, University of London (two miscellany articles), the Carl Winter Universitätsverlag, Heidelberg (two articles from *Euphorion*); in respect of one article each: the General Editor, *Forum for Modern Language Studies*, Naturmetodens Sproginstitut, Copenhagen, the Max Niemeyer Verlag, Tübingen, the Editors, *Reading Medieval Studies*, the Franz Steiner Verlag GmbH, Wiesbaden (*Zeitschrift für deutsches Artertum*). Full bibliographical details will be found in the introductory note to each essay, and under *Publications*, pp. 226ff.

Arborfield Cross   F. P. PICKERING
August 1978

I
TEXTUAL STUDIES:
ICONOGRAPHICAL APPROACHES

1. THE GOTHIC IMAGE OF CHRIST

THE SOURCES OF MEDIEVAL REPRESENTATIONS
OF THE CRUCIFIXION

A German prose tract of about 1350 on the Passion of Christ describes the Seizure and the Descent from the Mount of Olives in the following words:

> Then they seized Christ with raving violent devilish gesticulations, one grasped his hair, a second his clothes, a third his beard. These three were as foul hounds as ever might cling to him...and so he was pulled away, with violent wild raving abandon, with fierce blows of mailed hands and fists upon his neck and between his shoulders, on his back, on his head, across his cheeks, on his throat, on his breast...They tore his hair from his head so that the locks lay strewn around on the ground; one pulled him one way by the hair, the other pulled him back by the beard [*twelve further lines of print*]. So they dragged him down from the Mount... [*four lines*]. And they hauled him to the gate of the town in such a way that he never set foot properly on the ground...until they brought him into Annas' house.[1]

> In the Synoptic Gospels one reads: 'They laid hands on Jesus', or 'They seized him' (*tenentes* or *comprehendentes Jesum*), 'and took him' (*duxerunt, adduxerunt*) 'to the High Priest'. In John 18.12: 'So the band and the chief captain, and the officers of the Jews seized Jesus and bound him and led him' (*comprehenderunt, ligaverunt, adduxerunt*) 'to Annas first'.

No European text is known to me which describes in comparable detail, and with such insistence, the brutality of Christ's enemies on the way from Gethsemane, and then later during the interrogations, at the flagellation, the crowning with thorns and at the crucifixion. There are no pauses in the narrative account for prayers or compassionate outpourings, or for reflections on the significance for mankind of these sufferings. Far less disturbing is the treatment of the same subject at the level of the popular ballad in the stanzas of the so-called 'Hohenfurt

3

Songbook' for instance,[2] or in the longer Passion plays, [for there, despite all the mimed violence and the turbulence, the Jews are also caricatured and ridiculed]. The text I have cited offers no respite of any kind.

At the same time it is well known that in the Latin and vernacular devotional literature of the Middle Ages there are hundreds of works, major, minor and insignificant, which in their basic narrative content are similar to our text (*Christi Leiden in einer Vision geschaut*), so let us discount degrees of 'gruesomeness'. The works are similar in that they have in common a story of the Passion of Christ far more detailed and strangely specific, than the accounts of the four evangelists; it is also evidently in some way authoritative. In the work of medieval artists also, down to the Passion cycles of Albrecht Dürer, one finds the minutest details of the same story translated into pictorial terms. All this has long been known to literary and art historians. But nothing certain was known of the ultimate origins of this common tradition.

I

Many years ago I began to look for an explanation of the common 'new' elements in medieval Passion narratives, or rather to hope for some insight which would be more useful to me as a philologist than the customary appeals to medieval asceticism, the preaching of the mendicant orders, mystics, flagellants – and whatever other factors in the period down to the Reformation might be deemed to have made the ecstatic contemplation of the physical sufferings of Christ the foremost devotional exercise. I now believe that, from an insight, I have found an explanation and a method of textual study. I take as my material the words used in medieval texts and give them almost exclusive attention. It now seems to me that the 'religious feeling' to which our opening passage gives expression was itself in large part generated by a textual tradition which is firmly rooted in the teaching of the Fathers of the Church.

4

It is authoritative. It is ultimately Biblical. That is the thesis of this essay.

It is of course not possible in a first statement to refer to all the principal events of the Passion from Gethsemane to Golgotha. I shall therefore touch merely upon some of them, anticipating in part the method which will be demonstrated more fully when we consider medieval treatments of the Crucifixion.

The *Seizure* of Jesus and the *Descent from the Mount of Olives*. These scenes (our opening example) are treated in the Middle Ages 'rhetorically'. The text of the New Testament says, for instance, 'having seized Jesus, they led him. . .'. For reasons to be explained, this *means* at least: 'the hounds who had surrounded him, led him like a lamb to the slaughter, but he did not open his mouth'. That is to say, the prophetic words of the Old Testament which the Fathers of the Church had once and for all associated with the Gospel words 'they led him' are here (and whenever the Christ of the Passion was led) applicable, and immediately available, if there is to be any amplification of the Gospel text. The prophecies involved here are Psalm 21 (A.V. 22). 17/16, Isaiah 53.7 and Jeremiah 11.19. Beyond that there is the possibility of 'description'. The 'band', which according to St John seized Jesus, may be resolved, as in our passage, into 'one. . .', 'a second. . .', etc.

The *Interrogations*, the *Mocking of Jesus*. Medieval treatments follow the relatively detailed Gospel accounts of the interrogations ('Trial') and the mocking. Further charges, threats and humiliations may be incorporated from two apocryphal texts (the *Gospel of Nicodemus* or *Acts of Pilate*, and *Wisdom of Solomon* Chapter 2), or based on Isaiah 50.6.

The *Flagellation*, which the Gospels dismiss in virtually a single word (*flagellatum* or *flagellis caesum, tradidit*; *flagellavit*), becomes in the Middle Ages an elaborate ritual involving (in texts) up to sixteen soldiers,[3] wielding weighted scourges, rods, ropes and chains, notionally two for each of the charges (an inference from the 'two witnesses' required by the Law).

It should be possible to trace the development of this scene, century by century. Due attention will have to be paid to the marble column (see below) to which, according to belief, Jesus was bound before the flagellation. (There are other items of 'Holy Places lore' which determine the setting of this scene.) Otherwise, as in the case of the Seizure and Descent, the elaboration is rhetorical, or choreographical (e.g. in art and in the drama), with simultaneous exploitation of Old Testament prophecies, particularly Isaiah 1.6: 'a planta pedis usque ad verticem non est in eo sanitas'. In a fully developed description of the Flagellation, every part of Christ's body 'from the sole of the foot even unto the head' is enumerated, and duly said to have been struck and wounded.

I come now to a much more detailed consideration of the Crucifixion. One will scarcely find a medieval account of the Passion of Christ in which the Crucifixion is dealt with, as in the Gospels, in a one-word statement: 'crucifixerunt' ('they crucified him'). From about 1200–20 the medieval preacher, author or artist knew, almost as well as he knew the Gospel accounts, *two* narrative traditions concerning the Crucifixion of Christ, both evidently approved. Both are to be found in that compact corpus of Passion lore to which reference has been made, and for which the witnesses most commonly quoted by medieval scholars are:

1. The so-called 'Dialogue of St Anselm and the Virgin', one text of which is printed in Migne, *PL* 159, cols. 271–90: 'Pseudo-Anselm'.
2. The 'Meditations on the Life and Passion of Our Lord' ascribed to the seraphic doctor Bonaventura, text in *S. Bonaventurae Opera Omnia*, ed. Peltier, Paris 1868, vol. 12 (*Spuria*), cols. 509–630: 'Pseudo-Bonaventura'.
3. (In the form of a Lament of Mary) the *Liber de Passione Christi* etc., ascribed to St Bernard, a text in Migne, *PL* 182, cols. 1133–42.

Other narrative texts, the *Vita Rhythmica Salvatoris* for instance, and such non-narrative works as *Stimulus Amoris*, *Vitis Mystica* etc. need not be considered in this survey. We shall probably never know who wrote these works and most of the

6

countless adaptations and translations. Of the texts as we now read them in the commonly available editions it may be said in broad terms that, taken together, they present the fully elaborated medieval tradition of the Passion – of the period, roughly, 1200–50.

To illustrate the tradition of the Crucifixion I shall, where feasible, quote vernacular adaptations of the main witnesses. For instance, between 1315 and 1330 Robert Manning of Brunne translated Pseudo-Bonaventura's *Meditations* into English verse. Of the Crucifixion he writes:

> Beholde what werkmen þere wykkedly wroȝt:
> Some dyggen, sum deluyn, sum erþe oute kast,
> Some pycchen þe cros in þe erþe fast;
> On euery syde sum laddres vpp sette,
> Sum renne aftyr hamers, some nayles fette. . .
> [*Mary covers Christ's loins with her kerchief*]
> Twey laddres ben sette þe cros behynde,
> Twey enmyes on hem smartly gun glymbe,
> With hamers and nayles sharply whet:
> A shorte ladder before was fet (*var.* set),
> þere as þe fete shorte weren. . .[4]

In this form of the Crucifixion (*erecto cruce*) Christ is forced to mount a short ladder set before the erect Cross. There he turns, spreads wide his arms, and prays God to forgive his tormentors. Nails are driven through his hands, his veins burst. The ladder before the Cross is removed together with the others (see text), and then 'they hauled his feet hard':

> tyl þe cros kraked;
> Alle þe ioyntes þan brasten atwynne.

In the *Northern Passion* of the early fourteenth century is to be found 'the other' form of the Crucifixion. Here the tradition is that the Cross was made in advance, and 'the holes to receive the nails' had already been bored. Christ is then laid (or thrown) upon the Cross as it lies on the ground, and it is discovered that the holes have been bored too far apart:

> A drowen is fet ouer þe bor neith a span long.
> His schankes þe breken, wo was him begon.[5]

When Christ's limbs have been drawn to the holes and duly nailed there, the Cross is dropped into the deep hole dug to receive it. It is generally said that the Cross was dropped in such a way as to tear hands, sinews and veins, and rocked from side to side to add to the torments. This Crucifixion (*jacente cruce*), for which the source generally cited by editors is the 'Dialogue' of Pseudo-Anselm (see above, and section IV), is at least as frequent in medieval narrative tradition as the Crucifixion *erecto cruce* which always seems to us more familiar. Common to both modes is the pulling of Christ's limbs, in each case appropriately motivated.

Modern editors of Passion tracts and plays have generally been content to say that their texts offer, beside Biblical narrative, the 'accretions usually found in works of this kind'; they may add references to the editions of Pseudo-Anselm, Bernard, Bonaventura (etc.). There has not to my knowledge been any serious attempt to establish the precise source or sources of the evidently special knowledge of the Crucifixion transmitted by these latter works. The source can be established. More is involved in the case of the Crucifixion, however, than exploitation of the words of Old Testament prophecy, and elaboration. Before proceeding we must examine some still current surmises.

II

One must take seriously the suggestion that medieval scholars (theologians) had access to sources from which information concerning Roman crucifixions could be gleaned, to supplement the Gospel accounts. That is of course true: it was known in the Middle Ages that flagellation followed by crucifixion was part of Roman criminal procedure. As Peter Comestor says in his *Historia Scholastica*, 'sancitum erat a romanis ut crucificiendus prius flagellatur'.[6] But to establish how Christ was scourged and crucified there was no need for Christian theologians to consult pagan authorities, and it is surely significant that in his *Etymologies* (*c.* 622–33), under the heading 'De poenis in

8

legibus constitutis', Isidore of Seville cites only the crucifixion of 'two thieves' on Golgotha.[7] To have considered the flagellation and crucifixion of Christ as a normal case of capital punishment in the Roman world would surely have been blasphemous.

Medieval anti-semitism is no doubt a factor to be considered, but it is certainly not directly responsible for the way in which the Jews as enemies of Christ are portrayed, or for the gruesome detail in which their cruelties are described. As will be seen later, any reference to the Jews as 'hounds' (see the opening quotation) has its ultimate origin in Psalm 21/22. 17/16: 'quoniam circumdederunt me *canes* multi'. We shall refer repeatedly to this Psalm [the Good Friday Psalm]. The epithets 'wild', 'insensate' (etc.) are equally inferences from verse 14/13 of the Psalm or from 34/35.16: 'frenduerunt super me dentibus suis'. From the philologist's point of view, that is in the light of textual history and verbal tradition, these are the primary considerations. Add then anti-semitism: it does not discard, but carries forward with a special vehemence, the Biblical designations and epithets.[8]

Occasionally the idea is expressed, but not, I think, committed to print, that other passions and martyrdoms to be found in the ecclesiastical histories and legends of the saints may have influenced the depiction of Christ's sufferings. No evidence will be found for such a view.

Many students of devotional literature and art have had to ask themselves whether medieval descriptions and depictions of the Passion of Christ owe anything to the 'revelations' vouchsafed to ecstatic visionaries. That can hardly be the case. The *Revelations* of St Bridget and many mystics offer, from the moment when they describe the Crucifixion, nothing more than free adaptations of the commonly accepted accounts of Pseudo-Anselm, Pseudo-Bonaventura. The by now traditional accounts are recalled, perhaps with unusual fervour.

The only feature in the typical account of the Passion of which one can say with assurance that it has no other source

9

than the testimony of pilgrims to the Holy Places, is the marble column to which Jesus was bound at the Flagellation. By 'no other source' I mean that I have not discovered any attempt made by a Church Father or later theologian to 'justify' the column by reference to any Biblical text (there is clearly no Old Testament 'type' of the column). On the contrary, the principal authorities refer to the column 'which can still be seen', for instance Peter Comestor, again in the *Historia Scholastica*: 'adhuc columna cui alligatus fuit Jesus vestigia cruoris ostendit',[9] and fragments of the column were precious relics. Medieval descriptions and depictions of the Crucifixion itself owe nothing, it seems, to pilgrims' accounts (Holy Places lore).[10]

As for the 'influence of pictures' on narrative accounts of the Passion, particularly the Crucifixion, it should suffice that art historians regard it as axiomatic that ecclesiastical art derives its iconography for the representation of sacred story from written sources, the Bible and the exegesis of the Fathers.[11] It is only in the later Middle Ages that popular devotional literature can be shown occasionally to have been influenced by, or to have wittingly or unwittingly misinterpreted, pictorial conventions. Up to about 1250 the spoken word of the sermon, and the written word, are ahead of the artists.

A detail in the typical medieval account of the Crucifixion has in the past given rise to serious misconceptions: the statement, namely, that Christ's limbs were 'pulled with ropes' (see above). The following apparently rational explanation has more than once been advanced. In Passion plays the actor representing Christ could only be nailed to the cross in mime: in fact he was tied with ropes. Expressions such as 'bound with nails', or 'nail-bonds' in the ninth-century Old Saxon *Heliand*, *seem* to lend some support to this explanation, which continues: in order to justify the necessary ropes, the pulling was 'invented', and exploited in horse-play.[12] But that is impossible, for in the course of the evolution of the Passion-play texts, the pulling was taken over from earlier non-dramatic works.

It is also hazardous to speak of 'legendary' accretions to the

Gospel story. Legend-making proceeds apace during the Middle Ages, it is true, but it concerns itself, for instance, with the pre-history of the wood(s) of the Cross, with the subsequent history of the Cross; or with the eye-witnesses of the Way of The Cross (Veronica and others), or with Joseph of Arimathea. Legend-making begins in the apocryphal books of the New Testament, about which the following may be said at once. The Infancy Gospels trace in great detail the life of the Virgin, and the miracles of the infancy of Jesus. The *Gospel of Nicodemus*, which can be traced to the fourth century at the earliest, amplifies the role of Pilate (and of his wife, Procla), and names the thieves who were crucified with Christ. It enlarges on the charges levelled against Christ and adds the detail that Pilate ordered that Christ should receive the 'forty less one' strokes of which the Old Testament and II Corinthians 11.24 speak. It mentions merely the fact of the Crucifixion, adding no descriptive details.[13]

III

Let us now seek an explanation in positive terms. Medieval re-narrators of the story of the Passion knew that much of what they had to tell was not to be found in the Gospels:

'Unde wy daz sie, das sin vil in deme ewangelio nit enste. . . .', *Christi Leiden*, Priebsch p. 26, *12* [Pickering p. 60, *14f*.].

'Audi Anselme, quod modo referam nimis est lamentabile, et nullus evangelistarum scribit', *Anselm-Dialogue*, Chapter X.

They were, however, convinced that what they reported had in some way the authority of the Church, and that the formulations they used were as sacrosanct as the words of the Gospels were sacred. But Pseudo-Anselm would be astonished to know what effort is now required to rediscover his authority in the teachings of the Fathers of the Church. It is there, but not in codified form, and there are arguments in the following sections of this essay, and some of the evidence, which he might not follow!

The key is to be found in Christ's own words, his final teaching before the Ascension (Luke 24.44): 'quoniam necesse est impleri omnia quae scripta sunt in lege Mosi, et prophetis, et psalmis de me', 'All things must be fulfilled which are foretold concerning me', etc. Christ not only spoke these words, but had given guidance as to the manner in which the words of the Old Testament concerning him were to be understood. He had established the connection between his three days in the tomb and Jonah, and between his Crucifixion and the raising of the (brazen) serpent by Moses. Those further prophecies which the evangelists had recognized as having been fulfilled were incorporated in their Gospels, that was clear. But had the evangelists confirmed all fulfilments of prophecy? The learned Fathers had but a poor opinion of the abilities of the evangelists, particularly the authors of the 'synoptic' Gospels. In his *Ecclesiastical History* (III, 24) Eusebius writes that the fourth position is rightly assigned to John, for though the first three evangelists were worthy men, inspired by God, they were un-schooled and simple souls who neither desired nor aspired to declare the teaching of the Master in engaging language. Augustine says the same of the disciples and apostles (*Civ. Dei* XVIII, 49). This opinion is handed down in the form that the evangelists had 'not told everything' – the distinction between teaching and story is lost:

'Die fier ewangelisten schriben dan abe kurczliche und alleine daz daz notdurftig ist unde waz unde liezzin daz andere bliben', *Christi Leiden*, Priebsch p. 26, *16f.* [Pickering p. 60, *19ff.*]: 'The four evangelists wrote briefly of it (*sc.* the Passion), only what was necessary, and omitted the rest.'

Let us not dwell on these statements. What medieval writers on the Passion claim to be 'certainly true although not in the Gospels' is the outcome of some hundreds of years of study of the Old Testament: by the Fathers of the Church and later theologians, seeking the 'omnia' concerning Christ. Clearly the evangelists had *not* recorded and confirmed the fulfilment of 'all things prophesied concerning me'. 'Omnia' includes words, roles, events, things even. These could only be recognized in their relevance by such mortals as had been granted (among possible gifts) the 'discretio spirituum' of which St Paul wrote (I Corinthians 12.10, A.V. 'discerning of spirits') – and there are in holy scripture depths of prophecy concerning Christ to exercise the industrious, says Augustine, 'which they find out when they find Him whom they concern' (*Civ. Dei* XVIII, 32, Everyman translation).

It is difficult for us today to read and understand the Bible, particularly the Old Testament, *exclusively* as it was read and understood in early Christian centuries and throughout the Middle Ages. In addition to the 'fourfold sense of the scriptural word' we have to take account of a doctrine of Old Testament figures and 'types', foreshadowing (prefiguring) New Testament 'antitypes'. In examining the work of medieval writers and artists we must be prepared to recognize reflections and refractions of such originally patristic lore derived from the study of Old and New Testaments as prophecy and fulfilment. Some of this lore seems, with the passage of time, to have taken on a life of its own, as we shall see.

Generally we encounter the outcome of such study of the Bible in an ordered presentation; if it is in a pictorial programme, for instance, we have little difficulty in recognizing the standard pairings of type and antitype. In medieval tradition Isaac bearing the wood for his own sacrifice and Christ bearing his Cross were, as Old Testament and New Testament story, distinct; considered as type and antitype, the meaning 'sacrifice' is added to the Cross-bearing, but the images remain (generally) unaffected.[14] The typological mode of thought may, however, have had consequences which we do not yet generally recognize or care to notice. For instance: the brazen serpent raised by Moses in the desert and Christ on the Cross were prophetic image and fulfilled prophecy. The medieval artist's endeavour to allude to the serpent in his image of the Crucified may explain the S- or Z-line given to the pendent body, that rather than any 'stylistic' impulse. That would be not a juxtaposition, but an overlaying of type and antitype, the artist evidently having seen in the *sicut–ita* comparison of John 3.14 ('*Sicut Moses exaltavit serpentem, ita* exaltari oportet Filium hominis') an instruction for the representation of the Crucifixion.[15] A further, again different, example may illustrate the point already anticipated, that typological lore may take on a life of its own. Late medieval artists may show Christ mocked by children who throw stones and filth at him on the Way of the Cross.[16] That is clearly a motif transferred from the story of Elisha (II Kings, 2.23): the 'little children' who mocked him on the way to Bethel, crying 'go up, thou bald head' ('ascende, calve'). Compare the following texts:

(*a*) 'Exitur etiam in Calvariae locum, ubi verus Elisaeus ab insensatis pueris irrisus...Ascendit itaque crucem calvus noster.' This is St Bernard on the subject of Calvary (*De loco Calvariae, PL* 182, col. 932). The story of Elisha is present here in the sustained type-metaphor: Christ is 'the true Elisha', the Jews are the 'children'.

(*b*) 'Sequebantur etiam pueri projicientes lutum et lapides.' From the *Dialogue* of Pseudo-Anselm, Chapter VIII. The story of Elisha is not mentioned. The children are 'real children'.

(*c*) '...da du wurd von dem richter in den schamlichen tod des crutzes verurteilt...und von den kinden mit horwe under din antlut geworffen'. From the 'Minnebüchlein' attributed to Heinrich Seuse (Suso), ed. H. Bihlmeyer, 1907, p. 542. *Translation*: '...when thou wast condemned by the judge to ignominious death on the Cross [cf. Wisdom 2.20, 'morte turpissima condemnemus eum'] and children cast filth into thy face'.

IV

Let us now consider more closely than hitherto, the way in which Old Testament words were incorporated in accounts of the Passion because, in their simplest literal sense, they prophesied events. Here we have to consider particularly Psalm 21 (A.V. 22). The evangelists had already drawn on this source in their accounts of the Passion, notably for Christ's cry, 'My God, my God, why hast thou forsaken me?' Further, verse 17/16 ('they pierced my hands and feet') was exploited in the Gospel of St John (John 20.27), in the evidence offered to Doubting Thomas. The Fathers were to infer an actual 'nailing' to the Cross from the combined evidence of the Psalm ('pierced my hands...') and the Gospel ('the print of the nails'). The evangelists incorporated the head-shaking (verse 8/7) and the parting of the garments (verse 19/18), but there is a good deal more which the Fathers were to deem 'necessarily' fulfilled, notably the references to 'all my bones', verses 15/14 and, particularly, 18/17, which by the time we reach the *Anselm-Dialogue*, have yielded the following [my italics]:

> ...et nullus evangelistarum scribit. Cum venissent ad locum Calvariae ignominiosissimum, ubi canes et alia morticina projiciebantur, nudaverunt Jesum unicum filium meum totaliter vestibus suis, et ego exanimis facta fui; tamen velamen capitis mei accipiens circumligavi lumbis suis. Post hoc deposuerunt crucem super terram, et eum desuper extenderunt, et incutiebant primo unum clavum adeo spissum quod tunc sanguis non potuit emanare; ita vulnus clavo replebatur. Acceperunt postea *funes* et *traxerunt* aliud brachium filii mei Jesu, et clavum secundum ei incusserunt. Postea pedes *funibus traxerunt*, et clavum acutissimum incutiebant, et *adeo tensus* fuit ut *omnia ossa sua* et membra apparerent, *ita ut impleretur* illud Psalmi: 'Dinumeraverunt omnia ossa mea' (Caput X).

'So that the words of the psalm (*or* of the prophet) should be fulfilled': this is the formula which appears regularly at the end of episodes and scenes in the Apocryphal New Testament. It should, however, be noted in considering the text of Pseudo-Anselm, that only the antecedent ritual pulling with ropes, which explains in 'historical' terms how Christ came to be thus stretched on the Cross, is relatively new.[17] By contrast, the final static image of Christ 'so stretched' ('adeo tensus') has the authority of the Fathers who interpreted the 'counted bones' in this sense:

(a) '*et dinumeraverunt etc.*' (Gloss): 'in cruce distenta conspexerunt membra sua'. With this compare the same writer's (Jerome's) paraphrase: 'Fixerunt manus meas et pedes meos, numeravi omnia ossa mea, quae ipsi respicientes viderunt in me.' – Jerome, *PL* 26, col. 882 and 28, col. 1143.

(b) *'Dinumeraverunt in ligno crucis extenta omnia ossa mea.'* (Gloss on this paraphrase): 'Quando pendens *extentus erat* in ligno. Non potuit melius describi *extensio corporis in ligno.*'...'Ecce intellegimus quae passus est: dinumerata sunt ossa ejus, irrisus est, divisa sunt vestimenta ejus.' – Augustine, Psalm commentary, *PL* 36, cols. 169 and 175f.

We must note carefully what it is that Augustine says 'could not be better described'. It is the stretched limbs, not the stretching, see the *participles*, 'extenta ossa', '(Christus) extentus'. These, together with Jerome's 'distenta membra', show that 'extensio' too must describe a final state. The *finite* verbs in these quotations denote what was done: the counting, the gazing. The Middle Ages introduced motion and action by 'telling' what must have gone before to produce (or, so as to produce) this result. [The story is then of the kind called 'aetiological'.] But even in the late Middle Ages, when attention was focussed on the actual ritual of crucifixion, the correspondence with prophecy could still be pointed out and taught. This is done perhaps most clearly in the Brixen Passion Play, where, after a detailed enactment of the pulling of Christ's limbs with ropes, and the erection of the Cross, the prophet David steps forward, and, as Mary sinks down at the foot of the Cross, declaims:

> Als ich am 21. psalm zwar
> Gesprochen hab frey offenwar:
> Seine hend und fues sy haben
> Gar jemerlich durch graben,
> Das im alle seine gepain
> Gezelt sein worden allain:
> Secht Nu all zu diser frist,
> Ob ietz sölichs nit geschechen ist![18]

[As I said indeed openly and clearly in my 21st Psalm, 'They have most grievously pierced his hands and feet', so that 'every single bone has been counted'. Look now, all of you, has it not all happened at this very moment?]

But such open reference to the psalm was not necessary. In a sermon on the Mass, Berthold of Regensburg (*c.* 1270) says:

'Darnach [i.e. after the *elevatio*] strecket der prister di arme sere von ime, daz bezeichent daz unser herre gedent wart an das heilege cruce als ser, daz man allez sine gebeine gezelt mohte haben durch sin huet.' – Thereupon the priest stretches out his arms to their full extent. That means that our Lord was stretched upon the Holy Cross so direly that one might have counted all his bones through his skin.'[19]

In 'dinumeraverunt omnia ossa mea' from Psalm 21 we have a text of singular importance. It entered as fulfilled prophecy into the story of the Crucifixion in the form: 'Christ was stretched (*sc.* they stretched Christ) on the Cross so direly (with ropes) that one might count all his bones', and one may now recall that medieval artists drew the Crucified in Z- or S-like posture, *or* so stretched that the rib-cage, often also sinews and veins, are prominently displayed, see section VI, below. This second iconography is more 'realistic' in the sense that its source is a prophetic text literally and 'historically' understood, whereas the Z(S)-line, alluding to an Old Testament 'type' or prefiguration, is symbolical. Both iconographies have Biblical authority and are therefore 'true'. A 'stylistic' preference may here and there have determined the artist's choice.

We must of course again not forget the prophet Isaiah, of whom Jerome and Augustine, and after them Isidore, said that he was so rich in prophecies of Christ that many considered him rather to be an evangelist than a prophet ('evangelista potius quam propheta').[20] It is generally accepted that Isaiah 53 was held to prophesy the Passion (and 'describe' the Man of Sorrows); it had the status of a source, but the verses could not all be drawn on in equal measure. There were verses in other chapters which were equally predictive, for instance Isaiah 50.6: 'corpus meum dedi percutientibus, et genas vellentibus: faciem meam non averti ab increpantibus et conspuentibus in me'. These words (of Christ speaking 'through Isaiah') may be preferred to those of the evangelists. The evangelists in fact report the Mocking of Christ quite fully, but here as elsewhere Isaiah offers something more. Here it is 'dedi genas vellentibus' (the evangelists do not mention the plucking of Christ's beard);

and 'corpus meum dedi percutientibus', taken in conjunction with 'dorsum meum' of Psalm 128/129.3, determined the iconography of many medieval representations of the Flagellation: Jesus presents his *back* to the smiters.[21]

V

More striking than the use of Old Testament words in their simplest literal and 'historical' sense, and at least as important in the context of this study, is the dangerous play which was made with the metaphorical or otherwise figurative statements of the prophetic books. It may, for instance, to us seem merely 'poetical' when Bernard of Clairvaux (the real St Bernard) draws simultaneously on Old Testament and New Testament wordings to assert that Christ was 'obedient unto the Father, even to the winepress which he trod alone' ('obediens patri usque ad torcular crucis, quod utique solus calcavit') – and so incorporates Isaiah 63.3.[22] (One is apprehensive that 'the true vine' may eventually 'tread the winepress', but incongruities were generally avoided.) St Bernard did not fall a victim to his own ingenuity: Cross and winepress no doubt remained distinct in his mind. More questionable is the substitution of 'tread the winepress' for 'die on the Cross' in *Unum ex quattuor*, a 'Gospel Harmony': 'venit hora passionis. . .in qua solus torcular calcare habeo'.[23] Pious layfolk may not always have recognized the rhetorical flourish; or it may with repetition have palled, leaving in either case the images of Christ treading the winepress,[24] or of the true vine being crushed. These must inevitably have reinforced conceptions of the indescribable sufferings of Christ and the brutalities of his enemies at the Crucifixion. The words of Isaiah may also be used in describing Christ's appearance after the Crowning with Thorns and the Flagellation ('Ecce homo'), for example in the *Lignum Vitae* attributed to Bonaventura: 'et vestimenta ejus quasi calcantium in torculari' (Isaiah 63, 2).[25] In virtually every medieval Passion text it will be said that Christ's garments were drenched with *blood*.

18

The faithful thought of (or were reminded of) Joseph's coat, they heard Isaiah's words concerning the treader of the wine-press, and they saw the Man of Sorrows.

To continue: St Bernard does not name his Old Testament sources when in a sermon on the Passion he says:

Patientia autem singularis, quod videlicet cum supra dorsum ejus fabri-carent peccatores (= Psalm 128/9.3); cum sic extenderetur in ligno, ut dinumerarentur omnia ossa ejus (= Psalm 21/22.17); cum fortissimum illud propugnaculum, quod custodit Israel, undique foraretur (freely after Song of Songs 4.4 and Psalm 120/21.4-8); cum foderentur manus ejus et pedes (= Psalm 21/22.16): sicut agnus ad occisionem ductus sit, et tanquam ovis coram tondente, non aperuerit os suum (= Isaiah 53.7).[26]

This is admittedly (and first and foremost) a feat of rhetoric, but at the same time Bernard clearly considers that, by adducing Old Testament wordings only, he has demonstrated the degree of Christ's 'patientia' at the Passion (the Passion considered as an 'opus'). He goes on to assure his hearers that these things were borne by the Saviour 'non umbratice, sed corporaliter', 'non figurative, sed substantialiter', 'non cooperative sed personaliter' – all this despite the highly metaphorical language of some of the quotations.[27] Here I add only the observation that the text quoted from Psalm 128 (it is: 'supra dorsum meum fabricaverunt peccatores') influenced the medieval image, not only of the Flagellation, but also of the Crucifixion. Without implying any connection with Bernard's text I cite from *Christi Leiden*:

'. . .unde wurfin yn uf daz cruce, he mochte sin zu sprungen, unde zogin eme sinen verwonten rucke. . .ubir die knorren des cruces, daz die stumpe von deme hulze die wonden von eyn ander riezzin', Priebsch pp. 41f. [Pickering p. 74, lines 22-6]. '. . .and cast him on the Cross so violently that he might have burst open, and pulled his wounded back over the knots of the Cross so that the stumps tore his wounds open'.

The purpose of this section was to indicate (no more!) the fateful ease with which important and revered metaphors and figures of prophecy could be translated into 'realistic' incident. In retrospect it may seem that, in the period (roughly) 1200–50, the Church hoped to screen the Old Testament from such abuse by admitting the 'credibility' of the story of the Passion as this was told by Pseudo-Anselm and Pseudo-Bonaventura. If there was such an intention, it was only partially successful.

VI

We turn now to what I shall call the 'symbols' of the Crucifixion. They are to be found among the vast number of so-called 'allegories' of Christ and the Cross in a section of Migne's *Index de allegoriis*, PL 219, cols. 130–43.[28] By the period on which we have been focussing attention many of these had been stripped of much of their symbolism ('de-symbolized', if the expression is acceptable), and in the process yielded new traits to amplify the *story* of the Passion. I single out some which were drawn on by the Fathers and later theologians to justify and reinforce the image derived from Psalm 21/22, of Christ's body stretched on the wood of the Cross, so that all his bones should be counted. First, the *harp of David*. Of the harp in general, and of the harp of David, the royal musician and prophet, in particular, the Middle Ages knew a great deal which on our first acquaintance may seem as strange as the animal lore of *Physiologus*; among other things, the harp of David was mysteriously prophetic of Christ's death on the Cross.

There are in theory scarcely more than three ways in which a relationship between the harp and Christ's death on the Cross can be established. One may declare dogmatically that the harp (of David) is or means Christ's death on the Cross; or having evoked an Orpheus-like God-Father, a poetic spirit may declare the Crucified on the Cross to be his harp. In the first case the harp would be a symbol, in the second a metaphor. Or thirdly, a methodical exegete may undertake an analytical *comparison* of harp and Crucifix. The relationship was in fact established in each of these three ways.

Why invoke the harp at all? What is the meaning of the harp on early Crucifixes? To us today the words of verse 9/8 of

Psalm 56/57 [the Easter Psalm] 'awake psaltery and harp' ('exsurge, psalterium et cithara') are 'poetic' merely, because we know nothing about the *psalterium* and the *cithara*, or what knowledge we have is not relevant to the case. The verse had a deeper meaning for the Middle Ages. Psalm-commentaries, from Jerome's down to that of Bruno of Würzburg (12th century) and beyond, contain a body of harp and psaltery lore, in some cases scattered, but gathered together in a foreword by Cassiodorus and Bruno, under the working title 'why this book is called a psalter' ('quid sit psalterium et psalmi quare dicuntur').[29] The gist can be formulated as follows: 'The book is called a psalter after psaltery, the name of the instrument, which differs from the harp (*cithara*) in having the resonance chamber higher (above) than in the case of the harp (where it is below). Otherwise they are alike, and have the shape of a Delta (Δ).' As for the *meaning* of the two instruments: 'the harp is the human body of Christ in his Passion ('caro humana patiens cithara est'). When the *harp* sounds (understand that) Christ 'esuriat, sitiat, dormiat, teneatur, flagelletur, irrideatur, crucifigatur, sepeliatur', writes Augustine,[30] and this list of human 'frailties' reminds one of medieval extensions of the Creed to emphasize that Christ suffered on earth 'corporaliter, non umbratice'.[31] When, however, the *psaltery* sounds, Augustine continues, Christ's miracles of healing are declared. By comparison with Augustine's dogmatic equations, the gloss on 'awake (my) harp' (*exsurge* or *resurge cithara*) in the Psalm Commentary of Cassiodorus (d. 570) is distinctly enthusiastic: 'the harp signifies the glorious Passion which with stretched sinews and counted bones ('tensis nervis dinumeratisque ossibus') sounded forth his bitter suffering as in a spiritual song ('carmen intellectuale')'.[32] Augustine, in assigning a meaning directly to psaltery and harp, claims them evidently as symbols. Cassiodorus's use of 'harp' is more nearly metaphorical. Both uses and interpretations are to be found throughout the Middle Ages, but obviously more important developments are to be expected when the harp metaphor is used poetically and with a certain freedom, as for instance in a Middle High German poem of about 1300, *Die Erlösung* (Man's Redemption). The poet has treated the Harrowing of Hell, and now celebrates the redemption of 'David who sang *Surge mea cithara*':

Iâ der werde godes vrûnt	Wer sie gespannen stellet
in deme salter aber sprach	und slehet dar und aber dar,
jubilîrende unde jach:	ir sûzekeit wirt man gewar...
'*Surge mea cythara.*'	In aller wîze det alsus
Nû hôret, wie man daz verstâ	unser herre Cristus.
dief von sinne scharpe...	jâ sâ der hêre heilant
Die harphe und daz psalterium	an daz krûze sâzuhant
sint beide ungespannen dum,	gezwicket und geslagen wart,
sie sint ungeslagen doup	gespannen unde sêre gespart,
rehte sam ein lindenloup,	geslagen dar und aber dar.[33]
daz von dem boume vellet.	

[The worthy friend of God, David, declared in jubilation in his psalter: '*Surge mea cithara*'. Hear now how that is to be understood in its deep and penetrating meaning...The harp and the psaltery are mute when still unspanned, and, unless struck, silent like the linden leaf that falls from the tree. If anyone tightens them, however, and strikes them again and again, their sweetness will be heard...Thus exactly did our Lord Christ. Yes, immediately the Saviour was nailed and fastened to the Cross, spanned and sorely stretched, struck again and again.]

The poet does not endeavour here to distinguish between harp and psaltery, but he is clearly writing within a tradition of interpretation which can be traced back over the centuries to Augustine and Cassiodorus, see above. He associates David, his Psalm verse, harp – psaltery, and the Crucifixion. In the *Altes Passional* of the same date (*c.* 1300), a work attributed to the Teutonic Order in East Prussia, there is a slight shift of emphasis from David the prophet and psalmist, to David the court musician. After a description of the Crucifixion *erecto cruce*, in which Christ's 'snow-white hands were pulled wide apart' and 'they fell upon his legs and pulled them down hard (one could have counted all his bones)', the text continues:

In den nagelen er sich spien	Eya mensche nu vernim:...
als ein gedente seite...	Der vater des gewaldis, Got

22

nach der minne gebot	an des cruces harfe
din herze an sich locken wil	gespannen...
vnde hat dar vf sin seiten spil	[und wil] von suchten bosen
durch gedone vollen scharfe	als Sauln Dauit dich losen.[34]

[He stretched himself between the nails like a tautened string...Now hear, mankind: God the almighty Father would draw your heart to him, and with that intent has spanned his strings on the harp of the Cross (so that its penetrating notes may reach you): he would deliver you from evil afflictions, as David delivered Saul.] 'All nature was spellbound by the Father's music; he played until the strings broke and fell limp' ('sus wurden alle saiten slaff'), the passage concludes. We may later be reminded of these lines and their final image. There is in the *Zerbster Prozessionsspiel* of the year 1507, roughly a thousand years after the early exegetes, a simple dogmatic reminder of the meaning of David's harp. A herald proclaims David:

> David eyn konnig lobesam
> Dornach eherlich quam.
> Das kreucz ist in der harffe
> Dor auff gezcogenn alszo scharffe.[35]

[Then came the noble and worthy King David. The Cross of Christ is in the harp (there) so tightly strung.]

If the words of the herold were understood in this way ('is in' = 'is to be seen in'), the lines will seem to be a late reiteration of the old 'symbolic' equation of harp and Cross (or Crucifix).

Among the possible symbols of the Crucifixion, the *bow* is originally kept distinct from the *harp*, though both are in a manner of speaking stringed instruments. In a work of the exegete Gotfrid of Admont (Styria, d. 1169) on the allegorical meaning of the Blessing of Jacob, one encounters the following interpretation of the blessing spoken over Joseph, 'sedit in forte arcus ejus...' (Genesis 49.24):

A bow consists of a piece of wood or horn and a *chorda*, which worthily represents (*nobiliter demonstrat*) our Lord and Redeemer. The *chorda* may be taken to mean his most holy body (*caro*), which, in the various dire tribulations of his Passion, was wondrously spanned and stretched (*mirabiliter attracta et distenta*). By the wood or horn his invincible divinity is meant, which, as it were, remained rigid and unbending for the bearing of the sum of human miseries. Until the noble bowstring, his holy body, began to be drawn in mockery, spanned with insults and stretched to the *affixiones* [notches of the bow, nails of the Cross] for our salvation. This is the bow which the Father promised when he said: 'I do set my bow in the cloud' (Genesis 9.13).[36]

This possible interpretation of the words of the blessing, which must have been more frequently used by exegetes than I have been able to discover,[37] will have justified the application of the commonplace 'stretched like a bowstring' to the description of Christ on the Cross. The Viennese Heinrich von Neustadt describes the Crucifixion in his *Von Gottes Zukunft* (*c.* 1320) as follows:

(Er mûz die presse eine   Do worden sine reinen glider
treten, als die wissagen   und sin geeder uf gezogen
kûnten e vor manigen tagen. . .)   als die senewe uf den bogen.[38]
Man legte in uf daz cruce nider:

[He has to tread the winepress alone, as the prophets long ago declared. They laid him down on the Cross. Then his pure limbs and veins were drawn like the string on(to) the bow.]

Having now seen the stretched body of Christ on the Cross compared with a drawn bowstring (or the taut strings of a harp), and recalling the 'extensio' singled out by early exegetes as the final image of the Crucifixion, one can better understand the choice of words in two of the Church's most famous hymns celebrating the Cross, namely *Vexilla regis prodeunt* and *Pange, lingua*, attributed to Venantius Fortunatus (d. 600). I refer to '*confixa* clavis *viscera*' as designation of Christ's body on the Cross in the one; in the other the 'lofty tree' of the Cross is implored to bend its branches and (relax or slacken?) its 'sinews': '*Flecte ramos, arbor alta, tensa* laxa *viscera*'. The *tensa viscera* are here, though not unambiguously, the fibres of the tree (and J. M. Neale's translation is 'Thy too rigid

24

sinews bend'). The image is, I think, very roughly that of the archer's bow. Stripped of some of its symbolism the archer's bow has seemed to me more readily associable with the medieval Crucifixion *erecto cruce*, but it would be neither accurate nor useful to seek to equate the two modes (*erecto* and *jacente cruce*) with bow and harp respectively.

The de-symbolizing process began, these examples would suggest, when an original symbol ('allegory') of the Crucifixion was treated as if it were the *comparatum* in an analytical comparison: Christ on the Cross *is like* a harp or bow, *because*...The early exegetes were forced into such methods of 'proof' by unbelievers and the sceptical. Compare Augustine's lengthy disquisition on the *similarity* of Noah in his Ark and Christ in the community of the Church (*Contra Faustum Manichaeum*, Book 12, Migne, *PL* 42, cols. 207f.). The methods evolved in controversy will then surely have been used in the instruction of the clergy. The use of the comparison did not destroy the harp (etc.) as symbol, but it speeded the 'recovery' of the *historia* prophesied in the symbol.

In this section we have so far discussed texts, the authors of which, we may assume, still knew and understood the patristic interpretation of harp and bow. Below I shall quote lines from *Christi Leiden* in which the formulaic comparison 'stretched like a string' ('Saite') is fairly clearly used without knowledge of the patristic source (this is equally evidence of the astonishing stability of verbal tradition concerning the Passion). Towards the end of the Middle Ages one must suppose that only the outcome of the scrutiny of symbols was fully understood. If the theologians still wanted to recall the harp of David, or the bow in the Blessing of Jacob, well and good! What they said was illuminating, but only as a gloss on what *happened* on Golgotha.

Brief treatment only can be given here to one further nexus of symbols, from their origins to their resolution into incident (of some kind). I choose it because of the light which may be thrown on a number of otherwise enigmatic passages in medieval devotional writings. At the same time they require us to consider whether, in the world of symbols, similarity of shape

or outline may have led to uncertainties of recognition, ambivalence, and easier 'exploitation' by imaginative writers. Harp
and bow are only vaguely alike in shape (a straight line, a
curve), and a different range of words and expressions is
associated with the parts of each, and the manner of use: the
images could never fall into absolute register. The situation is
different in the case of 'serpent' and 'worm'.

Christ himself had declared the (brazen) *serpent* raised by
Moses in the desert to be prophetic of his own 'raising' (on the
Cross), see above, p. 12. This image can scarcely have been
reinforced and fixed in the minds of the Fathers by the discovery, among 'omnia de me', of a *vermis* and a *vermiculus.*
The former occurs in the all-important twenty-first Psalm ('Ego
sum *vermis* et non homo, opprobrium hominum et abjectio
plebis'); the latter, less important, is the 'tenerrimus *ligni
vermiculus*' in the Vulgate rendering of II Samuel 23.8 (entirely
different in A.V.). The exegetes necessarily associated *vermis*
and its appositions, 'opprobrium hominum' and 'abjectio
plebis'; they could scarcely ignore the reference to the Cross in
the case of *vermiculus.* There remains then the difficulty of
associating the 'abject' *vermis* (*vermiculus*) and the clearly
victorious *serpens* on the Cross [and Moses, one reads, raised the
serpent 'pro signo', which is 'as a standard']. But there were to
be still further complications!

Before examining the quotations, mainly from vernacular
poetry, which are to follow here, it must be recalled that in the
Germanic languages 'worm' can also mean 'serpent', and
indeed 'dragon', and that in Medieval Latin *vermis, serpens*
and *draco* are more closely related than today one would
imagine. For Isidore of Seville the *draco* is 'major cunctorum
serpentium'. (Elsewhere in the *Etymologies* he lists *draco* under
signa, i.e. standards, which explains why medieval artists may
represent Moses holding aloft, not a serpent on a staff, but a
highly decorative dragon on a column: that is not our subject
here.)[39] Serpent and worm, to repeat, could be designated by the
one word 'worm', and serpent, worm and the diminutive *ligni*

vermiculus, sharing an S-line, are more or less identical: the world of symbols disregards relative size! A different consideration is that in vernacular poetry 'worm' attracts, or has in time past attracted, the rhyme-word 'storm'. As for the meaning of 'storm' ('Sturm') in the extracts to be considered, it seems in some cases to mean a storm-wind, but its presence must surely imply some allusion to the storming of Hell and the conflict (*proelium, certamen*) of the Redeemer with Death, on the Cross. There are inevitably some ambiguities of image and meaning in the texts. How is one to understand and render the following lines of *Das alte Passional* (*c.* 1300, see above)?

Wande in betwanc ein herter *sturm*   sich wie er recht als ein *wurm*
daz er sich want als ein *wurm*   der in grozen wetagen
der do gespissen were...   ist mit negelen durchslagen
[Mary:] 'Sich an sine geberde   sich in den nagelen windet.'[40]
den dv hast bracht in diesen *sturm,*

The narrative statement is that 'a hard assault so assailed him that he writhed like an impaled worm'. Mary's (much later) reproach is a repetition with variation, stating that 'he twists and turns (*windet. . .sich*), pierced by the nails'.

In the Wolfenbüttel and the Bordesholm *Laments of Mary,* the Virgin, as she approaches the Cross with John, asks:

Johannes, mîn vil leve ôm,
Wat is, dat dâr hanget an dem bôm?
Wer isset, ein mynsche edder ein *worm*?
It windet sik unde drîvet groten *storm*.[41]

In the Redentin *Easter Play* the Jew Krummnase states:

Do horde ik van Jesu groten *storm*.
He want sik also en *worm*.[42]

(*a*) John, dear kinsman, what is it hangs there on the tree? Who is it, a man or a worm? It writhes and struggles violently.

(*b*) I heard of Jesus' great struggle. He writhed like a worm.

Without the compelling authority of 'Ego sum vermis et non homo' (which with 'opprobrium hominum' and 'abjectio plebis' could of course *also* be referred to the Man of Sorrows), the

27

Fathers, and the Middle Ages after them, would not have seen in the brazen serpent (the standard of the Victor over Death) an image of one writhing in the throes of death on the Cross. Hitherto I think that editors have considered only a possible immediate source, the lines, namely, of a Latin hymn:

> Recordare quod ut vermis
> ligni tener et inermis
> in altum erigitur.[42]

'Ut vermis', 'like a worm': the Biblical words were 'sicut serpens', and of that even a relatively unschooled author could remind his public. The beadle in the Augsburg Passion Play cries:

> Daz er am holcz des creutzes erhang
> Als hat bedeut der erin schlang.[43]

One notes, however, that despite the reference to the serpent, Christ's limbs are stretched: 'spannend im die saytten hoch' ('tighten his strings hard', line 1636). How, one wonders, did the player representing Christ enact the death throes?

This section may be brought to a close with a quotation from Frauenlob's *Kreuzleich*. His theme in the passage in question is 'Christ's Leaps', one of which (here the fourth) is to the Cross. This is not the more usual 'ascent of the palmtree' foreshadowed in Song of Songs 7.8, but a leap 'in the likeness of an eel':

> Got spranc ûz sînem vater in sîn êwikeit,
> dâ nâch sô spranc er in daz wort,
> der dritte sprunc was in die meit;
> der *vierde* kam *in âles wîse*
> spîse, kriuze, dîner hôhen wirdekeit.[44]

It required the febrile imagination of Frauenlob to see in the serpent (or the worm?) on the glorious Cross an eel as 'spîse', one assumes as a 'bait' to catch Leviathan.

VII

There was a residue of 'symbolism' in the texts just quoted. The use of rhyme, the naming of original symbols, and the echoing of sacred words (*mynsche, worm | homo, vermis*) ensured that even unpretentious works celebrated, however dolefully, the 'glorious' Passion. Therein lies the undoubted uniqueness of *Christi Leiden in einer Vision geschaut* with which we began. This work, more than any other, demanded an explanation, which must be that the anonymous author was determined to admit to his account only what 'really happened' on the way from Gethsemane to Golgotha and the Resurrection. He omits all subsidiary matter (and this includes Peter's denial).[45] The main events, whether these were prophesied by Isaiah and the Psalms, or had been recovered from Old Testament metaphors and symbols, he relates without any allusions to sources (they do not interest him). But even he adapts traditional word sequences where he may. Of the stretching with ropes at the Crucifixion he writes: 'unde deneten yn so sere, daz nye keyne *seyte* so faste uf ein *bret* wart gedeynt, biz sie daz loch gereichten' ('and stretched him so direly, that no *cord* was ever stretched so tight over a *board*'), Priebsch p. 42, lines 22ff. [Pickering, p. 75, lines 9ff.][46] This *bret* is no 'Hackbrett'; it is not a dulcimer! But the use of 'seyte' ('Saite') betrays the origin of the comparison. In *Christi Leiden* there are 'de-symbolized' symbols in plenty, the most startling of which, derived from *statera* = Cross, is the story of the 'falling Cross':

'unde bewarthin das cruce nyt wol, daz es fast stunde, unde da sie davon gegingen, da ubir weig der lyp daz cruce, daz er dar nyder fiel uff die erdin, das daz antlicze Xristus in der erdin steckete alse eyn Ingesiegele an deme wasse, unde daz die erde an deme antlicze clebete', Priebsch, p. 43, lines 3–7, [Pickering, p. 75, lines 24–8].[47]

'And they did not shore up the Cross properly so that it should stand firm, and when they went away, the body caused the Cross to overbalance, so that it [the body] fell to the ground, and Christ's face was depressed in the earth like a seal in wax, and the soil adhered to his face'.

That is by no means all that is to be said about 'de-symbolized' symbols as one source of medieval conceptions of the events of Holy Week. Readers of this essay will have little difficulty in seeing what could be made, by writers so minded, of some of the following prefigurative symbols, particularly when allowance is made for associative thinking: *ram, lamb, fleece, parchment, book, charter* (of man's redemption), or *parchment, drumskin*; the *vine* (on the trellis, in the winepress); the *grain of wheat, bread, wafer, host* (broken on the altar – of the Cross); the *rock* struck with a rod – etc. For each of these one or other exegete had an explanation, and for each explanation there was an author ready to exploit it 'realistically'. Not every narrative incident of such derivation entered into the common stock of motifs, but it should not be dismissed as 'legendary'. Each is the final precipitate of a *textual* evolution which can be traced back over the centuries to the initiative of the Fathers of the Church. In this essay I hope to have indicated the kind of investigation which the evidence requires, and I offer it for further consideration.[48]

2. EXEGESIS AND IMAGINATION

A CONTRIBUTION TO THE STUDY OF RUPERT OF DEUTZ

In submitting afresh (and in translation) only the final ten pages of a long article of 1971 (see prefatory note, p. 206), I concentrate attention on Rupert of Deutz (d. 1129), ignoring Joachim of Fiore with whom I had compared him, and by my new title I suggest that Rupert was an 'imaginative exegete' rather than, like Joachim, an 'aberrant historian'. Even so, one still has to consider, I think, what contribution Rupert may have made to medieval belief concerning 'what really happened' during the week of Christ's Passion: the facts and the circumstances of the various scenes and events.

Rupert was, of course, not satisfied with the eye-witness accounts of the evangelists; few people were in his day. The prophecies of the Passion in the Psalms, Isaiah, Lamentations etc., annually rehearsed in the Liturgy, were a constant reminder that the evangelists had not told all. To Rupert and his contempories they were 'simple and unlettered men' (*homines idiotae et sine litteris*). Unlike his predecessors and most of his successors, however, who were content to *supplement* the Gospel accounts, particularly of the Passion, by approved methods including the 'argument from prophecy', Rupert took it upon himself in his major work to *displace* them in a 'Testament of the Spirit' of his own composition. As a virtuoso of exegesis, he was able both to envisage and to undertake such a work, and in it to evoke the 'spectacle' of the Passion on a higher plane than that of simple *historia*. But does that amount to a story told? Literary historians will justifiably, after a brief glance at Rupert's texts, not hesitate to say that he does not narrate: 'nothing really happens'. Even so, though technically correct, that might still be a wrong judgment. Anyone who reads not a few short passages, but say a hundred consecutive columns in Migne's *Patrologia Latina*, vol. 167, will discover that the one treatment which the Passion of Christ seems to defy is that of non-narration. In other words, whatever Rupert's intention may have been, he generates by his exegetical procedures a version of the *story* of the Passion never previously told, and which though even now not really told, remains as a memory when his methods are largely forgotten.

In my own attempts to trace medieval elaborations of the story of the Passion down to the drastically 'realistic' versions of the later Middle Ages, I have so far not mentioned Rupert by name or tried to assign him a place.[1] For such reticence there were several reasons: the repute in which he is generally held, and my quite inadequate knowledge of his total *œuvre*, were long the foremost of these. Still important is the fact already noted, that Rupert never narrates the Passion story in a manner comparable with that of the better-known Passion tracts (Pseudo-Bonaventura, see previous essay). Whereas they offer only the assured 'historical' results of patristic and later Biblical scholarship (or they preface apocryphal, or established traditional details with 'fertur', 'pie creditur'), Rupert is still actively engaged in the search for Old Testament prophecies of the Passion, typologizing, spiritualizing, like a latter-day Father of the Church, and paying only formal attention to the first, literal sense of the Biblical word.

One may admire the audacity of Rupert's undertaking to write a Testament of the Spirit, and concede an intellectual achievement of some magnitude in completing it. There remains a doubt. Can an author quote and compare his sources, then by accepted methods of interpretation 'prove' a text purporting to transcend them, and yet deny the latter – his own text – a first and literal meaning? As for the objection that Rupert's words are and remain those of a visionary, by their sheer number and frequency his images become a continuing sequence to which the mind of the beholder adjusts itself. There is a sustained degree of remoteness from remembered 'historical' reality (e.g. the reality of the Old Testament story of Job) which is in the end (in fact soon) only dimly apprehended: one witnesses a new series of *quasi*-scenes and events. In other words, there are diminishing returns from the continuous appeal to the spiritual sense of the scriptural word: it yields a new historical sense. Add to these considerations the impact of Rupert's diction. It is preponderantly the highly figurative and often vehement diction of the Old Testament, used first in direct quotations of Old Testament prophecy, but then drawn into Rupert's own enunciation of what was the real course of events. The mind seeks respite from such rhetoric in the devotional image, the imagined enactment of all that was prophesied. If that may be said of the modern reader's response to Rupert's texts in convenient print, what are we to judge to have been the effect of his preaching and teaching over the years on his Rhineland audiences in his own day?

There could, therefore, scarcely be a greater contrast in methods of Biblical study in the Middle Ages than that between Rupert of Deutz, and Peter Comestor writing about fifty years later. This is a matter on which Beryl Smalley has written with great authority in her *Study of the Bible in the Middle Ages* (second edition 1952). The Comestor bases his *Historia Scholastica* on the words of the Bible, Old and New Testaments, understood in their first, literal and historical sense. He rarely offers the spiritual sense even for consideration. As for the argument from prophecy which Rupert uses (or considers) on every conceivable occasion, the Comestor eschews it: he seems indeed (on the evidence of the Migne text) to have suppressed the very words in Christ's final teaching of the apostles which were held to justify its use.[2] But clearly it was only in the West (Paris) that such a call to reason ('back to the letter') was heard. Elsewhere there was greater sympathy with the methods – or perhaps rather the product of the methods – of, among others, Rupert of Deutz.

Before illustrating his exegetical methods (below) I should explain why I have so far made no reference to the nature of Rupert's piety, and only just now allowed that his treatment of the Passion of Christ may have been congenial to his contem-

33

poraries. Firstly, the outline story of developments in religious sensibility – from Bernardine mysticism down to the openly emotional or even coarsely sensational outpourings (and pictorial art) of the later Middle Ages, which scholars have dignified as an emergent and finally dominant 'theology of suffering' ('Leidenstheologie') – is too well known to bear repetition here. Secondly, I think that that story, as conventionally told, under-estimates the role of a succession of *narrative* texts which en-larged the scope for the compassionate devotions of the faithful, and aimed to 'stimulate' these. No doubt such texts (and the pictorial cycles to which they gave rise) reflect or express a new kind of piety, but first and foremost they are *writings* embody-ing the findings of Biblical studies pursuing an increasingly historical line, seeking, and, having found, declaring the true facts behind the commemorative texts and ritual of the Liturgy of Holy Week. It is the events ('what they did to Our Lord') which spur the devout to ever deeper compassion. What Rupert of Deutz wrote contributed significantly to medieval apprehen-sion of those events. He offered a wealth of newly authenticated detail to add to the established facts, and to shape and colour these as he had imagined them. He invites his hearers (readers) to witness a series of 'spectacles', and these he 'stages' (see below). His imaginative (or even spectacular) findings had the authority of his undoubtedly scholarly method. We may find it excessively speculative. There can be little doubt that it was acceptable to many in his day. He and those who followed him may one day be recognized as at least in part responsible for the particular gruesomeness of religious art in the Rhineland. Now finally, let us examine some of the texts which led me to these views.

Job as a 'type' of the Man of Sorrows

The voluminous work from which I extract Rupert of Deutz's treatment of this subject was referred to above: it bears the title *The Works of the Trinity*,[3] and is predictably in three parts. The proportions are interesting. To the Old Testament (the

Works of the Father) Rupert devotes a text filling 1329 Migne columns, to the New Testament (the Works of the Son) thirty-five! The 'Testament of the Spirit' (the Works of the Holy Spirit) fills 256 columns. In all the work occupies 1630 columns. (As Herbert Grundmann wrote, Rupert 'brooded endlessly on the Works of the Trinity'.)[4] Our excerpts are of course taken from the third part.

The works of the Holy Spirit are those of each of the 'seven gifts'. We shall be concerned only with those of 'wisdom', for that is where Rupert deals with Job as a type of the Man of Sorrows. It is of course a *topos* of Christian teaching since patristic times that Job on his dunghill prefigures the Christ of the Passion. All the more amazingly Rupert will confess that, in an earlier review of the patriarchs, he 'forgot' to mention Job's prefigurative role (see below).

With connecting summary and some comments, I wish to concentrate attention on the 'devotional image' ('Andachtsbild') towards which Rupert is steering in this 'Testament of the Spirit', as he calls it. I can however indicate only the general course of his speculations and arguments, for to trace all the convolutions of his associative thought-processsses would involve writing out his text in full. What he envisages is an *image*, subsuming both type (Job) and antitype (Christ of the Passion). It is to be both derived from and glossed by a *new text*. For the latter Rupert recalls the words which, understood historically referred to Job on his dunghill, understood spiritually refer to Christ, conflated yield Job–Christ with whom the Testament of the Spirit deals. The image is therefore a 'montage', the text a mosaic. Whether in this process the Holy Spirit so guided Rupert's amazing powers of recall as to make him its *calamus*, or Rupert abandoned himself to the exciting outcome of his conflationary techniques, it is difficult for a modern reader to say. At any rate the remembered words of the Old Law, the prophets and the Psalms so commingle in Rupert's mind that his devotional image is confirmed. We now try to follow his arguments, accepting alike the subtleties and some of the

35

banalities of the spiritual interpretation, through four Chapters of *De Sapientia, Liber Primus, PL* 167, cols. 1605-9.

Cap. I. 'This first Chapter deals with the Holy Spirit through which, as the Apostle says, Christ offered himself [Hebrews 9.14].' That means: 'we treat here of the Spirit of Wisdom (*spiritus sapientiae*), that Wisdom which "none of the princes of this world knew: for had they known it, they would not have crucified the Lord of glory" [I Corinthians 2.8].'

With that as his basic New Testament text, Rupert now announces the battle which the 'spiritus sapientiae' joined with the 'sapientia saeculi', and in which the 'patientia' of the former was victorious.

Cap. II. 'That we shall forthwith see enacted' (*Hinc ergo ut proposuimus spectaculum jam nunc ingrediamur*).[5] The attack was led by the New Adam, whose role is thus characterized in the words of the prophet Isaiah: 'by his knowledge shall my righteous servant justify many' (*in scientia sua justificabit ipse justus servos meos multos* = Isaiah 53, 11 according to the text in Migne, Vulgate: *servus meus multos*). 'The New Adam was obedient. How obedient?' (Rupert withholds the answer until he has recalled the disobedience of the first Adam): 'obedient unto death, the death of the Cross'.

Cap. III De beato Job. For the gist of this chapter we may adopt the Migne heading: 'Job is a type of Christ in that he was a precursor in respect of wisdom, i.e. of suffering'.

Rupert has by now assembled most of the terms he needs, and mustered all the roles except that of the main adversary. He has rehearsed some of the texts which he will use for the *mise en scène* of the advertised 'spectaculum'. It is at this of all points that he confesses that on a previous occasion ('some way back' – *longe superius*),[6] when reviewing in succession the 'revered images and figures of the Truth, i.e. of Christ the Son of God, among the prophets, patriarchs and kings', he *forgot Job!* He forgot 'that exemplar of *patientia* whom the authority of the Fathers most certainly declared to have gone before as a type of that same Christ our Lord and his Church'. With bland effrontery Rupert now claims that the earlier regrettable lapse is a cause of joy; 'we shall find no better place than this to recall him'.[7] Rather than speculate how Rupert could have contrived to forget Job before, let us note how he proposes to use him now.

'By his example we may now see as in a mirror, less painfully (*tolera-bilius*) and more clearly (*certiore intuitu*) than in the blinding light of the Truth, the work of the Wisdom of the Spirit in Christ.'[8]

Cap. IV Here Rupert introduces the as yet absent opponent, Satan. Rupert's Satan is, properly, at first the Satan of the Book of Job, understood historically. But: 'the very exemplar of *stultitia*', Satan turned away from God to persecute Job 'and therefore Christ'.

Rupert is now ready to 'start the show' (*spectaculum. . . ingrediamur*, above). He quotes Old and New Testament texts in ideal order, the words of the prophets falling into their place. The roles and the words which one recognizes when they are first named or quoted, become, on their repetition, so interlocked that one is often left uncertain who persecuted whom in the battle of good and evil, and who was 'evicted' to sit in misery outside the city walls; and the menacing words 'morte turpissima condemnemus eum' (Wisdom 2.20) are reiterated, but with reference to whom, Job, Christ or Satan? – for in one way or another all were cast out or rejected by their persecutors: Job by Satan, Satan by Christ who cast out devils, and Christ by the Jews possessed of the Devil. What is new in the account (or on the evidence of this enquiry) is that, like Job, Christ was 'driven from the city'. That is a scholarly finding that was not forgotten. (Rupert elects to cut off his exploitation of prophecy at this point. He does not invoke Lamentations (1.12), 'O vos omnes qui transitis per viam' to refer to the Man of Sorrows, sitting outside the city, by the wayside. Elsewhere he finds in the Psalm verse 'lapidem quem reprobaverunt aedificantes' (117/118.22) sufficient evidence for the gloss: 'Christum quem ejecerunt extra civitatem', *PL* 170, 508.)

Rupert sums up: 'Satan intentabat in Job', that is 'Satan intentabat in dolentem, subauditur pro nobis Dominum Jesum', for Satan had possessed the hearts of those who cried out 'morte turpissima condemnemus eum', for which reason he was banished from God's sight. In this way Rupert aligns his texts to suggest a story of Job–Christ's eviction from the city, there to sit on his dunghill, scraping his sores with a potsherd, while the adversary is banished from God's sight. But he has not yet finished. He returns to Job, this time the Job of the Testament of the Spirit, as we must judge:

'Igitur cum hic dolens qui quondam dives et ut vere rex sedebat, circumstante angelorum exercitu extra portam ejectus morte esset turpissima percussus, quasi leprosus reputatus revera sedebat Job in sterquilino sanie coopertus: nam Dominus posuerat in eo iniquitates omnium nostrum.'

Thus the text. Whose picture is this? Who is this once powerful one, who had sat, a very king, on his throne, until before the eyes of the heavenly host he was cast from the city, there to sit like a leper upon his dunghill (etc.)? The picture is a 'montage' of Job, Christ, the suffering Servant (of Isaiah 53), the scapegoat, and indeed of Lucifer himself. It is over 'this man' that the sentence of a 'shameful death' is uttered. But despite all the rhetoric this is a finally relatively static image, on which Rupert meditates: 'Therefore it is rightly written that Job scraped himself with a potsherd, for. . .' but I spare readers Rupert's consideration of the spiritual meaning of 'potsherd'.

Today, with time to reflect on the printed text and consult a Biblical concordance, one can trace the outlines of the superimposed figures in this devotional image, and identify the exploited prophetic texts which are its captions, but the 'spectaculum' of violence we have witnessed still remains before the mind. At this point I may recall that we have considered the burthen of, in all, *four* columns of Migne text. What can have been the effect of Rupert's teaching at a time when the demand was to 'know more' and 'to know for certain' (*wizzen und niht wænen* in fourteenth century texts) – of the Passion of Christ? Therein lay the danger of Rupert's apparently so simple methods. Others were to speculate on similar lines after him: so at least one must gather from the narrative and dramatic texts and the pictorial art of the later Middle Ages.[9]

Some of the further content of Rupert's First Book (on the Spirit of Wisdom) may be indicated in briefest outline. He proceeds to a regular interrogation of the Book of Job, not for the sake of Job's story in itself, but in search of those words of

38

Job which might be more fully understood in a Christological sense. Here are examples from three different Chapters.

Cap. V Job had 'cursed the day on which he was born' and wished 'that he had died in his mother's womb' (3.3 and 11). The day of the birth (or the night of the conception) of sinful man is meant, Rupert suggests, but then argues at length that not even the most potent curse of a Job, or of any of the elect, can be effective, and of course the curse cannot be attributed to Christ on behalf of humanity (*Cap. VI*). Rupert passes on.

Cap. VIII Job spoke of God's justice as a balance: 'Utinam appenderentur peccata mea (A.V. my grief)...in statera' (6.2). Rupert will not have been the first exegete to have seen in the *statera* a figure of the Cross of Christ the Judge, but it is noteworthy that scholars have quoted passages from Rupert in their endeavours to elucidate certain 'allegorical' representations of the Crucified.[10] There was also a later medieval tradition according to which the cross on Golgatha 'overbalanced' and impressed the face of the Crucified like a seal in the soft earth.[11] Of Rupert's own lines on the balance-cross one will certainly say that they are more circumspect. He restricts his reflections to the rising and falling scales weighing man's sins; there is a final 'tipping of the scales', but it is the sins of mankind (not the Crucified on the Cross) which are plunged into 'the depths of the *sea*'. But when one reflects that 'plunged into the depths of the sea' has as its Biblical justification only 'heavier than the sands of the sea' (*quasi arena maris gravior*), one may think that Rupert had shown the way to some successor who adduced in addition 'infixus sum in limo profundi' (Psalm 68.3/69.2).[12]

Cap. IX–X Job was mocked, says Rupert, by 'the sons of folly' ('Interea deridetur tanta sapientia, deridetur inquam a filiis stultitiae'). He finds his authority for this formulation in the story of Job, also in a prophetic utterance in *Proverbs*, and in the Mocking of Christ as recorded in St Matthew. As for the 'filii stultitae', Rupert combines Job's comforters, the unnamed enemies of the prophetic text who cried out 'deglutiamus eum...viventem' (Proverbs 1.12), and the Jews who bade Christ prophesy ('prophetiza nobis', Matthew 26, 67f.). These together represent the ideal enemies of Christ to whom the ferocious words 'deglutiamus...' could be attributed. These enemies behaved, moreover, 'like drunkards' ('et errare eos faciet quasi ebrios', Job 12.25, see also below). That was all prophesied. And when Job asked, 'Who was ever so mocked as I by his enemies?' (cf. verse 4): 'whom can he have meant by *sicut ego* but him whose role I play before him?' (*Quid enim est 'sicut*

39

ego' nisi ac si diceret, cujus ego derisus ab amicis meis, typum praefero?).[13]

From this brief review of, by now, ten columns of Migne text it must surely emerge that the tendency of Rupert's use of the spiritual sense of the Biblical word (and of the argument from prophecy) is to tell *all* that can be verified concerning the sufferings of the Christ of the Passion. Herbert Grundmann was fully aware of this, but as a historian he had to record that Rupert of Deutz had 'no significant contribution to make to medieval historical thought' ('Die breiten Ausführungen Ruperts...haben keine grundlegende Bedeutung für die Bildung neuer geschichtlicher Anschauungsformen').[14] It was in that context that he said (see above) that Rupert 'brooded endlessly on the works of the Trinity'. We have been more concerned with the nature and the direction of the broodings, and I think we may now say with Rupert's misuse of the spiritual interpretation. Once an authoritative method of exegesis, it seems in his hands to have become a game played with *fiches* for the 'invention' of a quasi-historical account of the Passion of Christ. But before our argument becomes circular, let us say rather that all three elements are involved: exegesis, imagination and – religious feeling! In the passage which we next analyse we shall see all three again at work, perhaps all the more disturbingly in that Rupert is not writing a Testament of the Spirit of his own devising, but a commentary on one of the Minor Prophets of the canonical Old Testament.

The Mocking of Christ by the Jews

Rupert of Deutz did not hesitate to apply his imaginative methods of exegesis with full rigour when his 'findings' could not but seem to be of contemporary relevance. In the instance to be considered the initial impulse may of course have been given by his own hatred of the Jews – which I do not immediately impute. I stress rather the evident satisfaction with which, by use of the spiritual interpretation and the argument from prophecy, Rupert claims to find scriptural authority for such hatred. (Beryl Smalley has noted similar use of the 'sensus spiritualis' in the work of another, hitherto neglected Old Testament exegete.)[15] It was with reference to such dubious methods that I originally classed Rupert (with Joachim of Fiore) as an 'aberrant historian'. A fresh word of introduction will be necessary to establish a context.

In his *Commentariorum in duodecim Prophetas Minores Libri XXXI*, again a very long work,[16] Rupert devotes a passage of elucidation to a few verses of the prophet Hosea on which I wish to concentrate attention. Anticipating the more detailed analysis, below: Rupert first, but more or less as a formality or *captatio benevolentiae*, considers the possible historicity of the verses in an Old Testament context, but then goes on to exploit them as testimony of the wild and insensate behaviour of the Jews in the palace of the High Priest Caiaphas. He proves in the process that the Jews who mocked and tortured Christ throughout the night were 'sated and drunk with wine'. As we noted above, Rupert's vehement diction (derived from the quoted prophecies) lends lurid colours to the scenes he evokes. As an account of the atrocities committed against Christ, Rupert's differs little in respect of 'gruesomeness' from late medieval Passion narratives: mainly in its repeated references to the authenticating Biblical sources. It is then interesting to compare Rupert on Hosea with his commentary elsewhere on St Matthew's eye-witness account of the same events.[17] Whereas he clearly regards Hosea as a source of 'historical' information, he makes the Gospel account of Matthew the pretext for interminable spiritualizing interpretations. Is this not a more disturbing misuse of exegetical methods than the *reductio ad absurdum* some scholars have found in the work of Joachim of Fiore?[18] May one not charge Rupert with malicious fabrication of pseudo-facts? The few scholars (I am not one of them) who know Rupert's total *œuvre* in detail may not want to subscribe to such a view, but I myself doubt whether a scholarly and

41

'balanced' view of Rupert's work as a whole is of any relevance at this point. (Equally I have not felt any obligation to pursue my own enquiries further.)[19] There follows now, as indicated, a closer analysis of Rupert's commentary on Hosea 7, verses 3–7, with no final summing-up.

Old Testament scholars today are as unsure as was Rupert of the historical circumstances which prompted the diatribe of the prophet in Hosea 7, verses 3–7. It is interesting that Rupert makes a show of concern to know what *may* be the 'sensus historialis' of the passage: 'Before we consider the prophetic sense of the words in question, let us not fail to examine any reasonable conjecture' (more fully: 'Mysterium propheticum de nece Salvatoris, de quo nunc loquebamur, paululum differimus, ne conjecturam utcunque rationabilem atque probabilem nos neglexisse videamur'). At the length of a Migne column he interprets the passage in the light of the assumption that the King referred to is Jeroboam; at five times that length he elaborates on the contrary assumption, namely that the verses are prophetic. They run as follows in the Vulgate [A.V. and Luther differ mainly in omitting reference to the city, v.4.]

3. In malitia sua laetificaverunt regem, et in mendaciis suis principes.
4. Omnes adulterantes, quasi clibanus succensus a coquente; quievit paululum civitas a commistione fermenti, donec fermentaretur totum.
5. Dies regis nostri: coeperunt principes furere a vino; extendit manum suam cum illusoribus.
6. Quia applicuerunt quasi clibanum cor suum, cum insidiaretur eis; tota nocte dormivit coquens eos, mane ipse succensus quasi ignis flammae.
7. Omnes calefacti sunt quasi clibanus, et devoraverunt judices suos; omnes reges eorum ceciderunt; non est qui clamet in eis ad me.

For us today these words are prophetic only in the sense that they are the words of a (minor) prophet. For Rupert, on the assumption (which he will in fact make) that they belong to the 'omnia de me' which Christ had said must of necessity be fulfilled, they *had* been fulfilled. Theologians will say today that Rupert was wrong: the words have no such relevance. In the centuries after Rupert and to the end of the Middle Ages the view prevailed, indeed it is a commonplace, that the Jews caroused throughout the night before Christ's trial. How does Rupert proceed?

In his preamble Rupert quotes the opening words of the prophet Hosea's final verse: 'Quis sapiens et intelliget ista, intelligens et sciat haec' (14.9), i.e. the prophet himself warns us that mere intelligence will not suffice to understand his words. When Rupert says that 'we will now consider the verses [viz. 7, 3–7] "intellectuali oculo" as prophetic', the emphasis seems to be on the 'eye' of the exegete.

'Even in Isaiah [Isaiah 1, opening verses] the sacrilege perpetuated against our Lord is prophesied.' And: 'What they did that night to our Lord and his Anointed is not unlike the sacrilege of the Sodomites',...for on that night, after they had eaten the paschal lamb: 'Crapulati et ebrii circumdederunt Dominum, et tenuerunt eum ut traderent gentibus ad illudendum, ad flagellandum et cruifigendum'. [Note that the prophet's words, or synonyms for them, are progressively introduced into the narrative statement: it is still based in the main on Matthew].

Who was the King of whom the prophecy speaks? Was it Pilate, or was it Caesar himself? In his answer to this question Rupert adduces Psalm 2.1f. and Acts 4.26 (!). The answer must be Pilate! Caiaphas and Annas are (after a good deal of argument) determined as 'the princes'. 'While the city slept' (v.4, *quievit civitas*)...'the princes drank and raved' (v.5, *coeperunt principes furere a vino*). Rupert recapitulates: 'Veraciter animo coeperunt furere, quia non jejuni aut sobrii mane, sed crapulati et ebrii comprehenderunt illum.' Here Matthew's share is reduced to the final two words.

So Rupert continues until he can claim that 'omnia quae scripta sunt' have been fulfilled, as follows: 'Omnes calefacti flamma zeli et invidiae, quasi clibanus, omnes...principes sacerdotum et ipse Pilatus, Scribae et Pharisaei, persuadentes turbis Judaeorum,...et omnia quae scripta sunt peragentes.'

That should suffice, despite substantial abridgement, to illustrate Rupert's handling of the minor prophet Hosea. Bearing in mind the skill and accuracy he displays in arranging his evidence, one will hesitate to impute a 'flamma zeli' in Rupert himself. On the contrary, one can only be astonished that such a command of Scripture was squandered in such wretched 'inventions'. It remains for us, as indicated, to compare Rupert's treatment of the same episode on the basis of St Matthew's Gospel.

One should perhaps note first that, to the extent that he quotes Matthew at all in this commentary, Rupert adduces his words as part of his own continuous exposition: Matthew confirms Old Testament prophecy. The episode we wish to consider (the mocking of Christ by the Jews) is introduced by a modified quotation from the vision of Ezekiel (1.10): 'facies autem bovis sive vituli a sinistris et facies leonis a dextris', and 'it is of this that we shall be speaking'. Here Rupert introduces a combined summary and quotation of Matthew 26.67f. and 27. 28–31, in print about fifteen lines of text. This does not mean that Rupert tells the story of the mocking (crowning, flagellation and crucifixion) of Christ. Rather, he finds in Matthew a *summa* of the 'illusiones' to which Christ was subjected 'from the left'. It was a 'duplex illusio': by the Jews and by the Gentiles, as was prophesied by Christ himself in the Psalm: 'Circumdederunt me vituli, tauri pingues obsederunt me, aperuerunt super me os suum, sicut leo rapiens et rugiens. . . Canes multi circumdederunt me' (Psalm 21.13, 17/22, 12, 16). And this prophecy gives the true order of events (confirmed by Matthew). The passage is worth quoting:

'Miro modo prophetia haec ordinem tenuit historiae sive rei gerendae, ut sicut futurum erat, et sicut factum est, quod prius a Judaeis, et deinde a gentilibus illusus et male tractatus est', col. 1574.

The equation *vituli* = Jews, *canes* = Gentiles, responsible respectively for the mocking, crowning, and the flagellation, crucifixion, is explicit. Rupert then continues to quote Psalm 21 ('foderunt manus meas et pedes meos') and Isaiah 53 to complete the picture of the Man of Sorrows (still col. 1574). There is no need to trace the further course of Rupert's commentary on Matthew (ten Migne columns) in which he treats Christ's Crucifixion as the immolation of the 'vitulus' of Aaron's sacrifice. It is by now fairly evident that the Gospel provides little more than a thread of reference for Rupert's spiritualizing glosses: Matthew's account is more or less completely 'alienated' in the process. Perhaps a residual sense of the seemly or the absurd explains why Rupert did not on this occasion insist that, in addition to being 'vituli', the Jews were sated and drunk with wine.

3. *TRINITAS CREATOR*:
WORD AND IMAGE

This essay is an abridgment and clarification of two older articles of 1956 and 1964; written in German and published without supporting illustrations, they are no longer easily accessible, and bibliographically they are overlaid.[1] In them – in the course of a controversial exchange into which I was drawn by an enquiry of Otto Pächt (see below) – I urged and argued a completely new interpretation of the opening pages of the so-called *Altdeutsche Genesis*. By 'opening pages' I mean about five-hundred lines of text and an associated first series of pictures treating the Genesis story from the Creation to the Banishment from Eden. Two manuscripts are extant: W (Vienna) and M (Millstatt). They are in fact anthologies, both Austrian, of the period 1180–1210. The first work in each is the *Altdeutsche Genesis*, followed by a *Physiologus*, then an *Exodus*;[2] M has five further pieces. We are concerned here only with the *Genesis*, a verse paraphrase of the Biblical book written in Early Middle High German, the original composition of which is dated about 1080.

About manuscripts W and M the following further details have to be noted from the outset. For literary studies the archaic text of W is naturally preferred to the late adaptation found in M; but M is also edited, and is duly considered in the continuous narrative of German literary history.[3] As for the illustrations, the opening series of miniatures is probably complete in M (and must have been present in the postulated common source *WM). In W the series is represented – after six prefatory devotional images (see below) – by *a first picture* (not completed, see illustrations, W7) and *space*s reserved in the text for the remainder of the series, indeed for all the remaining Genesis pictures (seventy-six according to M).[4] My interpretation takes account of the German text, the pictures executed and the blank

46

spaces of W: I take the latter to be evidence of a medieval artist's dilemma. His failure to continue throws light on *something*, either twelfth-century notions of iconographical propriety, or the possibility that an artist was engaged for work 'not really his line'.

A more personal consideration in turning for the third time to this subject is the need I feel finally to persuade by a better presentation of my arguments: with the hitherto missing pictures, without polemics. For whereas my article of 1964 completely convinced a number of eminent scholars on both sides of the disciplinary divide (and of the Atlantic), there is no record in print of such agreement, rather the opposite.[5] I am therefore particularly grateful to Hugo Buchthal for so generously allowing me to print his comments of 1964.[6] Indeed, I regard his and similar testimonies as my authority for making only passing reference to other readings of the same pictorial (and textual) evidence. At this point I must say a word about the title I have chosen for this essay. My primary aim is still to interpret a specific series of Genesis pictures. I deal as fully with the announced subject as the circumstances allow. If my interpretation is correct, a hitherto unfamiliar iconography of *trinitas creator* has to be accepted. *Trinitas creator* is after all a Genesis theme which can only be treated in that context.[7]

To this last remark I append some general observations to serve as an introduction to our problematic *Altdeutsche Genesis*. First, about the repertory of medieval Christian art in relation to the Genesis *story*. The story required of the artist a cycle of 'historical' pictures reflecting Scripture as understood in its first 'literal' (historical) sense – rather than a selection of 'devotional' pictures for pious contemplation. Sacred story had to be so presented that it could be read into (and from) the images in succession, whether or not there was to be a supporting text or scheme of rubrics. Art history knows a number of early Genesis cycles (represented for example by the Vienna Genesis[8] and the Cotton Genesis); they were evolved by ecclesiastical artists in the older patriarchates of the Eastern Mediterranean. The particular problem raised by our manuscripts (W)M is that they are evidence of a picture-cycle of ultimately such (Eastern) origin,[9] brought *tant bien que mal* into register with a Western *literary* tradition (starting with Avitus, d. 519) of Biblical paraphrase, the latter necessarily reflecting Western exegesis concerning *inter alia* the 'persons' involved in the Genesis story as it unfolds.

Until relatively recently, art historians sought to exploit the *pictures only* of our manuscript M, and to interpret them in the light of other known Genesis cycles in whatever medium – e.g. whether they appear in illustrated manuscripts or in mosaics. To the extent that the German text of the *Altdeutsche Genesis* has (latterly) been considered, it has been imperfectly understood. Early Middle High German is not easy reading, even for specialists in Middle High German. At any rate it has not been allowed to influence the interpretation of the enigmatic picture-series, Creation to Banishment. This reluctance to consider evidence of the text which the pictures were deemed (by someone!) to illustrate, is of course understandable. Vernacular texts have in themselves no authority and can never have been the sole 'source' of an iconographical convention of any importance. Yet it explains the failure to recognize the teaching of the Western Church as this is reflected in the text, particularly its teaching concerning the Creation as the work, not of God the Father alone (or of the Logos), but of the Holy Trinity: *trinitas creator*. To be fair, the learned editors of the text have recognized it and annotated it with reference to other Early Middle High German *texts*. If they thought they should say something about the pictures too, they have set down what the art historians told them to: merely described the pictures; they have offered only some very tentative identifications of individual pictures, not of the series. The series *as* series is in fact the record of a bold essay in iconography, representing *trinitas creator* 'historically' through five scenes, deliberating, then acting. The very strangeness (to us) of the solution has led to some guess-work delaying final recognition. Other strange, even wayward

48

solutions have been recognized and have been duly registered in the more compendious handbooks of Christian iconography.[10] Briefly, in twelfth-century art we must in future be prepared to encounter *two* figures representing the Trinity.[11] On this more will be said in a moment.

Matters are further complicated in our Genesis series by the opening 'scene' (M1, W7). The basic drawing-pattern used here is one customarily used, particularly at the head of a work, to depict the dedication of the work itself to whoever commissioned or inspired it. The pattern is, however, so heavily modified that the appropriate reading cannot possibly be, even in W7, 'Moses dedicates his completed work to God (or the Logos)'. Doubts raised by a proposal of H. Menhardt (1954)[12] – that one should recognize instead 'God and an archangel' (conferring on the replacement of the Fallen Angels) – led Otto Pächt to consult me on the possibility of such a theme (did I know it from literature?). After a preliminary essay for Pächt (followed by my article of 1956 and a doctoral dissertation by Hella Voss of 1962 countering most of my suggestions in her complete survey of the pictures of M), I had by 1964 committed myself to the following account, to which I still adhere. Though the subject is known (indeed, is present in *Altdeutsche Genesis*, folio 2 recto in M, 2 verso in W), and a consideration of artistic tradition alone might permit such an identification of the two figures, the German rubric for the picture (folio 3 recto in M) reads: 'here ye shall note how God determined to create man'.[13] There follows, moreover, in the main text a verse paraphrase of 'faciamus hominem' and a lengthy description of man's body from head to foot, omitting nothing. Proper identification is not possible until we come to the verses after picture M2, stating 'this was a work pleasing to both, the Father and the Son; the Holy Spirit was...with Him'. The German for the last part is 'was al mit ime'. One may debate in what sense 'al' (adv. 'completely') is to be understood, see below, but not dispute the singular 'with him', though the editor Diemer thought the meaning might be 'with

49

W 6

W 7

M 1   M 2

Trinitas creator. Illustrations in the *Old German Genesis*, manuscript W (after Voss) and manuscript M (after Diemer), greatly reduced.

М 3   М 4

М 6   М 9

М 10   М 11

each'. Then follows the Trinity doctrine in the form: 'note in addition, the one has three names: He as the Wisdom of the Father acted with the guidance of the Holy Spirit'. This is surely the explanation of the *two* figures who create and then animate Adam (M2, M3), and in all probability of the two figures in M1, W7. Proof of this must, however, await the *rejection* of the proposed alternative, below, but let us assume the interpretation is correct. The text intended for the scroll is in any case 'faciamus hominem' – as in the long scroll held by *three* like, but differentiated figures representing *trinitas creator* in the *Hortus Deliciarum* (Alsatian, twelfth century) of Herrad of Landsberg.[14] I suggest that that may be a preferable formula in a *devotional* picture; but where, as in the *Genesis*, a narrative sequence has to be sustained, the theologically correct role 'the Son as the Wisdom of the Father' provides a welcome reduction of figures to *two*. With this amount of guidance readers may now wish to examine in a provisional way pictures M1 to M11. (Lacking in the illustrations are M5, 7 and 8, with the following conventionally treated subjects: Adam names the animals, Eve is tempted, Adam accepts the apple.) What 'persons' are represented? And if it is thought that the 'extra person' is the Holy Spirit, how shall that presence be justified in each case?

Before discussing the pictures in turn (and the series as a narrative sequence) I shall deal with the oddity which will have been noticed and which first seemed to me to justify interruption of a too exclusively art-historical discussion – to draw attention to the German text, see M4. What are those strange 'hanging' objects? (They hang, if from anything, from the rules for the two preceding lines of text.) Pächt (and Günter Bandmann) immediately declared themselves convinced by my explanation. They are a lower and a higher scale-pan (*cum* fruit-basket). A generously aimed photographic lens will pick up with the picture the lines: 'in the middle of the garden Mighty God planted two sturdy trees; he bade them bear an unequal yield' (*Wucher*, 'increase'). Menhardt's suggestion (followed by Voss in 1962) that these are purely decorative and space-filling 'hanging bowls' (*Hängekromen*), for which the model must be sought elsewhere, will surely some day be abandoned.

Let us now, finally, take the pictures in turn, M1 and W7 still at some length, despite what was said above, partly because the artist of W abandoned his task here, leaving even this first Genesis scene incomplete.

M1, W7. Left a youthful figure, lightly bearded, with cross-pattern on nimbus, enthroned. Right, a second figure (winged, with halo, in M). An unscripted scroll is held by both. [It is intended to receive the words of the enthroned figure (see gesture of speaking): 'faciamus hominem'.]

As an artist's exemplar, that is (before the identification of the figures by feature, attributes etc.) the formula for the dedication of a work, the conferment of an instrument (or insignia) of authority – to be read from left or right according to the case. The youthful, enthroned figure is, it was suggested, intended as 'the Son, Wisdom of the Father'. The figure to the right is, I believe, the Holy Spirit in the first of five appearances (M1, 2, 3, 6, 9; of these M3 is clearly the most important; the rest are graded according to the occasion). The Holy Spirit is of course 'normally' (and in general recollection) represented by a dove, particularly in the so-called 'Throne of Grace',[15] which, however, is a later convention. Here we have a winged figure. The hovering 'angel' in M2 is more readily acceptable as the Holy Spirit (text, context). Given that a picture-cycle is a cycle, the 'angel' in M1 may be claimed also as the Holy Spirit.

This interpretation of M1 has, I am sure, not yet convinced completely. We must therefore look just once more at the suggestion 'God and an archangel'. Even if not demanded by the German rubric and text, the words 'faciamus hominem' would still have to be assumed as the content of the scroll: the next picture represents the creation of man. But we should then have an angel included by God in the pronouncement '...in our image', *and* a combined intention to fill the empty choir.

The theologians had of course long ago had to answer the question 'in whose likeness?' Take Isidore of Seville for instance, of whose *De fide catholica contra Judaeos* there is a splendid Old High German translation:

> Quod si respondeant, ad angelorum. Num angelus aequalem cum Deo habet imaginem, dum multum distet imago creaturae ab eo qui creavit? Aut numquid angelus cum Deo potuit facere hominem? Quod *ita existimare magnae dementiae est*. [The likeness is 'with God'.]

That was Isidore's conclusion on the question of 'similitude'. On 'faciamus hominem' he had already said:

> Per pluralitatem personarum patens significatio *Trinitas* est.[16]

Now we have assembled most of the evidence for explaining the failure of the miniaturist of manuscript W to complete W7. (The missing wings are in fact said to be present in silver-point outline.) The exercise of a little imagination will be needed to make the points in a plausible order. He did *not*, for instance, say 'God and an archangel, that is a *magna dementia*', and flounce out of the scriptorium – at least not immediately. He seems rather to have assumed that at, or at any rate near, the head of the text, for we are at his fol. 5 verso, the drawing required was his rather strange 'dedication'. It must, however, have become clear (from the pictures and rubrics ahead in the immediate source?) that he was on unfamiliar ground. If the scenes to come were supposed to represent the Trinity they were 'not in the book' (*sc.* his pattern-book). He had already drawn *his* Trinity, see W6, the sixth of six prefatory pictures 'for this book':[17] *three* like, but differentiated figures, the Logos on the right, the unity of the Trinity marked by the single and 'special' nimbus for God the Father. Clearly hieratic images were this artist's *métier*, not historical cycles. He may in our estimation be the better artist, but he was less versatile than the illustrator of M – and their common predecessor. He was released, I suggest – and not replaced.

M2.   Together with M3 this represents the creation, then the animation of Adam. First, the creation. According to the text (see above): 'the Holy Spirit was with Him' (*sc*. the Father and the Son, or the 'Son as Wisdom of the Father'). Moreover the Spirit was present 'al', for which a gloss might be 'vi compare'.[18] Note that the Vulgate here has 'formavit igitur Dominus Deus hominem', singular verb for a narrative statement. The verse paraphrase on the other hand incorporates the Church's teaching concerning *trinitas creator*, while the matching drawing attends to representation of this teaching and 'continuity'. (The text is expansive on God as 'workman', taking clay, fashioning man.)

M3. At the animation of Adam the Son (Wisdom) blesses Adam and 'blows into him his spirit' (Vulg. 'spiritaculum vitae'). In this, its principal appearance, the Holy Spirit is ornately vested in high-priestly apparel and wields a trefoil sceptre. That the latter in this context alludes to the unity of the Trinity is a possible inference, or one may think of the 'alma sceptra' of the Holy Spirit held on behalf of the Trinity – in a vesper hymn of Alcuin.[19]

M4. Adam between the two trees in Eden, discussed above: from this scene the Trinity is absent; it cannot witness Adam's choice. [The artist has in fact drawn an Eve. All writers seem to agree to overlook this slip. See M6, the *creation* of Eve.]

M5. Adam names the animals (not in illustrations). This is a vivid picture (one of several in the *Genesis* to suggest that the artist of M knew that a *Physiologus* lay ahead). Here God the Father, with full beard and nimbus as in M10, leads Adam to the animals and invites him to name them. There is no allusion here to *trinitas creator*. One recalls that there is no picture in our manuscript to represent the *creation* of the animals (birds, fishes, reptiles).[20]

M6. The raising of Eve from Adam's side. In the medieval view this was a less important occasion for the Holy Spirit, and wings and sceptre have disappeared. According to the German text it was magnanimous of the Spirit to appear at all (not a quotation, an inference), when 'the maid' was thus raised from the body of 'the man' (a reflection of the usual etymology

55

'virago a vir', cf. Gen. 2.23). The retention of the Holy
Spirit, was, however, essential, for God had said 'faciamus ei
adjutorium', with the same use of the plural as in 'faciamus
hominem'.[21]

M7, M8. The Temptation and the Fall. The Trinity is
again rightly absent.

M9. What is to be said of the weeping figure (left) supporting the familiar youthful figure (the Son, Wisdom)?

I am relieved to be able to offer an improved interpretation of
this image. I no longer wish to see any 'possible allusion' to
Misericordia, one of the four 'Daughters of God', for that is an
exegete's allegory based on Psalm 84.11/85.10 and applied to
the lot of man at his Fall: the suggestion was unnecessary and
methodically unsound. I hope that the following explanation
will also be more acceptable to Buchthal.

It now seems to me that poet and artist here part company for
a while. The poet keeps to the *historical* line represented by the
German rubric: 'how, after nones, God reproached Adam and
his helpmeet Eve for their transgression of his commandment'.
He appends a short homily in which he of course bemoans this
outcome, but says nothing of the Trinity: he has already been
explicit on the subject. The artist on the other hand is concerned
with pictorial continuity, and must at the same time prepare for
the 'editing out' of his second figure. In a way it was a technical
necessity for him to draw a reduced form, but, at the same time
again, his choice of the *doctrinal* line is correct, for God's words
at this point are 'Ecce Adam quasi *unus ex nobis*'. He is,
moreover, not alone in asserting a continued presence of the
Trinity *or* in representing the occasion as 'grievous'. Though I
could have wished for a similarly complete statement of slightly
earlier date, I now find the following passage both helpful and
illuminating. It is from the *Historia Scholastica* of Petrus
Comestor (*c.* 1179) – our most reliable source always for the
sensus historialis (twelfth century) of the Biblical word:

'Ecce Adam factus est quasi unus ex nobis': ironia est, quasi voluit esse
ut Deus, sed in evidenti est modo, quod non est. Nec est vox insultantis,

sed *vox a superbia corrigentis*, et est *vox Trinitatis*. Vel est *vox Dei ad angelos* et est *vox plangentis*, quod patet, quia factus est a me ut esset quasi unus ex nobis, si stetisset.[22]

If we disregard the alternative 'vox Dei ad angelos' (which is 'wrong' according to 'similitude' teaching, but right in that man was meant to replace the fallen angels), we have here confirmation, if not the actual source, of what we see represented in M9: the addressing of words correcting pride, words of sorrow at the Fall of Man – by the Trinity. One may then recall Ephesians 4.30ff., 'Nolite contristare spiritum sanctum'. The artist identifies the Holy Spirit by halo alone; the last vestiges of priestly apparel have gone.

M10. The banishment from Eden by God the Father – alone. The Holy Spirit's role is, for the time being suspended, i.e. until the appearance of the three angels to Abraham (folio 27 recto) where the 'angel' to the right in the group of three at table is recognizably the Holy Spirit, carried forward from M9, and the group is unmistakably the Trinity, not so much prefigured as postfigured.

M11. To guard the Tree and the gates of Eden the artist draws not the difficult 'engel cherubin' of which the German text speaks, but presumably an angel (with halo), versatile no doubt, as Scripture says, and wielding a 'fiery sword'. Whether one needs (with Voss) to invoke specifically St Michael, or see rather a final use of a drawing-pattern which has become available for other employment, may seem in retrospect to be a merely residual problem. A properly-drawn cherub would have been a startling image in this context.

If and when this interpretation is generally accepted by art historians, it may be appropriate for a fresh scrutiny to be made of Western Genesis cycles, and among the tasks to be tackled will be the identification of the prefatory pictures in manuscript W, the five which precede the Trinity (W6). Hella Voss confessed herself unable to identify these. This led to her strange caption 'Christ between two saints' for W6 (her illustr. 23).

As one of the pictures (folio 2 recto) has already been tentatively claimed as a 'Fall of Lucifer', the question of the pictorial content of the hypothetical common source *WM is raised afresh: had it too a sequence of prefatory pictures, prefatory because the text of *Altdeutsche Genesis* moves too fast in its opening sections? These are, however, matters for separate treatment. For the rest, will art historians now wish to adduce other instances of the representation of *trinitas creator* by two figures, a youthful deity and a supporting winged figure?

ADDENDUM

On some six occasions in recent years (in North America, and at the Conference of University Teachers of German in Canterbury, March 1977) I have delivered a lecture-version of the above contribution, displaying a fuller range of illustrative material than I am able to reproduce here. I showed *inter alia* all six of the Vienna Genesis pictures, and offered and invited comment. It may therefore be helpful if I state that I shall limit any further contribution of my own to suggestions concerning these, and the opening series of pictures in the postulated common source (*WM) of manuscripts W and M.

4. JUSTUS LIPSIUS' *DE CRUCE LIBRI TRES* (1593), OR THE HISTORIAN'S DILEMMA

Officially and finally, that is to say some twelve years after its publication, Lipsius' *De Cruce* of 1593 had been classed as one of his many works 'on Antiquity'.[1] There seems to be little doubt that when it was first published the additional hope had been entertained by Lipsius and his Jesuit friends that it might be accounted a work (at least in part) on the Christian Religion. We cannot overlook the fact that *De Cruce* was written by one brought up by the Jesuits, but who had spent his most brilliant and public years in Jena, outside the fold (by turns Lutheran and Calvinist). He had been brought back to Louvain by persuasion and some official pressure. It was expedient that as a re-convert he should again be seen to be a good Catholic after all.[2]

De Cruce was accordingly offered to the *Tres Ordines Brabantiae*, the Church, the Nobility and the Magistrature in that order. Beside Lipsius' own dedicatory epistle there are the usual commendations, including an *Epigramma* by Maximilian de Vriendt which acclaims Lipsius, *quasi* a second Constantine, as having rescued the true Cross from partial oblivion. The full title moreover – *De Cruce, Libri Tres ad Sacram Profanamque Historiam Utiles* – suggests a devout work. But if it was hoped in 1593 that *De Cruce* might contribute usefully to the required image of Lipsius, this 'Rehabilitationsschrift' must be deemed a failure. At any rate, about ten years later, Lipsius took more drastic steps, which some of his friends thought dubiously helpful and seem to have regretted. These are his short monographs on two local shrines, and the miracles attributed to them, the so-called *Diva Hallensis* 1604 and the *Diva Aspricollis* 1605.[3] We should probably want to classify them as early examples of 'Kitsch', the more distasteful in that the learned

59

author is at such transparent pains to shed the scholar in favour of the simple devotee. As if this were not enough, Lipsius also dedicated to the former shrine his author's quill, with the customary lines; to another shrine his doctor's gown – the occasion evidently of still further scandal.[4] He died in 1606.

But what may have been the impact of *De Cruce* on any devout contemporary who opened it, not at the title-page, but at one of the engravings? A cupid strung up in a tree (say Fig. 1); or, against an ideal landscape background, a heavily-built, muscular male in loin-cloth, gazing open-eyed at the point of the stake coming out of his gullet, and on which he is in fact impaled (Fig. 3), and so on; malefactors under the *patibulum*, or crucified head down, or assailed by wild beasts, or being burnt at the stake. The victims mostly show a stoical calm. It is not the kind of work one leaves lying around. It is of course easy enough to say that Lipsius is a *bona fide* historian, that evidence is evidence, a drawing is clearer than a description and that *De Cruce* really means 'concerning capital punishment' etc. There remains an element of doubt, as with the genus 'Sittengeschichte'.

As for the complete work – all the detailed, scholarly enquiry with copious quotations from the Fathers, and the sacred subject to which Lipsius had on the whole quite seriously bent his mind and devoted much of his book: it is surely significant that friends and supporters could never claim more than that Lipsius had 'published a study on the holy cross' (*monumenta sacrae crucis celebravit*) and had 'read widely in the Fathers'. (We shall have to look at this 'wide reading' in a moment.) Even when the theme was Lipsius 'of pious memory', as we find him treated in part of the *Fama Postuma* of 1607, there are only about half a dozen references in all to the work. They are in roughly the same sparse terms. One is a statement that he 'wrote it here' (in Louvain).[5] It is with greater confidence that his friends listed *De Cruce* as one of Lipsius' works 'on Antiquity'. The case, such as it was, for his piety had to be made instead on the basis of the *Diva Hallensis* and *Diva Aspricollis*, the 'wide reading' and the undoubted orthodoxy of his death-bed conversation with his Jesuit confessor.[6] Had there not been calumniators to answer and a broadsheet to be discredited,[7] it is possible that his friends would have kept to the 'great example' Lipsius had given of devotion to scholarship, which was his *métier*, and his Stoic resignation – in the spirit of his own Foreword to *De Constantia.*

With those reservations we may now consider more closely at what point *De Cruce*, as a work 'on Antiquity', fitted into Lipsius' economy of historical studies. We may be guided by a famous letter of December 1600 to Nicolas Hacqueville (*Epist. Cent.* III *Misc.*, No. 61). Lipsius's correspondent had evidently begun to flounder in his study of history. Lipsius gives him a programme, indeed a complete theory of historical study. Some of the statements concern us directly, and precisely because they were written after *De Cruce.*[8]

Lipsius begins with a long series of distinctions between the different kinds of history. First between *Mithystoria* and *Historia*, of which the former is a mixture of fact and fiction, the province of poets *et id genus*; the latter with 'true and noteworthy facts'. Though the poets, particularly Homer, delight us, they also transmit much that is important for the historian; but that line of study is 'not to be embarked upon yet'. *Vera Historia* sub-divides into *Naturalis* (e.g. Pliny) and *Narrativa*; *Narrativa* (treating *gestas actionesque...sacras et profanas*) comprises *Divina* and *Humana*, the latter *Privata* and *Publica*. Of all these *Historia Narrativa* should take precedence, but 'one will need a grounding in *Geographia* (a general knowledge of places and regions) and *Chronologia* (*notitiam communem...non exactam exigo*)'. Here there are difficulties: 'I often wish someone would provide us with a brief but comprehensive and critical survey of world history (*breviter et compendia, et quod caput est, judicio*) by periods (*velut Fasti*)': 'just the dates and main events, noted, briefly touched upon'. The attempts that have so far been made are 'unselective or muddled (*aut confundunt nimis, aut diffundunt*), or have missed the most important things out'. Until there is such a survey: 'use Eusebius and various of the more recent writers'. Having prepared in this way we can then proceed to 'history proper' (*age ad ipsam historiam*). Piety would suggest that we start with *Historia Divina*. 'This is easy and will not detain us long.' For *Judaica* use Holy Scripture, and Josephus with Hegesippus' commentary. For our *Historia Christiana*: 'we used to get it from Eusebius and Sozomen, but now one uses Cæsare Baronio.[9] But what is lacking in the work of this most assiduous scholar? Very much, I am afraid, especially for those who are not trained theologians. . . .It is enough for us historians to know the main facts: origins, developments, the principal figures. I don't deny that Baronio's history is a work of exact and compendious scholarship, but *Humana Historia* is the thing to go for (*Humana superest*).' The moral value of historical studies is stressed, but Lipsius presses on to give a select bibliography for the study of *Humana Historia*, under the four headings Oriental, Greek, Roman and Barbarian. On Oriental he is brief, on Roman eloquent, the Greeks he rushes. Under the fourth heading he offers cautious advice on editions of 'barbarian' historians to supplement Jordanes and Procopius etc. Next come exhortations to care and assiduity: there must be no planless browsing. Notes are to be entered under four headings: *Memorabilia* ('outstanding' events etc.), *Ritualia* (ceremonial, rites, public and private), *Civilia* (law and government) and *Moralia*.

Lipsius gives more detailed guidance under *Ritualia* where he distinguishes *sacra* and *profana*. Notes on 'gods' should include: *nomina, cognomina, insignia, munia, cultus*; and *templa, sacerdotes, sacrificia* (etc.), even *verba solemnia*. (*Ritualia*) *profana* are either *publica* or *privata*. *Publica* include: *leges, judicia et eorum ratio, supplicia, tormenta, poenae*.

This, then, is the point where Lipsius' *De Cruce* belongs: under *Ritualia-profana-publica*. Immediately after, and still under this heading the following topics call to mind other works by Lipsius: *ludi et spectacula* (*De Gladiatoribus* 1582, *De Amphiteatro* 1584). Lest it be thought frivolous of me to point out that *De Cruce* is to be placed according to this scheme of things in close proximity with *ludi et spectacula*, I cite a testimonial of 1607 written by a Jesuit 'in the antique style'. It lists *De Cruce* as one of Lipsius' 'gifts to the people'; Lipsius, we learn, was therefore himself a *Munerarius* (a provider of public spectacles), but with one difference: *sanguine ludus caruit*.[10] I am insufficiently acclimatized in the conceits of the Humanists not to find this latter observation somewhat startling, and I react in much the same way when the same *ritus priscus* requires Lipsius' Christian orthodoxy to be referred to as a *cura Tonantis*.[11] But fortified by these examples of the Humanist's fancies, one will perhaps more readily accept

Lipsius' characterization of some of the more wayward notions of the Fathers as *inventiculae Patrum*.

The purpose of the remainder of this essay is to review the contents of *De Cruce* with particular reference to what I have called the historian's dilemma. Since the work was published under such ambiguous auspices we shall be wise to be critical, even sceptical. The 'wide reading of the Fathers' will have to be looked at. We shall find in fact that the quotations from the Fathers are copious rather than discriminating. Lipsius is in addition occasionally flippant, perhaps contemptuous of patristic lore. He seems unable or unwilling to distinguish between patristic statements based on the 'historical' and on the 'allegorical' sense of Scripture. This of course makes nonsense of many of his quotations [and denies him access to the real sources of Christian Crucifixion iconography]. In practically every case where 'hallowed tradition' and historical evidence are at variance, he becomes sanctimonious and says that 'the Fathers and Christian art are right'; as a historian Lipsius capitulates! Should he not have seen, and said boldly, that the 'truth' and 'historical facts' are the concerns of two systems of enquiry, different branches of knowledge – exegesis and historical research? As for his efforts in the latter field, it is worth noting that Lipsius is still quoted, in New Testament Commentaries and elsewhere (*Konversationslexika*); whether he is read is another matter. (It would surely be wiser to quote, if anything, the article *crux* in Pauly-Wissowa, which already contains the historian's necessary *captatio benevolentiae* for ignoring 'hallowed tradition'.)[12] The conclusions which Lipsius drew concerning capital punishment in Antiquity are in the main no doubt still acceptable. He obscured the issues, however, by his *mélange des genres* [...]

There remains a doubt. Could anyone in Lipsius' day have explained the iconography of the Crucifixion? The fallacy that failure to 'find the place' in the Fathers must be evidence of historical reminiscence (or the growth of legend) was probably well established by Lipsius' day. It is at bottom a failure to distinguish between and segregate *historia profana* and *historia sacra* in a scholarly way. Lipsius elected instead to make his operatic gesture of submission to the Fathers which seems to have convinced nobody.

De Cruce libri tres

For convenience I have reported on L's appended *Notes* in their intended context. Spellings are adjusted; references are to Book and Chapter only. Except where I use square brackets I am quoting or summarizing Lipsius' arguments.

PREFACES etc.

(i) L's own dedicatory address to the Bishops, Nobility and Magistrature of Brabant.

(ii) L's *Ad Lectorem* disowns previous *schedia* (drafts) and *opera*, and anything on this subject printed without his formal approval: 'for we do not wish such things to be deposited in the Temple of Memory'.[13] He has been concerned not to write anything *præter religionem moresque veterum.*

(iii) An *Elegy* by Joh. Bochius addressed to all *Principes Christiani* calls on them to 'join hands beneath the "banner of Christ" lest all should perish'. [There is in this most eloquent but conventional invocation a good deal of typological play upon the ignominious *lignum* of the O.T. and the glorious *arbor* of the new dispensation, with allusions to the 'harrowing' of the forces of discord.]

(iv) De Vriendt's *Epigram* (see p. 59) compares L to Constantine in the form: *Fallor? an et JUSTUS sive Cæsaris æmulis, atra/Nocte laborantem tollit ad astra Crucem.* [*Cæsar* is glossed as *Constantinus* in the margin.]

(v) An *Epigram* of Michael van der Haghen of Antwerp commends the work for describing the *supplicium crucis* 'to a nicety': *Supplicium Crucis ille vetus describit ad unguem/Quale fuit, nostram salvificamque crucem.*

(vi) A *Verse* by Balthasar Moretus.

BOOK I

CHAPTER I is an *Avis au lecteur* (*precatiuncula*) giving the plan of L's investigation according to the traditional pattern *quid Crux, cujusmodi. . .ubi. . .quare,* etc. He invokes to his aid Christ (*qui*) *infame illud lignum instrumentum fecisti publicae salutis;* 'grant me to write the truth to thy honour and the glory of thy Cross and our benefit'. In CH. II the

64

range of meaning of *crux* is discussed, which more loosely may refer even to killing by drowning. In the *Notes* to this Chapter, L says that according to Mart. Antonio Delrio [del Rio] *gabalum* is a Hebrew word (*gab* = *excelsum*, *gabal* 'boundary post'). He now thinks of German *Galgen*; in the main text he had been reminded rather of *Gabel*. [His first thought was correct; Med. Lat. *gabalum* is based on the Germanic; the Hebrew word in the Deuteronomic code, *Deut.* 21.22–3 is *ets*, Vulg. *patibulum* and *lignum*.] Because of the meaning 'touchstone', Greek *basanos* will be 'enquiry by torture'. In Cicero, Seneca and Livy occur *lignum infelix*, *damnata crux* [this information may be intended as a gloss on the *lignum infame*, *mors turpissima* of Christian idiom]. *Crux* can be used of any *fixio*; Tertullian uses *cruces Caucasorum* of the fate of Prometheus. Ch. III deals with the verbs associated with *crux*: – *figere*, *cruciare*. The *Notes* interpret (with Isidore, *Etym* X, 49) *cruciarius* as 'fit to be, having been, crucified'. Ch. IV deals with Greek nouns and verbs. L lists *stauros* and *skolops* which he glosses as 'pale' and 'stake' (*palus*, *vallus*). (A *Note* adds *ikrion* 'mast', to the list of nouns.) After a passing comment – *jocosa derivatio!* – on an attempt of Lucian [of Samosata] to derive *stauros* from *Tau*, L proceeds to the Greek verbs for to 'nail' and 'fasten', *proseloō*, *kremannumi*, and the verbs derived from *stauros* and *skolops*. In the quotation of sources he keeps to the historians and poets, and arrives at the conclusion that *stauros* and *skolops* are indeed *single* stakes or pales, set upright, and that malefactors were nailed or hanged or impaled on them. [What is here so remarkable is L's absolute silence on the fact that *stauros* is used for Christ's cross throughout the Greek N.T.; that *xulon* is used in the Greek N.T. in any reference to the 'hanging from a tree' in the spirit of the Deuteronomic code; further that in considering *pendere* he does not note the Vulgate use of *pendere* in these same contexts: Matthew 18.6, 22.40, Luke 23.39, Acts 5.30 etc. Instead he insists that a *stauros* consists of *one* stake or beam. Later he will accept the *crux immissa* (of *two* beams) as the 'real cross', and heartily agree in this with the Fathers. This is indeed a dilemma. Could L rely on his Catholic readers' adherence to the Vulgate only? With *crux* he could harmonize Christian Cross-lore; the evidence in the case of *stauros* silenced him. Why did he not say that *stauros* is used in the N.T. in a sense 'not found in *historia profana*'?]

In Ch. V Lipsius passes from 'words' to a closer consideration of 'things', but first restricts himself to *affixiones* and *infixiones in uno simplicique ligno*. Dealing with the crucifixion of Cupid by Proserpine (in Ausonius), he provides an engraving, and the negative comment: *nec manibus expansis...nec clavis sed funibus*. [This is an *argumentum ex silentio*, betraying L's anxiety to establish the Christian crucifixion (*with* extended hands, with nails) by 'distinctions'. Again, when he says that, according to the Martyrology, Paphnutius was hanged from a palm tree, we should take his comment, 'other trees were also used', to be an anticipation of 'Wood of the Cross' questions, on which he will have something to say.]

CH. VI is notable for its engraving of an impaling (anal) and notes on *ana-skolopizō* ('to impale'). CH. VII brings us to the artefact – the *crux compacta,...manufacta e duplici ligno*, the 'cross proper', the *xulon didumon* of the Septuagint, where however, as Lipsius notes, the Vulgate uses common terms such as *lignum* [or *patibulum*]. He cites Joshua, 8.29.

L next runs through the possible crosses consisting of two beams: *decussata* (X), *commissa* (T) and *immissa*. [Here L's attitude to any kind of cross-symbolism and typology is mainly one of levity and irreverence. Jerome's comparison of the *decussata* with the letter X surely merits more serious annotation than a ponderous reference to Isidore: not to Isidore on capital punishment, but on the alphabet! One readily concedes that the Fathers are 'often less clear' than this.] L claims not to be sure how to deal with the Fathers' association of the cross [the *decussata*] with Jacob's blessing with crossed hands of Ephraim and Manasseh [Gen. 48.13f.]: *et sic mihi libido aliquando legere: sed refraeno et accipio Christum crucifixum*. Typology of this kind he evidently finds 'rather amusing'. In his discussion of the Tau-cross in CH. VIII (his authorities are various early Fathers and Isidore) he finds 'some support in art for this'. [Indeed he should; but this does not *appear* to be associated in his mind with the smearing of the Blood of the Lamb, with Moses raising the brazen serpent, with the serpent on the historiated *Te igitur* initial of his Missal. This is of course all irrelevant in a historian's enquiry, but it will be seen that when it suits him, L considers other senses of the scriptural word than the first, historical sense.] At the end of this section there is a fatuous contribution of L's own to cross-symbolism; he pretends to note a formal resemblance between the Tau-cross and homely crutches, 'which moreover we call *cruckas*'. [This flippancy is probably meant to serve as an *Auftakt* to his performance in the next Chapter. Thinking again of the note-book he kept for *Memorabilia*, one imagines it must have had a sizeable section for *Lascivia!*]

The title of CH. IX states the conclusion of this part of the enquiry: *Crux immissa e scriptis maxime Patrum affirmata*. [This is of course true, but Lipsius' procedure is pretty scandalous. Knowing that his Roman and Greek historians provide him with no evidence for such a cross – in the same way as they had proved that a *stauros* is not a cross in the conventional sense at all, but a pole – he fills a couple of pages with all the silliest Cross-imagery he had found, or had pointed out to him, in the Fathers, from breast-stroke swimmers to the *orans*, from birds in flight to the points of the compass; the shaft of a wagon for a team of oxen, yokes, ploughs, etc.; *fasces, tropaeum* and so on. I have put the *orans* into this list in imitation of L's lack of discrimination. The *orans – Christus orans* ('pater ignosce illis') – is the starting point of Christian Cross-iconography. Much of the rest of the imagery was about due to be discarded, or allowed to rest, even by Catholics.] As L again finds these things 'rather amusing', he gives good measure: *quae pluscula posui, quia me quoque inter exscribendum delectarunt inventiculae istae Patrum.* [His struggle in this section to understand patristic interpretations of the O.T. *cornu* ('horn of salvation' etc.), and the 'unicorn' as it is occasionally exploited in Cross-allegory, are referred to below, in the summary of Book II, Ch. X, 'footrest'.]

In CH. X Lipsius asks: 'on what kind of a cross did Christ die?' He is now necessarily (in the light of Ch. IX) involved in a *petitio principii*, annotating the Fathers and the Christian Latin poets by references to Christian art, and *vice versa*. He chooses his idiom accordingly:[14] *in qua earum* (of the three kinds of cross, *decussata*, etc.) *ille mortuus, qui morte suâ nobis vita? In illâ inquam [inquam!] quae quattuor finibus universum orbem complexa est, non sine mysterio.* For this he gives as his authority the fifth-century poet Sedulius: *Neve quis ignoret speciem Crucis esse colendam;/Quae Dominum portavit ovans.* The 'four ends' of the Cross lead naturally to the words of St Paul (Ephes. 3.18), on its *latitudo, longitudo, sublimitas* and *profunditas*. Next comes St Augustine on Psalm 103/104. The Fathers, the poets and the artists agree! 'Winged genii support a Cross of just this shape in the monuments of Constantine; one cannot well doubt a tradition of such antiquity' (*Nec meo sensu, ambigi profecto potest in tam veteri Christianorum sensu*). 'But some adhere to the belief that it was a Tau-Cross, nor is this entirely blameworthy, for Pilate's added *titulus* would complete the *crux immissa.*'

In CH. XI Lipsius returns to his History. He refers briefly to the 'cross' of the Syrians (Esther), the Jews (Josh. Ch. 8 – the King of Ai): it occurs 'often in Scripture'; on then to Thucydides, Herodotus (*Thalia* III, 25 – Polycrates) and Plutarch (Alexander's crucifying of Glaucus and others). 'If Livy is to be believed the custom goes back to the earliest Roman kings.' Tacitus writes of the Germani: *proditores et transfugas arboribus suspendunt*, 'but this may mean death by strangulation'. A *Note* quotes from the Law of the Lombards: *si servus...Morth fecerit...super fossam mortui appendatur* [as in Grimm, *Dt. Rechtsalter-thümer*, II, 263f.].

CH. XII. The Roman evidence suggests that the *crux* was a *supplicium servile*; according to Livy there may have been a form of capital punishment for each man according to his station at a given time (his *fortuna*):

67

crux, gladius, securis in ascending order; 'but for serious offences only, in any case'.

CH. XIII. Lactantius had asked why Christ, if he as God wished to die, should have chosen this, the vilest form of death, which even a guilty freeman would have been spared. One can limit this statement, says L, for even a guilty *civis* could, within the law, not be condemned to the *crux*. Thieves (witness the Gospels), murderers and forgers *could* be so condemned.

In CH. XIV Lipsius goes through the motions of asking, *pie non curiose*, on what pretext, 'for cause there was none', Christ was condemned to the *crux*; he provides the commonplace answer: *Mihi videatur et respondeam*, he begins, *damnatum innoxium nostrum agnum*. [His use of *agnus noster* in an ostensibly historical work raises the question whether L is inviting his readers to see his dilemma and exonerate him (or to recognize the tongue in the cheek?). If so, I should say he does so convincingly at this and one or two other points only.] L runs through the charges brought against Christ by the Jews, quotes a bit of Roman law on sedition, looks at the Deuteronomic code, refers to the *rex* in Pilate's *titulus*, and pretends to quarrel with Philo on a point of detail. Suddenly he breaks off and says: 'but this is a complicated dance-figure for theologians only'. There is, however, here and there evidence (CH. XV) for irregular use (*ex ordine et more*) of the *crux*. Alexander crucified Kings; Quintilian and Josephus also cite examples. [He takes the chance of referring to Josephus' dubious story of the procuress Ide (*Antiqu.* XVIII, iii, 4), and the high rank of sundry martyrs in the Martyrology.]

BOOK II

CH. I is a summary of Book I; *quid, cujusmodi, ubi,* and *quare* have been dealt with; the *crux* was the *supremum supplicium*. CH. II foreshadows the discussion of two 'modes' of crucifixion, *vulgaris* and *rarus*. Meantime there is the 'scourging' and the 'beating of the victim on the way' to be considered. A *Note* is added to refer to the occasional blindfolding of victims. CH. III examines the distinction between scourges and rods. *Flagella* are often mentioned by the historians; *virgae* are evidently a milder punishment and less humiliating, *honestiores*. After a lexical survey of the terms *flagrum, lorum, scutica* (lashes and whips), L discusses the weighting with 'dies' of various shapes and sizes (*flagra talaria, taxillata*), or animals' bones. 'Were such weighted lashes used on our Lord?': *imaginantur aut pingunt per pietatem nonnulli*. [He is thinking of paintings of the Flagellation and of the iconography of the Instruments of the Passion, Mass of St Gregory etc.] The Gospels say (simply) *flagellis*

68

caesum, 'he was scourged'. L notes Matthew's *phragelloō* (27.26), a corruption of the Latin term.

In CH. IV Lipsius' dilemma becomes acute; so acute that he does *not* seek to evade the issue. He seems to accept the fact that Christian tradition does not accord with the historical evidence at all. The Flagellation, Way of the Cross and Crucifixion of Christ were in their *modus* individual. [He is now able to speak on the one hand of the Flagellation etc., on the other of the Roman *ludibrium, deductio, crux*.] He finds little evidence for a flagellation *domi*, within the precincts of a building. 'There are some texts in the historians of uncertain interpretation'; 'there is no doubt in the case of our Saviour, although the Evangelists are not clear on the subject'. [This passage is important]: *Etsi enim Evangelia non exprimunt* [a familiar preamble in medieval commentaries]: *tamen secuti Patres. Prudentius clare, et cum ritus quoque prisci attestione: atque columnae/annexus, tergum dedit, ut servile, flagellis.* [There is of course no need to quote Prudentius; what L means, but for some reason will not say, is 'see Isaiah 50.6 and 53'; he prefers to use the 'argument from prophecy' as he finds it used in an authority; see the next comment.] He quotes, as countless writers had done before him, Jerome's letter to Eustochium on the subject of the revered Column of the Flagellation, that *Columna, Ecclesiae porticum sustinens infecta cruore Domini, ad quam vinctus dicitur et flagellatus.* 'It was possibly used as a supporting column in the construction of the Temple. Prudentius says it is still there.' [This is not strictly 'patristic', despite the authority of Jerome and Prudentius, for there seems to be no Biblical text in any of the discussions of this subject. I class it as a piece of Holy Places lore.[15] L does not claim that part of the column is elsewhere venerated as a relic. Nor does he find texts to show that victims for flagellation were 'in fact' fastened *over* a whipping-block. He leaves it that the Flagellation was *sui generis*, and as the artists represent it.]

CH. V. The bearing of the *crux* in antiquity was part of the *deductio* (see Ch. VI); only one beam of the *crux* was carried by the victim. The testimony of St John, however, is sufficient to show that Christ carried *plenam crucem*, 'otherwise why should he have needed help from Simon?' [John does not mention Simon; in an added *Note* L remembers that Christ 'at first' carried his Cross alone. Jerome is his authority; this is a Gospel-harmonizing solution.] 'John's phrase alone (*bajulans...crucem*) justifies reference', says L with Tertullian, to '*vetera quaedam vaticinia aut imagines*'. [It is interesting to see Isaac's carrying of the wood of his sacrifice, and Isaiah's prophecy – *factus est principatus super humerum ejus* – referred to in this way; the latter prophecy (Isaiah 9.6) was never familiar in the same sense as the prophetic *image* of Isaac. Since L uses the plural *imagines*, we may well believe him to have had in mind, and to have disdained to mention, the Widow of Zarephath and her wood-carrying; he clearly dislikes typology and the argument from prophecy, but is prepared to cite it *via* Tertullian, or *via* Prudentius – see above, when the Gospel evidence requires support.]

CH. VI deals with the *ludibrium* and *tormentum* of victims on the way to execution. Dionysius [Halicarnassus, fl. 30–10 B.C.] appears to have a description of such a *deductio* referring to an order to 'pull' or 'drag' victims (*trahere eos jussit*). This prompts L to annotate: *Nec dubium est quin impulerint, deiecerint, erexerint, per saevitiam aut per lusum.*[16] [This is patently an attempt – 'there cannot be any doubt' – to provide a historical note to justify the brutalities of the Way of the Cross so un-compromisingly represented in the later Gothic. L betrays no knowledge of the patristic origin of this scene — the exploitation of the taunting and stoning of Elisha, of Isaiah 53, and phrases of the Passion Psalms – beyond the use of the term *saevitia*, a dim reflection of *circumdederunt me canes multi* etc.] Next: 'Our pictures show an *asserculum* or a *tabella* attached by Christ's tormentors to the hem of his tunic to impede his progress.' He recalls 'goads' of similar construction, but is defeated by this *destimulatio!* 'I am not the inventor nor would I be the interpreter of any such an *inventicula.*' [I suspect that L had been asked to discredit this 'innovation'. The origin of the spiked tripboard is, in the main, Matthew 23.4–5; it must be interpreted as a typical 15th century vulgar-ization of Scripture to gain a further 'proven' example of the brutality of Christ's enemies. See J. J. M. Timmers, *Symboliek en Iconographie* etc., 1947, para. 519f.][17]

In CH. VII Lipsius approaches the vexed question of the two kinds of nailing to the cross, namely *erecto cruce* and *jacente cruce*. The title of the chapter states at once that 'both methods are attested'.[18] [As the Church admits both traditions we may assume that L was free as a historian to favour either, *or* to 'prove' each.] There is no doubt from the description of the martyrdom of St Pionius [d. 250 A.D., Eusebius, *H.E.* IV, xv, 46f.], which L reproduces, that the victim might be nailed to a cross on the ground; the cross was then raised. [He adds the 'reasonable' argument that this 'would be easier'; the usual reasons are given.] 'But many believe the cross was erect'. He quotes Cicero, *in Verrem* [V, lxvi, 69], Josephus, and Ezra 6.11. The verbs *tollere, agere, ferre, dare (in crucem)* can all be used, he says, equally of an *elatio (erecto cruce)*, or *mollitio (jacente cruce)*. With the same objectivity he lists *excurrere, ascendere* and *salire (in crucem)*, though his examples are taken from sacred and profane literature indifferently: Plautus, Prudentius, Nonnus [c. 400, Paraphrase of Fourth Gospel and] 'Nazianzenus': 'I doubt whether the Tragedy [*Christos Paschon*, see Migne, *PG* 38, 133f., now believed to be 12th cent. at earliest] is really his'. [This is in

70

the main a historian's chapter, involving few of the ambiguities of method
so often observed in the foregoing sections.]

CH. VIII enquires 'how were victims fastened to the cross?' L's conclusion is 'with nails or ropes, but more often the former'. The array of
texts consulted is somewhat mixed: Seneca, Ausonius on the *crux* of
Cupid, Artemidorus [*Oneirocritica*, 2nd cent. A.D.] but the evidence for
nailing seems adequate. 'It is wrong', he says, 'to represent the two
thieves as roped'. [Most medieval artists seek to represent the crucifixion
of Christ and of the Thieves *differently*; nails for the thieves cannot be
'proved' from Scripture, and are often consciously denied them]: the
argument Lipsius advances is based on Nonnus' verse paraphrase of the
Fourth Gospel – which he translates: *In cruce praeduris clavis fixi inque
ligati*. He continues 'What need had Helena of a miracle to distinguish
Christ's cross if the thieves had been bound?' [What, therefore, had
started as an apparently serious inquiry again ends with a flippancy.]

In a long *Note*, L returns seriously to the topic 'nails or ropes?', and
becomes involved in the evergreen compromise solution that 'ropes will
really have been necessary as well'. [On balance I think that this is a
relevant historian's note on crucifixions in the ancient world, for the
'mercy seat' will not have been universal. Despite a quotation from
St Hilary and reference to Christ's prophecy of Peter's end (John 21.18 –
et alius te cinget) the Christian Crucifixion seems indeed *not* to be L's
subject here; he is trying to get at the historical facts.]

As for the number of nails used at a crucifixion (CH. IX), L quotes on
the one hand Christian poets and patristic interpretation of Psalm 21/22;
on the other Plautus! His conclusion is: *frustra litigemus*, 'it is not for me
to judge the Fathers'. In a *Note* he decides in favour of four nails.
[The problem of four nails or three – the reason for the abandonment
of four in favour of three in Christian art from, broadly, about the end
of the thirteenth century – seems not to admit a solution satisfactory to
all investigators. There is a recent summing-up in the article 'Dreinagel-
kruzifixus' in the *Reallex. z. dt. Kunstgechichte*. Reference to the
factors involved would not help in our inquiry into *De Cruce*, because
Lipsius has in any case mixed the two kinds of history again.]

CH. X attempts to deal with the 'footrest' (*suppedaneum*), which not
unnaturally defeats Lipsius. *An lignum aliquod in Cruce suppedaneum?*
he asks. [L denies himself a solution of this problem of Christian iconography – he is not the last to do so – by his complete neglect of Biblical
prophecies of the Crucifixion, and his abhorrence of typology and symbolism. Here there is space only for the briefest reminder of the considerations which produced this quasi-real piece of Cross furniture.
Its antecedent (in a pragmatic series) is the *step* on which the prophecy
ascendam in palmam could be carried out, and the step or *platform* from

which Christ as Aaron the High Priest could arraign or pardon, and the *altar* of the Lamb of Sacrifice. All these things had been represented in hieratic Christian art and *required* the *suppedaneum*.] His conclusion is, properly, 'the *suppedaneum* occurs in the oldest pictures and I shall not rashly disregard it'. [His historical evidence points of course, as he sees, not to a *suppedaneum* at all, but either to a 'mercy seat' (a *horn*, or a *parva tabula* with a *pes*, to be fitted into the upright beam, so that the victim was supported by a kind of saddle or seat); *or* to a rope sling, to take the weight of the victim. A long added *Note* shows how L struggled to get this point right. A difficult section in Bk. I, Ch. IX involving comparisons between various Old Testament *cornua* or even the unicorn, and the structure of the Cross, should have been included, if anywhere, here.]

According to CH. XI the custom of advertising the offence of a victim by some inscription 'was known'. He provides ample evidence. [The inquiry is naturally intended as an annotation of Pilate's I.N.R.I. *titulus*.] Beginning CH. XII with a cheerful '*bene jam et fideliter fiximus*', L now examines the causes of death, which were gradual loss of blood (*a stillante paulatim sanguine*), or starvation (*vel a fame*). St Andrew survived two days (*ô athletam Deo dignum!*), Victorinus three, other martyrs nine days, some living, according to Seneca, to spit on their mockers, and some, L reads, to earn a reprieve.

In CH. XIII Lipsius lists (death on the *crux* through) attacks by birds of prey, wild animals: 'which means that some crosses cannot have been very high'. [This implies a discreet questioning of the excessively high crosses which wayward exegesis had brought into favour in the later Gothic.] For the lance-thrust he refers to the New Testament [not to the prophecy in Psalm 21/22]. As for the breaking of the bones of the thieves, 'it is a common mistake to generalize from the Gospel report of that incident'. L says boldly in his next heading (CH. XIV) that the *crurifragium* is a distinct form of execution (*à cruce remotum*), more brutal and more vile. It was their (the Jews') custom which required that victims be taken down and buried before nightfall (and therefore the breaking of the bones of the thieves). He adds a *Note* to remind readers of an example of observance in the Old Testament, II Samuel 21.9-10. There follow several passages from Roman writers and the Martyrology to give a clear impression of what *crurifragium* involved. Normally, according to CH. XV, bodies were left to rot on the cross; the only setting of guards attested by the historians (CH. XVI) was to ensure that relatives did not remove victims to bury them (Petronius). L wonders in passing whether indeed Pilate's command: *habetis custodiam, abite*, was not intended in this (Roman) sense.

BOOK III

In Book III Lipsius presses on to the discussion of less frequently employed methods of capital punishment (*crux*), and for many reasons – mainly because he is concerned almost exclusively with *historia profana*, has few iconographical problems to delay him, and is dependable – we may be briefer in reporting on him. His first major subject is the *furca* (CHS. I–III), the older Roman, and the more recent *furca*. [According to the article *crux* in Pauly-Wissowa the old term *furca* may have been revived under Justinian to shield the sacred term from misuse; its shape, the conventional 'gallows', may have been evolved in such a way as to avoid any association with the Christian Cross.] The earlier *ignominiosa furca* was a pair of beams (halter-stocks) assembled about the wrists and neck of the victim, to expose him to public ridicule; the *furca poenalis*, similar in shape, could be hauled up by ropes over a branch of a tree or the protruding arm of an upright pole, to form 'a kind of cross'. The latter would be, 'to all intents and purposes, a *patibulum*, and this would account for the phrase *patibulo crucis affigi*'. In CH. IV Lipsius makes a show of perplexity in trying to visualize these various forms of *furca*, and offers several engravings for our appraisal. From CH. VII on, the subject is *de nova furca, nostrum patibulum*, the 'Tribonianum' [so-called after one of Justinian's jurists], in fact 'the gallows'. [The 'gallows' which so often *seem* to appear in our medieval texts in association with, or as a synonym for the Cross are to be explained otherwise. What is in fact involved is the use of the modern term *as a translation* of the O.T. *patibulum*, the 'ignominious cross' of the old dispensation, which was displaced by the Cross of the Redemption.] Capital punishment is henceforth 'by strangulation', says Lipsius. [It is interesting to see that he uses in the main text and in the *Notes* a good deal of the material which we find in Grimm's *Dt. Rechtsalterthümer.*] From CH. VIII Lipsius discusses still rarer forms of *crux*, variations on a theme, like Peter's (*inversa figura*); flayings, burnings at the stake [his sources still use the word *crux*; he is still 'on the subject']. In CH. XIII the Wood of the Cross comes up for consideration. To substantiate *quercus*, L refers to the plentiful supply of that wood in Palestine, and to relics! With CH. XIV ('until when did the *crux* continue to be used?' 'Constantine abolished it, and the *crurifragium*', says L) we begin to suspect that a pious conclusion is being prepared. Quickly indeed we pass to the use of the *crux* as ensign, Constantine's *labarum*, the Chi-Rho monogram. 'The Byzantine Emperors bore a Cross in procession. So also does Rudolph –'

– the Rudolph who provided the *Privilegium Cæsareum* for this strange, and in so many ways disturbing work. Before leaving

73

it, it is interesting to compare the formal words of the official *Approbatio: – nihil. . .(continens). . .sacrae ac orthodoxae fidei repugnans aut ab ea dissistens,* with the broadside of 1606 from George Thomson of St Andrews addressed to Lipsius himself: *– Crucem, quam tribus libris, magna gabalorum, furcarum, paxillorum, et infelicium arborum accessione suffulsisti, non nos violentis manibus deripuimus, sed tutemet in extremâ ad eos libros notâ, levi venti in maximam egisti malam crucem.* George Thomson had clearly read the work, right to the last *Note,* where he indeed found a reference to 'Christian crosses blown down by the wind', and whence he derived his own polemical image of Lipsius the iconoclast. It was possible for us, remembering Lipsius's dilemma as a Catholic and as a historian, to be more charitable. Even so, in considering him primarily as a historian we noted (beside much that was impressive and is still quotable), shall we say – certain inadequacies, in respect of method and in the handling of sources.

5. GOETHE'S 'ALEXIS UND DORA' (1796)

AN INTERPRETATION

Klage dich, Armer, nicht an! So legt der Dichter ein Rätsel,
Künstlich mit Worten verschränkt, oft der Versammlung ins Ohr:
Jeden freuet die seltne, der zierlichen Bilder Verknüpfung,
Aber noch fehlet das Wort, das die Bedeutung verwahrt;
Ist es endlich entdeckt, dann heitert sich jedes Gemüt auf
Und erblickt im Gedicht doppelt erfreulichen Sinn.

(Alexis und Dora, lines 25–30)[1]

Goethe's 'idyll' *Alexis und Dora* has in its time attracted relatively little critical attention. The poem appears, for instance,
not to have been treated in any of the many post-war volumes
devoted to principles and examples of literary interpretation.
Goethe's editors refer, as they must, to the few (but important)
discussions of the poem in the correspondence and conversa-
tions, and they may quote in addition a perceptive remark from
a recent 'Goethe book'. But no matter where one reads, one
senses that writers are inhibited when they come to the subject
of *Alexis und Dora.* The six hexameters quoted at the head
of this essay are, I am convinced, in part responsible: they are
'awkward'. There can of course be no complete interpretation
of the poem if the lines are ignored. In this essay I take account
of them. Whether they are thereby made more acceptable, I
doubt; but Goethe scholarship will surely acknowledge some
incidental gains from this renewed approach. In prose translation the lines run:

Do not reproach yourself, poor fellow! The poet often presents his
attentive audience in this way with a riddle, cunningly framed in words.
All are delighted by the unusual way in which graceful images are joined
together, but the word which holds the meaning is still lacking. When
finally it is found, everyone becomes cheerful again and is doubly
delighted by the [revealed] meaning of the poem.

75

Schiller received the poem in May 1796. After a second reading, in a letter to Goethe of 18th June,[2] he praised it for its 'simplicity and great depth of feeling', but, as is well known, he was unhappy about the concluding passage (about lines 137–54). He found the change from the delirious happiness of the lovers in the brief moment before their separation, to Alexis' 'fear of loss' and his outburst of jealous passion as he sails away, too abrupt. To this Goethe's reply (22nd June) was: 'in reality, hot on the heels of unexpected fortune in love ('Liebesglück') there must follow fear of loss'. Had Goethe left it at this 'natural' explanation, as he calls it, or said that one of his intentions in the idyll was to treat such a simple moralization artistically, this essay (to mention only a certain consequence) would not have been necessary. It served, however, as a mere preliminary to an 'artistic' justification formulated to match the terms of Schiller's objection. The upsurge of jealousy in Alexis was 'necessary'. It was necessary 'because the course of the idyll is throughout an emotional progression, and passion had therefore to be intensified ("gesteigert") until shortly before the end, where the poet withdraws with a bow and allows the idyll to revert to sentiments which are more bearable, even serene'.

This first exchange between the two poets set the tone and the course of further discussion of *Alexis und Dora*. It has concerned itself primarily with questions of genre (the epic, dramatic and lyrical elements in the 'idyll'); or it has taken some lead from Goethe's appeal to his principle of 'Steigerung'.[3] And of course most critics and ordinary readers still have, like Schiller, their misgivings about Alexis' quite intemperate jealousy. But one may suspect that Goethe was himself affected by the course discussion had taken from the very outset, and persuaded, for instance, not to speak again of the theme 'unexpected and unmerited fortune in love' (how could anyone think the lovers in the poem undeserving of their happiness?) And why was Goethe so evidently reluctant to quote in his defence the hexameters (above) which speak of a riddle offered by a poet to an assembled company, and of a single word revealing the meaning of his poem? (The word, one gathers, must be found, and no doubt triumphantly declared, before there can be relief from the uncertainties the poet has created.) Are these allusions to the poet's occasional role as composer of charades, masques, tableaux, not part of the poem's own economy? One cannot avoid the conclusion that after Schiller had spoken, Goethe (and his later commentators) preferred to treat the poem as though the lines were not there; perhaps the suggestion of a riddle to be solved had been an unfortunate idea.

In seeking to restore lines 25–30 to the poem, we must note that the words are clearly initially Goethe's. In apostrophizing Alexis ('Klage dich, Armer, nicht an!', line 25a), Goethe makes, for our benefit, a comparison, involving on the one hand Alexis's bewilderment and, on the other, the often perplexing allusions of 'the poet'. As for the function of the lines, we must surely see them as in some way related to the concluding lines in which, as Goethe put it, the poet 'bows himself out'. Gundolf, paraphrasing Goethe, suggests that they are 'a kind of epilogue addressed to the Muses, mitigating the tragedy of the final scene, so that the poem may remain an idyll'. (He added, however, that the epilogue was 'rather an appendage to the poem than its proper conclusion'.)[4] If the concluding lines are a kind of epilogue, may not the first words spoken by the poet on his own account be understood as 'a kind of prologue'? (We must at any rate dismiss the notion that the lines could be part of Alexis's own monologue.)[5] In the following pages I shall treat the lines as a delayed prologue. In so doing I imply that Goethe's original intention or hope was that his audience would indeed be delighted by his manipulation of familiar images, and make a show of solving his riddle. There is perhaps even evidence that he never completely forgot that intention, for when, fully thirty years later on 25 December 1825, Goethe referred in a conversation with Eckermann, evidently for the last time, to *Alexis und Dora*, it still rankled that 'people' ('die Menschen') had found fault with Alexis' fit of jealousy. With touching zeal Eckermann praised the 'unfailing fidelity of observation' throughout the poem ('als ob Sie nach einem wirklich Erlebten gearbeitet hätten').[6] One cannot know with what inflexion of voice Goethe replied: 'es ist mir lieb, wenn es Ihnen so erscheint', but without malice one may translate: 'I am content that you should think that the case.' Goethe was still mindful of the extent to which he had committed himself to Schiller's approach. *If* he had once attached importance to the motif of 'fortune in love' as a clue, and if he had hoped that his hearers (readers) would enter into the spirit of the charade, he kept his disappointment to himself. At any rate he did not enlighten Eckermann. But the words of the prologue are still there. With their help we may, I think, uncover other merits than 'simplicity', 'depth of feeling' and 'fidelity of observation' in *Alexis und Dora*. Whether their discovery will confirm or upset a cherished 'Goethe-Bild', I cannot predict, but I am certain that they are of relevance in Goethe studies. They associate the 'idyll' more closely with the 'elegies' on the one hand, and on the other they open up a considerable gap between it and *Hermann und Dorothea*.

II

To repeat, in lines 25–30 Goethe compares the state of mind of Alexis with the perplexity of an audience whom 'the poet' has set a riddle. This may seem to be a strange notion, but it is almost immediately *we* who are the audience, and we do not yet know what is really happening in this poem. Alexis cannot grasp what has happened to him, neither can we put a name to his case. But from the disposition of in some way linked images (contained in the words of the poem) we are expected by the poet to find the elusive word which will put an end to our uncertainty. In relief and delight at discovery we shall, it is implied, find his poem doubly enjoyable. Meanwhile Alexis will come to terms with his present lot. All these things the poet seems able to promise at the point where he 'works in' his delayed prologue. But events (changes in Alexis' emotional state) overtake the lover, the poet who is chronicling them, and us. None of us can know how all this is going to end. The poet himself can finally do no more than dismiss his Muses, for it is, he says, beyond their capacity to describe the wild fluctuations of despair and bliss in the lover's heart:

> Nun, ihr Musen, genug! Vergebens strebt ihr zu schildern,
> Wie sich Jammer und Glück wechseln in liebender Brust.
>
> (lines 155f.)

The assurance of the poet, who in his prologue proposed to tease us with words and images in a guessing game, yields in the epilogue to the dismay of a compassionate witness – of a grief beyond his power to describe. He can only hope that in further time the Muses will afford Alexis some solace, for they cannot heal the wounds inflicted by Amor. In other words, the progressive 'intensification of emotions' ('Steigerung des Leidenschaftlichen', see above) shatters the conventions of charade and riddle; Schiller, thinking rather in terms of the higher and more serious genres (and verisimilitude) had misgivings about the outcome. It seems that within the compass of this poem there could be no happy ending to Alexis' case, or to our endeavours to 'solve' it by putting a name to it. Do we then still wish to know what 'word' Goethe had in mind as he fashioned his poem? I think it important that we should.

A word that is to be revealed by inter-related images must itself be in some way pictorial, the name of a goddess, one surmises, or a personification of an abstract idea. Goethe in fact gave the word away in his 'natural' explanation, see above. It is 'Glück' (fortune, happiness), iconographically 'Fortune'. Goethe also specified which of the many possible 'fortunes' fits the case of Alexis and Dora. It is 'unexpected and unmerited fortune in love'. The complementary 'Unglück' which must immediately follow such 'Glück' is 'fear of loss' expressing itself as anxiety and despair, 'Sorge' and 'Jammer' in the poem. The *artist's* image of Fortune – since about 1500 a naked female precariously poised on a ball, driven along by wind and waves[7]

79

– implies the imminence of sudden reversal and disaster, and indeed the special image available for Misfortune is relatively rarely used or invoked. The image differed only in a choice of attributes when fortune was seen in the context of 'time' or 'moment': the 'fleeting' and 'favourable' moment which must be seized. The figure is then 'Gelegenheit' (Occasio, Opportunity). The 'correct' answer to the poet's riddle was therefore in all probability simply 'Glück', which, with its negative aspect and associations, in fact in its characteristic ambivalence, survives to beyond the end of the idyll. This answer then leaves open the possibility – later, in relaxed discussion – of arguing the case for 'Augenblick', 'Gelegenheit', possibly other words, see below.

But is the presence of variants of the image ('Glück') sufficient to warrant the expression 'die seltne, der zierlichen Bilder Verknüpfung'? There are many other images of the same order (they are all emblematic) in the poem, but we have not yet reached the stage in this analysis where they can all be convincingly identified and named. I mention, however, two which are relatively easy to isolate. First, 'Reue' (*metanoia*, repentance, remorse).[8] Artists may depict 'rue' in the figure of a youth vainly stretching out to seize and detain Occasio (a female figure) who has escaped from his grasp or is evading it: all in a 'fleeting moment'. It is in just such a situation and posture that we encounter Alexis at the beginning of the poem. He is filled with self-reproach and helplessly strives to recapture and re-live the moment of happiness. He is the embodiment of remorse. At the same time he sees in his thoughts – and that is a second, related picture – the girl Dora staring into the distance as the sails of his ship recede. This is 'Sehnsucht', a rather more modern image, when so named, than the others we shall mention. Closely related, already implied, and unmistakable, is the image of Opportunity (Occasio), but it is almost completely enciphered. Occasio is present in everything but name – and one important attribute, see below.

Before examining Goethe's treatment of Occasio ('Gelegenheit') in greater detail (in section III), we may usefully dispose of a formal question. Why did Goethe not give his poem a more specific title than the genre designation 'Idylle'? If we ignore for the moment the conventions of the riddle (concealment, mystification): the poem has no evident single subject, and the themes 'Glück', 'Reue', 'Gelegenheit' follow in swift succession, and are matters – contingencies, states of mind – of the 'moment' ('Augenblick'). The 'moment' for most of these already belongs to the past and can only be recalled elegiacally. For Alexis (and Dora) they are out of the story; Fortune, for instance, appears to favour the seafarers and their venture. In short, the final title ('Alexis and Dora') is correct, because Alexis is still there at the end of the poem which is 'again an idyll'. He is, it is true, a prey to despair, but that cannot be a lasting state of mind. He will in further time either recall Dora's 'Ewig!', or the wounds struck by Amor will cease to smart (lines 157f.)

III

In saying that 'Gelegenheit' (Occasio) is present in *Alexis und Dora* in everything but name, I have so far assumed familiarity with little more than the idiom 'die Gelegenheit beim Schopfe fassen'. Before proceeding further we must clearly consider again – with due caution – one of Goethe's 'Roman Elegies' (*Fromm sind wir Liebende*), fully half of which he devoted to 'Göttin Gelegenheit' herself. The goddess is, one learns, the particular concern of lovers. They are her devotees; and she requires silence of them, both concerning their own love and concerning her.[9] Goethe then proceeds in hexameters to what is very nearly a formal handbook entry, beginning with a genealogy of the goddess ('she claims to be the daughter of Proteus', etc.) and a specification of her behaviour (she teases those who slumber, speeds past the alert, but will surrender to the resolute man of action).[10] There follows then a 'description' of the goddess as she once appeared to him!

81

Die Haare
Fielen ihr dunkel und reich über die Stirne herab,
Kurze Locken ringelten sich ums zierliche Hälschen.
(lines 25f.)

Goethe modifies the conventional iconography of Occasio ('Gelegenheit') in only one detail. His Italian lover did not seek to evade his embrace, but hastened towards him; he seized 'die eilende Geliebte'. Otherwise she appeared to him in the likeness of Occasio, with (dark) long flowing hair falling over her forehead, the nape of her neck graced by tiny ringlets only. The lovers embraced and held each other fast, seeking by their silence to defeat the passing moment and so avoid remorse. The words 'die Zeit ist vorüber' are spoken without regret.

In the idyll *Alexis und Dora* we are enjoined by the poet to discover the pictorial allusions for ourselves, and the role of Dora is certainly not a light-hearted adaptation of that of Occasio. But it is in the guise of Occasio–Fortuna that Dora approaches Alexis, greets him, tempts him (one may fairly say) into her garden, and is there embraced by him. Alexis, in other words, siezes the opportunity (and good fortune) which unexpectedly presents itself. But after a fervent exchange of vows with Dora (the picture changes and) Alexis answers the last call to the ship, now ready to sail with favouring winds. He leaves behind the happiness ('Glück') vouchsafed him in the fleeting moment. Almost immediately follows the *metanoia* of the two lovers, remorse in the case of Alexis, Dora's forlorn longing for her departed lover. Dora has promised to wait 'always' for Alexis' return. Such behaviour is anything but that of an Occasio. It is not Dora who escapes but Alexis who hastens away. One will search the poem in vain for even the common noun 'Gelegenheit', and in Alexis' description of Dora, whom we see only as he remembers her, there is no trace of an allusion to the flowing hair of Occasio:

Wir sahen einander
In die Augen, und mir ward vor dem Auge so trüb.
Deinen Busen fühlt' ich an meinem! Den herrlichen Nacken,

82

Ihn umschlang nun mein Arm, tausendmal küßt' ich den Hals.
Mir sank über die Schulter dein Haupt: nun knüpfen auch deine
Lieblichen Arme das Band um den Beglückten herum.

(lines 89–94)

Goethe studiously avoided throughout the poem any reference to Dora's hair: *Hals, Nacken, Busen, Augen, Haupt* (lines
43f., 74 and 89–94 above), but never her hair. This silence
serves as an ironic or melancholy comment on Alexis's lack of
resolution. Dora's role is that of Occasio, but of an Occasio
seized and then immediately relinquished. The both deliberate
and necessary omission of reference to Dora's hair is the clue to
the identity of the unnamed 'graceful image'.

But *Alexis und Dora* is more than a catena or cento of familiar
images. It is a highly artistic and poetic (dramatic) reworking of
these, which engages the poet to the limit of his capacities. For
the time being, however, our concern is to demonstrate their
presence, perhaps in a setting, in a grouping of characters, or in
the rhetorical figures of descriptive or reflective passages. It must
be stressed that to Goethe and his contemporaries the images
were familiar enough to be alluded to. Goethe will have known
them from engravings of the Italian Renaissance, but when he
spoke of 'zierliche Bilder' he no doubt included the modest
derivative and stereotyped versions to be found in favourite
emblem-books.

IV

Occasio and Fortune exist only in the world of human time,
indeed Occasio's brief span is the single moment. Ruefully
Alexis seeks to recall the unique moment of his encounter with
Dora in every detail. The poet helps him to isolate the moment,
and, by dwelling on it in fond recollection, to 'lengthen' it, and
so save it temporarily from the passage of time. The structure of
the poem is in fact largely determined by an endeavour to
represent time *as* time, so that Occasio may be seen as a
'momentary' contingency. The story of Alexis and Dora is

thereby made to seem 'dramatic' (there is in fact virtually no 'action').

Time was the context of the 'years', 'days' and each 'hour' that Alexis in his monologue is now able to recall, even 'that unique moment' in which he first began to live (line 15), and which makes all the rest of his days seem 'void'. As that moment of time recedes, Alexis, now on board ship and under full sail, resolves to 'repeat' it. Until time resumes its rule. Subject to the same rule of time is the poet of the prologue. His initial assurance is soon lost. He can do nothing for Alexis when the past, its events, and its daydreams have been recorded. But also the poet still outside the poem, Goethe, has only a limited control over the span of time in which he has set the moment of the lovers' encounter. He exercises that control with astonishing skill, so that the happiness of the brief remembered moment suffuses Alexis' whole life with its light. That is: Alexis' life *up to* the fortunate moment, and *since* the moment, to the extent that he now chooses to recall it. But, like Alexis, the poet must finally surrender the moment he had sought to recapture and hold. In the 'Roman Elegy' the poet and his lover, through observance of Occasio's precepts, enjoyed a more than momentary happiness. Alexis, having of necessity relinquished the moment to inexorable time, is suddenly unable to hold fast even the memory of it (see below); he is inconsolable. The poet in his turn is just as surely at the end of his skills as the puppeteer who has brought his two characters face to face with a locked door. He can let them knock, and then wait with them. It is not in the poet's power to help Alexis, or to tell us what his later fate will be. In that sense time, rather than the 'plot', determines the structure of *Alexis und Dora*.

V

This analysis, following the indications given in the prologue, began with the identification of certain 'pictures' in *Alexis und Dora*. Of these 'Gelegenheit' (Occasio) held our attention for a

time, but we found it not readily distinguishable from the fleeting moment ('Augenblick') and inconstant fortune ('Glück',
'Liebesglück'). Let us now leave these and many other vignettes
which pass before us in fairly quick succession (we return to
them finally in an Appendix, pp. 88–92), to consider the poem
as a whole. In its narrative content it is of course 'the story of
Alexis and Dora' – and there are sounder reasons than mere
convenience for the now accepted title, see above. But the story
has been referred to as the merest 'anecdote';[11] or: Goethe
provided some quayside leavetaking he had witnessed in Naples
or in Sicily with the simplest of narrative settings.[12] Clearly the
story is not told for its own sake, or merely so that Alexis and
Dora may be shown in a series of recognizable 'pictorial' situations and postures. Goethe seeks rather through the story to
represent time itself. The poem depicts time in the only way in
which time can be represented, namely as it is experienced, for
instance by an Alexis – and his chronicler. The picture of time
which the poem unfolds is certainly not one of the 'zierliche
Bilder' which the prologue advertises (to avoid misunderstand-
ings: it is not Father Time with hour-glass and scythe). It is too
vast a picture to be referred to in such terms.

Each reading of the poem renews the picture of time. It must
suffice here to indicate some technical details of Goethe's
handling of time. The 'real present' is treated explicitly in the
first ten lines of the poem. It is the present of Alexis, and of the
poet at his elbow, and to this we are returned as often as Alexis,
recalling past events, pauses to compare or contrast his present
state: 'Noch schlagen die Herzen' (lines 13f., cf. 19, 21a, 36);
'Nun trennt uns die gräßliche Flut' (line 53). But Goethe has
by various devices ensured that we abandon attempts at a time-
scale, for instance by the ambiguities of tense in which Alexis
compares 'then' and 'now'. He exploits the 'aspects' of the perfect tense and the conditional: Alexis believes (or now persaudes
himself) that he can remember having been anxious that the
pitcher might slip from Dora's head ('Oftmals hab' ich gesorgt,
es möchte der Krug dir entstürzen', line 45). Over line 57

('Schon erhebt sich das Segel, es flattert im Winde') one hesitates: this is *not* the historical present, it *is* direct speech, as one learns a moment too late ('so sprach er'). At what point does Alexis cease recalling the past and address himself to his new present? Goethe leaves us to infer this. It is roughly from the point where his dreams of the future become more sensible, for it is only when he has begun to think about the future hearth and home (line 129) that he can fall a prey to anxiety and 'fear of loss'; and finally to the despair in which the poet and we have to leave him.

More intricate are Goethe's indications of relative time (intervals) within Alexis' often interrupted monologue. Obviously we must accept the monologue in its first function, as a psychological study. It reflects states of mind, fluctuations of mood, entirely credible responses and reactions, given this hero and his present situation. But Goethe also uses the monologue as a means of representing time as man experiences it, strives to understand it, and seeks to escape from its tyranny.

Alexis failed to seize and hold fast the good fortune (in love) which unexpectedly crossed his path. He is now torn between happiness and remorse. He proposes to 'repeat' the precious moment of happiness in fond recollection (see IV, above), but his re-living of the moment in memory is interrupted by *remembered* calls to make haste to join the ship. The years of his youth, and the dreams of the future he dreamt as a youth, 'shall now be forgotten' (lines 35–7); today itself is hateful (line 20), etc. But Alexis *cannot* recall the precious moment as he experienced it. In the moment of separation Dora gave him her vow ('Ewig!'). He is thereby a changed person. The moment is also now coloured by memories of the Dora of days and years gone by, whom he had scarcely heeded. The recollection of her modest request in the garden, that he bring her 'ein leichtes Kettchen' from his travels, restores his contact with the present, whereupon he promptly lapses into new dreams of the future. These are at first fantastic dreams: in a moment he has been to distant lands and returned laden with his purchases.

He then considers more sensible gifts for the future home (etc.) where Dora will deceive him with a stranger. The precious moment so laboriously and imperfectly recalled is now lost, possibly for ever. Alexis has learnt, but not yet accepted the truism, that one cannot 'swim a second time in the same river' (cf. Goethe's *Dauer im Wechsel*).

In the light of these observations I find it difficult to offer anything towards a more conventional discussion of *Alexis und Dora*. If there is in the poem a 'fusion of dramatic and idyllic elements', I cannot recognize it as having been a preoccupation of the poet. Similarly, the intricate structure of the poem, the identity of the 'images', and the choice of an interior mono-logue as virtually the sole means of representation, all indicate some other (or further) purpose than the fulfilment of the demands of both epic and drama.[18] This further purpose is, I have argued, the adequate representation of our experience of time. The theme of time completely absorbs 'Glück', 'Gelegen-heit' and other 'momentary' themes or motifs. When seen in this way the story of Alexis and Dora serves primarily as exemplification. It is the upper voice in a more complex com-position representing time as the common lot of mankind.

One's admiration of Goethe's mastery as a poet is not diminished by increased awareness of his sources. On the con-trary, it is surely enhanced by consciousness of the limits (the 'Beschränkung') within which his mastery is displayed. Each image (scene) and narrative motif, that is to say the 'plot' of *Alexis und Dora*, is *given* in the emblem books. (Goethe pro-vided the characters with names.)[14] In Goethe's day the emblem-books were old-fashioned, but they were still cherished: their stock of images and motifs was familiar. Goethe recalls them elegiacally, and keeps them before our eyes for the duration of the idyll. He not only restricts himself to the one source: he seems to have drawn upon it to the extent that discretion allowed. One should therefore, I think, not be misled by Goethe's statement in the letter of 22nd June[15] that his only guide in working out the story of Alexis and Dora had been an 'unaccountable instinct' ('ein unerklärlicher Instinct'). In the context of the early discussions, Goethe was possibly being evasive. He could scarcely tell Schiller that he had consciously accepted the commonplace philosophy and the images of the emblem-books. The hallmark of Goethe's artistry (and artifice) is its apparent 'naturalness', and of his mastery, the self-imposed restraints on imagination. As for the 'blossom of poetry' ('die Blume des Dichterischen')[16] plucked by the poet in his idyll, are we disappointed to find it a metamorphosis of the 'gracefulness' ('Zierlichkeit') of the emblem-books?

APPENDIX

Images of Fortune in *Alexis und Dora*

Of writings on Fortune see A. Doren, 'Fortuna im Mittelalter und in der Renaissance', *Vortr. d. Bibl. Warburg* 2 (1922–3), Part 1 (1924) pp. 71–144 with 20 illustrations; R. van Marle, *Iconographie de l'art profane*, 2 vols., The Hague 1931 (repr. New York 1971), vol. II, pp. 178–202, figs. 207–28; [F. P. Pickering, *L & A.*, Ch. III = pp. 168–222 with illustr. 1–8b and 32a].

There are many allusions to fortune (Fortune) in *Alexis und Dora* which could not be pointed out in the foregoing essay. They will be dealt with below in the order of their occurrence, with reference where necessary to other images. But first Goethe's remark (see p. 76 *et passim*) 'unexpected and unmerited fortune in love'. This is a quotation from standard fortune lore. Since Antiquity the moral philosophers and satirists have complained that Fortune pays no heed to merit: 'fortuna caeca, vaga, inconstans, volubilis errans indignorumque fautrix', Pliny, *Hist. Nat.* 2,22; 'et caecam appellant, eo quod passim quoslibet incurrens sine ullo examine meritorum et ad bonos et ad malos venit', Isidore, *Etym.* VIII, 11,94. Unmerited good fortune need not, of course, be transitory, but Goethe's themes include Opportunity and Moment, and he is committed to the 'fortune of the fleeting moment'.

LINES 1–6 *Alles deutet auf glückliche Fahrt.* The image is that of the 'fortunate' ship under full sail, as one finds it represented in engravings and medallions of the Italian Renaissance, and, for example, in the arms of the Florentine Rucellai, see A. Warburg, *Ges. Schr.*, vol. I, pp. 145ff. and pl. XX, fig. 38, Doren, *loc. cit.* pp. 134f., 144 and fig. 19. Dolphins as a sign of good luck: see Pauly-Wissowa, *Realenzyklopädie* IV, 2, cols. 2504–10. The Middle Ages knew the same image, but without dolphins: 'ze wunsche im das êrste jâr/sîne segelwinde duzzen/und sîniu schef ze heile fluzzen', *Meier Helmbrecht*, lines 684ff. (Helmbrecht did not go to sea!). The word 'Beute' is possibly an allusion to the 'chase' (pursuit) of fortune. Compare a note, below, on line 154.

LINES 6–10 *Segel...*, *das sich für alle bemüht* (var. *statt seiner bem.*). All are 'in the same boat', but Alexis's gaze, as his joy 'sinks', is directed to the vanishing coastline.

LINES 11–13 The complementary image of Dora's 'Sehnsucht' (see pp. 80, 82). The lines are at first the words of the poet, apostrophizing Dora. They become those of Alexis at the apposition (*Freund/ Bräutigam*).

LINES 15–18 The 'moment' descended from the gods is Kairos (= Occasio or Tempus), cf. W. H. Roscher, *Ausf. Lexikon d. griechischen u. römischen Mythologie*, vol. II, col. 897–901, with illustr. of the famous Torcello relief *Kairos and Metanoia* (representing *missed opportunity, and remorse*). See also R. Wittkower, 'Chance, Time and Virtue', *Journal of the Warburg Institute* I (1937–8) pp. 313–21. The original 'Kairos' of Lysippus shows *kairos* as a youth standing on a sphere; his attributes are shears and a balance. In Renaissance art and the emblem-books Kairos (Occasio) is approximated to Fortune: a naked female figure standing on a ball, with a knife (rarely, if ever, shears), generally not with a balance. Occasio is mainly recognizable by the shorn nape of her neck (she shares windswept flowing hair – the 'Schopf' or 'forelock' – with Fortune). Alciati quotes Lysippus as inventor of the personification, and characterizes Occasio as 'cuncta domans capti temporis articulus' (the seized moment of time giving control over everything), cf. Alciati's *Emblematum Flumen abundans*, Lyons 1551 (Holbein Soc. facs. ed. 1871), 133: 'In Occasionem'. For Alexis the 'one moment' which now 'outweighs' all his previous life (lines 15f.) was 'the last' in at least two senses: 'most recent' and 'last possible', cf. 'so spät', line 31. He now enacts *metanoia*.

LINES 24, 32 Alexis accuses himself of 'stupidity' and 'blindness' (in fact of having been blindfolded). These are qualities usually attributed to Fortune and Amor, rather than their victim(s).

LINES 25–30 The lines claimed above as the poet's delayed prologue. This is probably the first point where a break could be made.

LINES 33f. *Lange schon harrte...das Schiff*. This line recalls the time spent waiting for 'favourable winds', until: 'endlich strebte der Wind glücklich vom Ufer ins Meer' (the opening lines of the poem had described the 'glückliche Fahrt' already under way). While emphasizing that Goethe is here concerned with the fortune of the merchant venturer, as Cassius in *Julius Caesar* was *not*, it is interesting to compare (Act IV, sc. 3): 'There is a tide in the affairs of men,/Which, taken at the flood leads on to fortune;/Omitted, all the voyage of their life/Is bound in shallows and in miseries./On such a full sea are we now afloat;/And we must take the current when it serves/Or lose our ventures'. The co-incidence of 'time' and 'tide' in English obscures the reference to Opportunity (which is not tidal!) – Compare Goethe's poem *Glückliche Fahrt*, ed. cit. I, 43, for a very breezy treatment of the subject.

LINES 36f. *einzig die Stunde* is more or less synonymous with 'einziger Augenblick'. Line 37 is completely ironic: neither the hour (moment), nor the happiness it held, 'remains'; Alexis does not 'hold' Dora.

LINES 39–52 These lines are devoted to the 'years' (line 51) which preceded the moment ('Stunde', line 36) of recognition. Alexis is only gradually able to compose a picture of Dora as she was in the settings he can recall: church, market-place, or at the fountain. The resultant genre picture suggests the peaceful life of a Mediterranean coastal town (cf. 'Tempel'). To that extent there are perhaps suggestions (as in *Werther* and elsewhere) of a patriarchal age. Franz Schallehn made surmises concerning the locality Goethe may have had in mind, in: 'Ursprung und Entstehung der Elegie Alexis und Dora', *Jb. d. Goethe-Gesellschaft* 17 (1930), pp. 166–82. See also, below, lines 64–88 ('golden Age').

LINES 59–62 A scene of leave-taking. It is natural enough to wish a happy and prosperous journey and safe return: 'Glucklich kehre zurück! riefen sie, glücklich und reich', but it is proper to recall that 'Fortuna redux' (a ship, or Fortune herself afloat on her ball, approaches the shore) is a subject of Renaissance artists. The finest example is Nicoletto da Modena's engraving of c. 1500, see van Marle, *op. cit.* fig. 125, [*L. & A.* pl. 5b]. A German variant is Virgil Solis's *Forthuna 1560*, Edm. Schilling, *Nürnberger Handzeichnungen*, 1929, pl. 55. – 'glücklich und reich' introduces the theme, later expanded in lines 115–28, of 'untold wealth' (*fortunae*).

LINES 64–88 *Mauer, Türe, Garten, Laube.* The court and the king-dom of Fortune were familiar ideas in the later Middle Ages (the most expansive treatment in Alan of Lille's *Anticlaudianus*, c. 1181–4); similarly the Garden of Love (*Roman de la Rose*). Middle High German knew the 'gate to fortune' (*der Sælden Tor*), and the 'castle of love' (*Minneburg*). Goethe's allusions are many and various, and not easily disengtangled. There are suggestions of an enclosed garden (as in the *Roman*) into which Alexis is enticed by Dora as Fortuna–Occasio (Alexis will later claim he was seduced, lines 142–5). There are sug-gestions of life in the Fortunate Isles, or in the world of a Golden Age. (In a letter of 7 July 1796, Goethe had to comment on an objection that it was unseemly for Alexis to arrive at the gate carrying his own 'Bündel', lines 61 and 63. That was intended, he writes, to indicate 'das

einfach *goldne Alter* [my italics]...wo man sich auch wohl selbst einen
Dienst leistete'). As for the superabundance of fruits (oranges and figs –
twice! lines 77 and 85f.) which pour as from a cornucopia into Dora's
apron and her basket, Goethe made certain that no one should take this
scene completely seriously, for after all Alexis did not pick up the basket
(line 89); he *did* remember to give it and and its contents to the lad sent
to call him for the last time to the ship (line 104). But the reference to
Fortune is clear. The cornucopia is one of Fortune's attributes: she shares
it with Ceres, and she is related to Hebe (both daughters of Jupiter)
according to Goethe: 'Es faßte/Hebe den Wandrer und zog mich in die
Hallen heran...Deine Tochter Fortuna, sie auch! die herrlichsten Gaben/
Teilt als ein Mädchen sie aus, wie es die Laune gebeut', *Roman Elegy*
VII, lines 15–21, cf. also *Elegy* XII. [Fortune is characteristically intem-
perate. Medieval artists may show her restrained by Providence's bridle;
Albrecht Dürer's 'Nemesis' holds a goblet representing, in my interpreta-
tion, intemperance, and a bridle, see *L. & A.* p. 122 and pl. 7a.].

LINES 89–94   See the quotation, pp. 82f. The Occasio image in
these lines was fully discussed. The two lovers immediately weep at the
prospect of parting. They are torn between 'Jammer' and 'Glück'.
That is also Alexis' state at the end of the poem, line 156.

LINES 115–28   Dreams of fortune (the fortune of the merchant
venturer). This theme was announced in Dora's words some fifty lines
ago: 'Fremde Küsten besuchest du nun, und köstliche Waren/Handelst
du ein, und Schmuck reichen Matronen der Stadt', lines 67f. It is now
treated rhetorically, first in Alexis' fantastic daydream – of commission-
ing a goldsmith to make Dora's 'Kettchen' (she had wanted something
inexpensive), and the settings for all the gems (ruby, emerald, sapphire,
hyacinth) he will 'acquire'; next in his more modest thoughts of 'jewelry'
and domestic gifts: woollen blankets (with purple hems), and household
linen (exquisite quality); these he will obtain by purchase and barter for
the nuptial 'couch' ('Lager', line 1131).

LINES 130–4   A picture of 'domestic bliss' which the author of the
'Roman Elegies' (as opposed to *Hermann und Dorothea*) can only have
intended ironically, to provide maximum contrast with the scenes to
follow. Very strangely, Korff wrote in *Geist der Goethezeit* (vol. II,
pp. 332f.): 'Die Liebe, die in *Alexis und Dora* verherrlicht wird, ist vor
allen Dingen die gesunde, normale, naturhafte Liebe...ihr schöner
Höhepunkt...die auf Liebe, Haus und Kinder gegründete Ehe', see
next note.

LINES 135f.   This is the point where Goethe begins that final 'intensification of passion' which will allow him to link two picture-book
scenes: 'domestic bliss' and 'the faithless wife', as Alexis appropriates
them. Alexis turns from the former, one of his 'Bilder der Hoffnung', to

91

the gods – and is soon comparing his lot with that of the despairing criminal pursued by the Furies and the hounds of Hell (a picture-book image again).

LINES 138–41   The image of Care ('Sorge'). The spectre of Care – the epithets are 'kalt', 'gräßlich gelassen' and 'gelassen' – is more fully evoked in the words assigned to her in *Faust*, Part II, Act V, from line 11453: 'Wen ich einmal mir besitze,/Dem ist alle Welt nichts nütze,/ Ewiges Düstre steigt herunter/...Und er weiß von allen Schätzen/Sich nicht in Besitz zu setzen./Glück und Unglück wird zur Grille,/...Ist der Zukunft nur gewärtig/Und so wird er niemals fertig.' These may be supplemented by the following from *Faust*, Part I, lines 643–8: '...Wenn Glück auf Glück im Zeitenstrudel scheitert./Die Sorge nistet gleich im tiefen Herzen.../Sie mag als Haus und Hof, als Weib und Kind erscheinen.' These lines provide a complete commentary on Alexis's despair. On 'Sorge' see also Wolfgang Kayser's notes on *Egmont*, Hamburg edition, vol. IV, p. 581f. As for the fortune which 'comes to grief in the whirlpool of time', artists represent a Fortune afloat on a horizontal wheel (= whirlpool). She may be heading for disaster in the turbulent waters surrounding her own island and kingdom. See also Lines 150–4, below.

LINES 141–8   This intentionally overdrawn picture of the 'faithless wife' throws light on the previous passage, lines 64–88. Alexis now believes that he was enticed (seduced) into the garden through an ever-open door. Fortune characteristically beckons to her intended victims; she is also, as Alexis now imputes of Dora, *meretrix*. It is interesting to compare Tasso's reflections on the behaviour of Lenore Santivale, *Tasso* IV 3 from line 2488, and V 5 from line 3333.

LINES 150–54   Here finally the image of Disaster (Misfortune, *infortunium*), as the shipwreck of but recently 'fortunate' seafarers: thunder, clouds, broken ('unglücklicher') mast, wreckage, lost cargo, with perhaps a variant designed to prepare us for some final relief: Alexis exaggerates when he sees himself devoured by dolphins. Their normal role would be to ferry him back to the safety of the shore. In this trait, and in the 'piling on of the agony' ('Steigerung des Leidenschaftlichen'?) in the picture of the 'faithless wife', I see an 'avoidance of tragedy' ('Abbiegung des Tragischen'). For the image of Infortunium in art (Fortune holding her torn sail is stranded, or a ship has broken up, on a rock or reef) see Doren, *loc. cit.* illustr. 17 (right); a Florentine engraving dated 1465–80 in Hind A IV 38; or an engraving of Gian Jacopo Caraglio (d. 1565), Bartsch, *Peintre graveur* XV, 91, 56 '(Fortuna innocuos cladibus afficit/Fortuna immeritos auget honoribus'), etc. Compare finally the much-debated final speech in Goethe's *Tasso*.

II
TEXTUAL STUDIES:
HISTORIOGRAPHICAL APPROACHES

6. NOTES ON FATE AND FORTUNE

For some time now I have been using an unorthodox formula in the discussion of medieval works of literature. I myself find it useful in dealing with major and minor points of interpretation. On the whole it solves more problems than it raises, and it puts a new complexion on much that is familiar. It takes the form of a simple question, 'Augustine or Boethius?' I shall be writing more fully under this heading elsewhere.[1] Meanwhile: what this formula implies is that, in the days before philosophy was made the handmaid of theology (that is to say until about 1250), medieval writers wrote in the main *either* on Christian subjects in accordance with the teaching of St Augustine, *or* as Christians, on secular subjects in accordance with the only approved Christian secular philosophy – that of Boethius in his *De Consolatione Philosophiae*.

It is better to begin with this clear disjunction, either–or. It helps one to disentangle the strands in a minority of important works which attempt a synthesis of Augustinian and Boethian modes of thought, and provides a useful rule-of-thumb when one suspects that a writer is merely digressing from his chosen genre. But how are we to recognize the basic choice an author has made? Clearly not by his quotations and borrowings in the customary sense. What we have to look for is the 'hierarchy of instances' to which he refers his subject, or, in other words, his view of history.

The philosophy of Boethius (and his philosophy of history), in the simplified form in which it exerted its pervasive influence, operates with 'instances' which correspond only in the upper echelons with those of St Augustine and the later theologians, and indeed with those used by Boethius himself in his own theological tractates, *De Trinitate*, *De Fide Catholica*. It shares with Augustine's scheme: God (*deus omnipotens, omnisciens*) as supreme instance, and Divine Providence; but there the

95

correspondences virtually cease, because Boethius is concerned, as Augustine was not, to account for history in the commonly accepted sense of the term. That is history as the vicissitudes of *fortune* of mortal man here on earth.[2]

Below *Providence* which is inscrutable, come, consequently, according to Boethius, *Fate* (as the temporal aspect of God's Providence) which is inexorable, and *Fortune* which is unpredictable. Man as a free agent (to Boethius too, man is a free agent) and Fortune together make history. This Boethian scheme is, one should note, both paradigmatic and exclusive. We have seen what it includes; it *excludes* Christ, the Holy Spirit and the Virgin; the Devil; Heaven and Hell as reward and punishment; the sacraments and the Church. These belong to a different order, or system of knowledge, involving faith and dogma. Boethius is, it is true, concerned with eternity, but in relation to time as experienced by man. He is on the other hand not concerned with the Ages of the World, Antichrist and the Day of Judgment. Not in this work. It is, therefore, by comparison with Augustine's, a restricted economy of ideas, and one which is no longer familiar. Indeed we may fail to recognize it as a system at all when we encounter it in use elsewhere, for instance as late as 1400 in the *Ackermann aus Böhmen*, where apart from one slip (a solitary ejaculation 'Jesu' in the concluding prayer) the Boethian scheme is rigorously adhered to.[3] *Ackermann* editors cannot get over this, and clearly feel that a Christian work ought to allude at least to the Trinity, and – in the later Middle Ages – Mary. They do not recognize the Boethian 'order'. Boethius and thousands of medieval writers after him held that the Christian faith and 'Heilsgeschichte' were properly dealt with in other works. Have not most of our medieval writers their 'other works', Heinrich von Veldeke, Walther, Konrad von Würzburg, Rudolf von Ems, Oswald von Wolkenstein?

There are therefore two distinct medieval philosophies of history: Christian 'Heilsgeschichte' (Augustine), and history pure and simple as it is written 'after Boethius'. Any medieval author writing dynastic history (Widukind for instance),[4] or any poet retelling the tales of heroes of long ago, or indeed inventing adventures for a chosen hero – having decided, that is, in some way to mirror terrestrial history, is *ex hypothesi* committed in all essentials to the Boethian interpretation. This means the use of his order of instances – God, Providence, Fate and Fortune – and avoidance of St Augustine's terms.[5]

It is for this reason primarily, and not because of a profound and compelling belief in a kind of salvation through chivalric enterprise that the Arthurian romances keep religion in the background. Chrétien and Hartmann are concerned, and can, as laymen writing secular narrative, only be concerned with the fortune (*fortuna – sælde*) and the final 'happiness' (*beatitudo –* also *sælde*) of their heroes and heroines.[6] These, then, the fortunes and the happiness, are the story; and as story the narrator 'tells' them. The Christianity of the Arthurian hero is in these circumstances a minimal, formal observance, generally at daybreak before the events of the day; and a few or frequent pious asseverations, and more or less trivial blasphemies. The hero may of course think like a Christian, and seek to resolve moral dilemmas in a Christian sense (generally he can – the story allows him), but all these things go to the account of characterization, and have only a superficial bearing on what he does. Easter and Whitsun are left as synonyms of Spring and Summer; or they are dates in the social calendar – high-class Bank Holidays. A Christian aside on the meaning of Easter would be alien to the genre. As for the souls of the heroes and heroines, and their hopes of salvation (alas for us, again *sælde*! or *der sêle heil*), the most the narrator can do is to assert that they were saved. He can show that this assertion is a reasonable fiction, no more.[7]

The writers of such romances were understandably in the last resort dissatisfied with their efforts within this economy, and spoke disparagingly of them. They made amends where they could – in other works, which, if narratives, were generally legends. Equally naturally we (who wonder how Arthurian romances could have had so long a vogue) are more deeply engaged when a writer of genius applies his talents to a romance involving a heaven-sent *quest*, and uses it in an endeavour to escape from the limited world of Fortune, to portray an ideal world in which the claims of knighthood and those of the Christian faith are, at any rate tentatively, reconciled. But let us not conceal from ourselves that the Grail Community, like the 'Turmgesellschaft' in *Wilhelm Meister*, is in the last analysis *quasi* a Church, significantly and wishfully entrusted by Wolfram with the preservation of dynasties and the elimination of mere Fortune – a rationalization of history. The *Parzival* is, however profound, and when all has been said that can be said, a mystifying and unprofitable fiction, as Wolfram seems himself to have acknowledged. In the *Willehalm* Prologue he invoked no Kyot, but the Holy Spirit;[8] for the duration of this one unfinished work, he forsook the world of romance and kept to memorable history and the then-known world. *Parzival* is, on this interpretation, like the *Divine Comedy* (and indeed *Faust*), an attempt to do justice to Augustine *and* Boethius in one and the same work. All these works imply the bold (possibly true) assumption that the Western world is not irrevocably Christian; the poet seeks to mediate between an evolving world and a relatively timeless Church, or to 'accommodate' the demands of the faith to those of an idealistic secular philosophy.

To sum up and to continue. For the treatment of the fame and fortune of dynasties, of kings and heroes, St Augustine offered the medieval author little or no useful guidance; for, *pace* Augustine, fame *is* the spur, earthly glory is only in the end a vanity, man is God's noblest creature and life on earth must have a purpose. Though Boethius' real aim was to offer to posterity philosophy's consolation for those who like him had fallen into *infortunium*, he had, incidentally, in the course of the five books of the *De Consolatione* provided a complete philosophy (of history) and the terms with which the moralists of the future, chroniclers and poets could argue about the good life, praise famous men and commemorate the deeds of heroes of old. The lesson was quickly learnt. See Otfrid's preface *Cur scriptor hunc librum theotisce dictaverit* for an example of the Boethian choice! And all this, it should be noted, without any necessary reference to what the Church might in *its* jurisdiction consider to be uncharitable, sinful or to merit damnation. Otfrid's preface is not exactly an object lesson in *ôtmuati* [humility].

When one recalls that most medieval authors had read and been examined on the *De Consolatione*, it seems strange that we so rarely quote it in our footnotes. I have myself reluctantly come to the conclusion that many medievalists do not know the work as they should, or imagine it to be just another *Ars moriendi*. These matters will, as I indicated, all be argued at greater length elsewhere. Meanwhile let us take a look at two or three medieval works of particular interest to Frederick Norman. Let us suppose that my formula 'Augustine *or* Boethius' is relevant and see how the works fare when it is applied to them, and at the same time let us put the formula under some pressure.

In his most recent article on the *Hildebrandslied* Norman commits himself to the view that the *irmingot* first invoked by Hildebrand is the Christian God:'Grosser Gott. . .denn Dichter und Zuhörer sind Christen'.[9] It is useful to have this stated categorically, on the basis of the more difficult term *irmingot*, and by Norman. The *waltant got* later called upon, when Hildebrand sees that he must fight with his son, will be more readily and generally accepted as the Christian *deus omnipotens*. So far, so good. Let us now apply, experimentally, the formula 'Augustine or Boethius?' and I think that we shall find that, 'Augustine' being obviously out of the question, 'Boethius' leads to a suprisingly complete gloss on all that is done and said (if not always on the manner of the saying) throughout the lay. Not only is the Christian God invoked at two crucial points in the 'story', but the actions of Hildebrand seem dictated by a view of fate and of the human lot which is in keeping with the

99

teaching of the *De Consolatione*. Now in more detail, the evidence.

Norman says that there is a 'stattliche, völlig nutzlose Literatur' on the subject of the no longer legible word *wettu* in Hildebrand's *wettu irmingot obana ab hevane*. That being the case, there can be little harm in considering what may be involved, if, as I suggest, the poet had in mind the Christian idea of fate. *wettu* would then have to be the subjunctive of (some derivative of) 'wissen', and should allude to God's foreknowledge (his Providence, which becomes man's fate). Paraphrasing roughly: 'may it be foreknown of (almighty) God that Hadubrand will never fight with Hildebrand (*sus sippan man*)'. The customary translation 'I call upon God to witness' will still serve, though the gloss is now 'may God in his prescience have ordained. . .' Let us continue the argument, for none of this can be proved. If Divine Providence *had* ordained that Hadubrand should recognize his father, that would have been the *fatum* or *wurt* of both and each. When it had become clear to Hildebrand that *waltant got* had ordained otherwise, that was still *fatum*, but, from the point of view of the victims (Hildebrand says this on behalf of both) – *wêwurt*, a 'cruel' fate.

This must all sound very strange to students of Old High German literature, and I admit it is wayward of me not to have prefaced my remarks with a thumb-nail sketch of 'germanischer Schicksalsglaube'. I do not want to waste my readers' time. But *is* it so scandalous to be looking towards Boethius? Before saying that there can be no possible connection between our heroic lay and Boethius, let us remember that, as the lay itself assures us, Hildebrand was the faithful follower of Dietrich. Dietrich was, we know, and no doubt the poet knew, 'really' the Theodoric who, in a manner of speaking, provided Boethius with the leisure in which he wrote the *De Consolatione*. (In the fiction of the lay, of course, Dietrich is still on his way to oust Odoacer, and has presumably not yet met Boethius.) It would at any rate be a strange irony of history if the Christian poet, whether Langobard or not, did not know at least in its basic outline the Christian interpretation of secular history written in Pavia by 524, and known from about that date throughout the whole Christian West;[10] i.e. if he did not know the basic paradigm: God, Providence (Fate), Fortune, man. Fate as the temporal aspect of Providence must have absorbed and superseded all older traditional ideas on fate at one telling. It was 'in order', one learnt, to be a Christian and to believe, as one always had done, in fate. With relief one learnt that Boethius's ideas are moreover in line with those of St Augustine, who, 'though he abhorred the world itself' had to admit that 'if *fatum* is derived from *for-fari*, it must be accepted as synonymous with the will of God'.[11] Both Boethius and Augustine say that God's foreknowledge of events is reconcilable with man's free will. I myself find it inconceivable that a poet, in or near Lombardy, could, in the time-span we can allow for the *Hildebrandslied*, still have had his mind encumbered with pre-Christian ideas of fate.

Poet and audience, then, were Christians, *wêwurt* refers to a malign fate (or fortune) in the Boethian sense. The characters too, as Goths coming from the East, are Christians – to the poet at worst heretics. All in all, there seems a fair chance that in *wêwurt skihit* the poet expresses his idea of a fighting man's Christian sentiments under stress. What then is Germanic in the *Hildebrandslied*? That depends of course on how we define 'Germanic', and that is not the purpose of this essay.

But we have not quite finished. We have looked at Fate. What about the Fortune of the Boethian scheme? This is an intricate point which I cannot deal with at all, unless I am taken partly on trust. Fortune is a very vividly conceived if totally enigmatic figure in Book II of the *De Consolatione*, responsible for all that man calls either fortune or misfortune. Unfortunately for her, she had no proper opposite number or name in native Germanic tradition, and was not easily assimilated into it. 'Luck' and its cognates were too closely associated with the purely fortuitous, or the gambler's throw. She had, however, a great future before her – once she had usurped an available, rather lofty title, *Sælde*. In the *Hildebrandslied* she is present by her workings, but not by name; she is not invoked or cursed; she is, in her negative aspect (as *infortunium*), contained within *wêwurt*. Let us now put her into her context.

What, according to Boethius, makes fate 'cruel' and inflicts suffering which to mere man appears 'unmerited' – the old opposition *virtus/fortuna* of Antiquity in Christian guise – is the work of Fortuna – *infortunium*. In his *infortunium* only a philosopher, particularly if he is incarcerated, can think rationally, and find 'consolations' or 'remedies'. Henceforth he will eschew the making of history. Of ordinary mortals, action is invited by Fortune, not after rational thought, but on the strength of an appraisal (appreciation) of the situation at a given moment. Sooner or later the man of action – acts. A free agent but a fallible judge, he makes history – with Fortune. The outcome is success or disaster, *fortuna* or *infortunium*.

Looking again at the lay, we may ask what share that instance has, which Boethius calls Fortune, in the staging of the encounter of Hildebrand and Hadubrand. Why must, of all possible champions, a father and a son have to meet between opposing armies? Why do all the circumstances conspire to ensure that Hadubrand will, within the space of five minutes, come to prefer mariners' tales to the living evidence before him? Why do the artificial conventions of the warrior caste to which father and son happen to belong, require the truth to be established by the utterly inappropriate means of an exchange of boasts, taunts and innuendo? It is indeed a malign *Fortune* which in all these chance circumstances invites Hildebrand to act – when he is ready. Were he a twelfth-century hero he would exclaim *unsælde sî verwâzen* – an outburst of sentiment and a display of sophistication inconceivable in a heroic situation 'long ago'.[12] Hitherto Fortune has favoured Hildebrand in thirty years of perilous campaigning. Now (it may be that the *nû* in *welaga nû waltant got* is more important than we dare to make it) she is about to desert him. But there is, as I say, no word in the text but *wêwurt* which may be said to allude to chance and coincidence, and the main function of Hildebrand's *wêwurt* is to acknowledge the workings of the higher instance, Fate. *wêwurt*, closely associated as it is in the text with *waltant got*, means fate as God's decree, and as such Hildebrand accepts it. He accepts it grimly and stoically but, I think, without defiance. He enacts what he conceives to be his *fatum* and God's will – voluntarily. His invocation of *waltant got* implies a soldier's *fiat voluntas tua*. Hildebrand knows what is being done through him. It will be his and Hadubrand's *wêwurt*, whoever kills whom. This thought he couples with the mere statement (or admission) that God's verdict will be made manifest in a *judicium dei*. We also know, as the poet of the lay could not, what would be the further fate and fortunes of the Hildebrand lay, down to – indeed *wêwurt*! – a modern translation into the original Langobardic.

Having devoted so much space to the immediate and wider implications of my 'Augustine' or Boethius?' question, and having illustrated them by reference to what is perhaps only marginally a Christian work – the *Hildebrandslied*, I can now show more briefly what problems arise when we turn to undoubtedly Christian literature. With 'fate' still uppermost in our minds we have but a short step to the *Heliand* – and a real poser! The *Heliand* re-narrates *sacred* history. But as everyone knows, the poet makes extensive use of the idea of fate, and has dozens of words and idioms to express that idea. And yet Fate belongs to the hierarchy of instances posited by Boethius for the interpretation of *secular* history only. What is to be said of this?

We need hardly stop to remark that anyone (including myself) who has hitherto discussed this matter, has considered only Germanic poetic tradition as the source for the words and idioms, and for the 'idea' of fate. This is pretty damning, I now think. There is a sizeable *Exkurs* on fate in the most recent (and unnecessarily long) book on the *Heliand* by Johannes Rathofer.[13] What Rathofer tells us again is that the *Heliand* poet uses *wurd* and its synonyms in order to make the patently 'impossible' desertion of Christ by his faithful henchmen comprehensible to his North German audience. 'This had to be; this was prophesied.' Secondly, the poet seems obsessed by the prophesies of the Passion in their relation to the *venit hora* of the Gospel narrative. I have, as I have indicated, written briefly elsewhere on these matters, and am duly noted by Rathofer to have contributed to the discussion. (He finds me at fault in thinking that preoccupation with *wurd* led the poet into unorthodoxy.)[14] Suffice it to say that Rathofer does not consider Boethius at all.[15] This is in itself interesting. The modern theologian considers Boethius' *De Consolatione* outside his purview, even when the subject is fate. A welcome, late confirmation that '*either* Augustine *or* Boethius' is relevant.

It will of course not be possible to attempt any real reassessment until the critics have summarized and appraised Rathofer's volume, but for the purposes of this essay I will risk the following. In his endeavour to make his re-narration of sacred story acceptable to recent converts the poet exploits an idea familiar to them, fate. He is thereby able to deal both with the fulfilment of prophecy, of which the evangelists themselves so often speak, and to represent the Passion and death of Christ as fore-ordained at a certain hour: *venit hora*. Desperately he tries by this same device to account for the defection of the disciples, and finally grasps at the words *spiritus promptus* to assert Christ's eagerness to obey the Father (and so dismiss his Agony as a weakness solely of the flesh). So much for the concessions which the poet made, perhaps was forced to make, to the prejudices of his audience. There remains the likelihood, that so far as he and his co-clerics were concerned (if they approved of his efforts at all), the terms used for fate bore a Boethian gloss. But the solecism also remains; for great as may have been the agony suffered in Gethsemane, and however completely Christ as man 'shared our common lot', it cannot be predicated of him that he was subject to Fate; that is, was *only* human. The term fate was not available for sacred history; not even, I think, for the story of the disciples. As for the words with which the missionary poet bodied forth his tale, these he had to find where they were to be found: in an existing rhetorical tradition. In using them afresh he contributed substantially to the evolution of their meaning in a Christian sense.

So far the emphasis has been on Fate. We come now a half-step down in the Boethian scale to consider Fortune, of whom Boethius had spoken with massive authority (see above), and whose image – *Fortune and her Wheel*, derived from the text of Book II – was to become perhaps the most important didactic image in the whole of medieval art. At the same time we move forward to the High Middle Ages, and are able to witness her operations in at any rate one of her main spheres. (We must leave aside dynastic history on which I shall be writing elsewhere.) In imaginative literature, particularly in romance (as opposed to *chanson de geste* and heroic epic) she is ubiquitous – our *Sælde*, bestower of *sælde*, or *unsælde*. We should dispel from our minds any idea that she is a trivial force. If the historians made Fortune responsible for the end of the Carolingians, the Saxons [see however note 4] and the Hohenstaufens, she is a sufficiently important governess for the Erecs and Iweins of fiction. (Conversely, as histories become longer and more intricate, fate becomes a vague idea impossible to sustain; and in the world of fiction one will not presume, except with a certain flippancy, to impute to the hand of God or Providence the vagaries of *âventiure*.) Let us ignore entirely the fortune or fortunes of the purely conventional Arthurian knight and his final disappearance into some unspecified bliss (*beatitudo – sælde*), just beyond the confines of the imagined ideal world (the 'happy ever after' solution).

*Sæld*e is responsible, as a quick glance at our texts will show, for the wealth, standing and earthly glory (Boethius' *opes et honores*) of Lord Henry and Gregorius. From the moment things go wrong for them, however, they become complicated for us. These heroes are not merely deserted by Fortune; they fall into *sin*, and each story in its unfolding passes out of the initial genre which is clearly Boethian, and beyond the proper province of the layman who is writing. Hartmann can, like any intelligent layman, deal according to his lights with problems of moral philosophy; he is not strictly entitled to treat theological issues, and yet he tries: sin and some kind of conversion in *Der arme Heinrich*, sin and penance in *Gregorius*.

What, applying my formula, we are now asking, is: given that a medieval narrative work is an expression of *Laienfrömmigkeit*, what view of history does it reflect? Is it mainly Boethian, or mainly Augustinian? I think the former. Here are a few pointers. When Heinrich falls into sin it is said that God closed *der sælden tor* on him. This is a suitably ambivalent statement: misfortune begins; hopes of passing through the gates of *Sælde* (vaguely, but not in any strict sense, Heaven or Paradise) vanish. When Heinrich's conversion has been effected he is restored to an enhanced *sælde*, which we infer to mean happiness (*beatitudo*) with, presumably, renewed hopes of salvation (see below). The outer framework of the story is thus clearly Boethian. The inner story meanwhile runs roughly parallel to that of the sacred story of the prototypical sufferer, Job. Of Job's plight the term *unsælde* is however not, and I believe could not be, used. (Luther seems to me to make a complete and conscious break with all tradition in this matter: his foreword to the book of Job speaks of Job's *Unglück*.) As for the miraculous healing of Heinrich, let us not be too subtle. It is the work of God. But, then, God and Providence are the supreme instances in the Boethian scheme. As for the maiden, her role is not compared or contrasted with that of any character from sacred history; in her early inspired teaching of her parents she reminds Hartmann of a Saint – St Nicholas; little more than an aside: amazing! I think the answer is that Hartmann strains somewhat at the limits imposed by the Boethian genre, attributing as much as he must, or dares, to God and Providence, and enlarging the province of *Sælde* as far as he may. He clearly associates a generously conceived Fortune (*Sælde*) with man's hope, or perhaps better *chance*, of 'beatitude' (*sælde*), or even salvation.

Now, as next step, we could consider the element of *chance* and coincidence in the career which leads Gregorius to the brink of (we infer) *damnation* and back. In the Augustinian scheme there is no such thing as chance, therefore the *Gregorius* cannot be basically Augustinian in conception.[16] Is it Boethian? I won't retail the story, but merely remind us of a few turning points, and ask whether we can say at once to 'whom' all these chance meetings, discoveries and rightly or wrongly seized or neglected opportunities are attributed? This very specification strongly suggests Boethius's Fortune, but the story is going to produce, after all, a – fictitious – Pope! Who guided Gregorius's barque to the abbot, led him to his mother's country, was responsible for the restoration of the key; who led Gregorius back to the spot where he discovered the tablet giving him details of his incestuous birth? Whatever nouns or verbs Hartmann uses, they must, I think, be brought as far as possible within the paradigm God, Providence (Fate), Fortune, of Boethius. Yet at the same time Hartmann has, through making his hero *sin*, invoked the Devil (*des tievels rât* 339). Having brought in the Devil he has access to a wider range of Christian terms, if only to keep the Devil under observation – a favourite device of amateur theologians.

I am, *nota bene*, discussing only narrative motivation and the powers governing the course of Hartmann's story. Here, at any rate, are answers to a few of the questions just asked. Gregorius's mother, having discovered that she is incestuously married to her son, complains of a malign Fortune (*mir ist diu Sælde gram*), and states in the same breath that the curse of God was on the day of her birth; Misfortune (*Unsælde*) had pledged itself to grant her no further happiness (2556f.). Gregorius (already called *der guote sündære*) inveighs against God, and attributes their common plight to him. This is the God of the Boethian scheme, I think. It is clearly Divine Providence which apprises the Romans who should be the next Pope. But the emissaries consider it 'fortunate' (*ze sælden*) that they come upon the fisherman's house when they are exhausted. Then – a clear departure from the Boethian scheme, and possibly to match the intrusive Devil – it is the Holy Spirit which sustained Gregorius on his rock, says Hartmann.

The recovery of the key is a tricky point. Gregorius demanded that it *should be* found if he was to be convinced; he demanded a miracle, but in fact the key had been found before he demanded that it should be. Very neat! – and no miracle, but coincidence. As for the recovery of the tablet, Gregorius prays that he may find it 'or else. . .', and is said by (unspecified) onlookers to be a 'fortunate' (*sælic*) man when he does find it. 'And that was no lie', says Hartmann. Fortuna – *Sælde* is indeed a difficult term! It extends all the way from happy chance to beatitude, even salvation – see *der sælden strâze* in Hartmann's Prologue, l. 87 – and makes one wonder whether the basic idea is not '*chance* (or hope) of salvation' – the most that mere mortal man can state with confidence that he has: something tenuously associated with the theologian's 'grace'.

It looks as if in the context of ordinary history or story, *sælde*, until one has and holds it, moves with the fleeting moment: as if, for all Augustine's teaching, salvation is a chancy business, rather than a matter of grace. There is in *Gregorius* a tiny episode which illustrates in a simple and touching way that man's hopes of salvation indeed depend on chance, and the recognition of the propitious moment. What one would never dare to assert of Parzival's missed opportunity, buried as it now is under libraries of often sentimental nonsense on the 'Mitleids-frage' (the words are *owê daz er niht vrâgete dô* – the keyword is *dô*!) one can with a clear conscience state of the behaviour of the surly fisherman and his wife. When the husband proposes to let Gregorius go on his way, his wife intervenes vigorously. Out of the kindness of her heart? The text says that what she fears is that the two of them, precariously poised as they are between bare subsistence and starvation, may miss their *opportunity* of earning salvation by helping the needy, as the New Testament enjoins; there may be only this one *armman* – the first and possibly the last, to come their way (2842ff.).[17]

The opportunity (*sælde*) must be seized, or their *heil* will be jeopardized. This more optimistic view of 'fortune' as something associated with the fleeting moment (*occasio*) – as an opportunity or a time to be seized by the audacious, is notably (and with good reason) not part of Boethius's own teaching. It is only dubiously amenable to a Christian interpretation. But that ultimately all fortune lore would come to be associated with man's hopes of salvation was inevitable.

I close with an instance which after ten years of 'Fortune' reading I still find somewhat bewildering. I offer it as a *curiosum* to an old friend and colleague who has spent a good deal of time on literature devoted to the Virgin Mary. The poet of the Middle High German poem, *Die Erlösung* (about 1300), speaks of, and can apparently visualize, the passage of the Wheel of Mankind's Fortune through the ear of the Virgin when the Word was miraculously made flesh in her womb.

> Die hêre gluckes schîbe
> Marien durch ir ôre scheip (= *rollte*, Maurer)
> dô sie die wâre minne dreip
> in der reinen maget schôz.[18]

If this article might have gone on for twice the length I should, as next logical step, have shown where over-zealous medieval exegetes found evidence of Fortune in the Bible. Of that perhaps more elsewhere.

7. THE 'FORTUNE' OF HARTMANN'S EREC

It is now some fifteen years since Arthur Hatto helped me with the final draft of 'Notes on Fate and Fortune',[1] the essay in which I first declared an historiographical approach to medieval literature. That commitment has meantime survived the completion of a monograph[2] arguing, and I hope demonstrating, that the terms 'fate' and 'fortune' belong in medieval consciousness to an economy of *historical* ideas which is systematically set forth in the medieval handbook of Christian moral philosophy, Boethius's *De Consolatione Philosophiae*, Book IV, Prose vi.[3] More directly and widely influential was the dramatic presentation of a personified Fortune in Book II of the same work: by the High Middle Ages Fortune at her Wheel had become the image of terrestrial, particularly dynastic history. More familiar to medieval scholars is the Church's scheme of universal history, based on St Augustine's doctrine of the 'Two Cities' (and the Six Ages) in *De Civitate Dei* – in which fate and fortune play no role. These discrete patterns of historical thought can perhaps most strikingly be illustrated by a renewed comparison of Bishop Otto of Freising's two great historical works: more is involved than pessimism in the one and excessive optimism in the other. In *De Duabus Civitatibus* (completed *circa* 1146) Otto writes as a Cistercian. He adapts the Augustinian scheme for the narration of universal history down to (and with projections beyond) his own times. In it he at one point expressly rejects 'the Wheel of Fortune of the philosophers'.[4] In the *Gesta Frederici* which followed Otto writes as a Hohenstaufen. He celebrates the glorious reign of his nephew Frederick I 'on whom Fortune never frowned'. The whole work (and that of his continuator Rahewin) is 'Boethian' in conception and in detailed execution.[5]

More controversially I have contended that it is the Boethian view of history as fortune which is reflected in virtually all works of medieval narrative literature, even in Wolfram von Eschenbach's *Parzival*, a grail romance, and in Hartmann von Aue's *Gregorius*,[6] a so-called 'courtly legend'. The two authors undoubtedly show a deep concern for the salvation of their respective heroes; they nevertheless as laymen tell and gloss their stories in terms of medieval fortune doctrine. But all this Hatto already knows! Is it then fair if, in an essay for him, I take another of our medieval classics and seek in it further support for the same line of argument? On balance I think it is. For one thing, I shall be 'looking for Boethius' this time in a typical Arthurian romance, i.e. one in which Arthur's (King Arthur's) court sets the seal on a completed knightly career: the hero does not set out in pursuit of a still higher goal symbolized by the Holy Grail; still less does he renounce the world. I have moreover elected to examine Hartmann's *Erec*,[7] a work in which Hatto's interest is of long standing. Will he agree, I wonder, that its real subject is 'the fortune of Erec'?

I

Hitherto, anticipating greater difficulties elsewhere, I have restricted myself to the bald assertion that a typical romance of chivalry can only be Boethian.[8] Here, taking *Erec* as example, I hope to show that it is – and not vaguely so, but as Boethian as the literary genre and the identity of the hero allow. A statement of the case in general terms would run as follows. Chivalric (Arthurian) romance is not concerned with universal history, the Christian faith, or even in any real sense with the Church and its sacraments, institutions, or history. Any allusions must fall to the account of characterization (e.g. of the hero) or be descriptive of a generally Christian world; they are not story. It is therefore not Augustinian, though anyone so minded could doubtless write an Augustinian gloss on the hero's progress to perfection. Chivalric romance (for instance *Erec*) is, however, equally not concerned with the destiny of nations, or real or imaginary peoples; at most the idea is present that dynasties make history (Erec is 'fil de roi Lac' and succeeds Lac), but this does not shape the stories, which are those of individual heroes, each of whom succeeds in the end, achieving a personal *fama*. The hero goes out of set purpose into the unknown in search of *âventiure*, to be tried in a series of chance encounters. He readily accepts hazards known to be impossible, even for the bravest. But as each hero in turn is for the duration of his own story the bravest, the fortune (*sælde*) which he 'has' must hold. Success brings the recognition which (conventionally) Arthur's court alone can bestow. The consummation of the hero's career, now completed as story, is a state of 'happiness ever after' (i.e. until death), shared with the heroine. The final setting is often the hero's home country, in Erec's case an inherited kingdom. In an epilogue the poet may confidently assert hero and heroine now to be in heaven, their souls saved. – How, it may well be asked, can a story following such a course reflect a Boethian view of *history*? Is it not, as the handbooks say, simply the rationalization of an original fairy-story (*Märchen*)? That is precisely the point I seek to make. Hartmann's final rationalization falls within – well within – the entirely rational scheme of secular history which the Middle Ages had from *De Consolatione Philosophiae*. What other norm for story was there? Hartmann treated Erec's case, as any other schooled writer would have done, 'normally'.

How does this claim fare, however, when tested, not against such a general statement but against the ten thousand lines of Hartmann's text? All I can say at this stage is that I have reconsidered *Erec* in such a light and find Hartmann *at least* as concerned to deal adequately with Erec's fortune (*sælde*) as he is to illustrate his knightly prowess and pay homage to chivalric ideals, or to criticize the 'Minnedienst' of the Red Knight (Mâbonagrîn), Erec's final opponent. Erec is, in other words, successful, not because he is or becomes in the course of his trials a perfect knight with a social conscience, and so deserves his success. He succeeds because he takes his chances, and because he recognizes when the moment has come to risk the gambler's throw, all or nothing! That is a statement requiring immediate expansion. Putting his trust, as always, first in God, Erec dares to be brave when bravery will not suffice without fortune. He puts his fortune to the test, and, 'by the grace of God', wins. (Good fortune is ultimately in God's gift; it is reward, but it is not in any strict sense earned.) Does such an emphasis on *fortune* suffice to make *Erec* a 'Boethian' work? I have already made qualifications to which we now turn.

We clearly need to consider what modifications of the Boethian philosophy of history were required to match the reduced scope for serious historical thought dictated by the two premises 'world of King Arthur' and 'story of Erec'. (There are of course compensatory enlargements of scope for fantastic story.) Moreover, we must make due allowance for the prejudices and the milieu of Hartmann and his aristocratic audience, their shared belief, for instance, that God was disposed to favour them and their kind, their *mores*: he too was courtly (*hövesch*). The full Boethian hierarchy of historical forces (God, providence, fate, fortune, man's free will) is thereby almost automatically reduced, or is reducible, to the following: a courtly God, fortune (in the abstract, or personified as Dame Fortune), the personal fortune of Erec, and Erec as man. Let us start with Erec himself. Is it primarily as a knight that Erec first fails: 'Erec verligt sich'? Or is it as a man, who, forgetting his true nature, as moral philosophy would put it, wallows in sensuality until he is shamed by the reproach (*itewîz*) which such conduct earns him?[9] Merely to rationalize a fairy-story as a tale of knighthood, it would surely have sufficed to show Erec content after marriage with the domestic life, a stay-at-home. One could of course say that here, as in the description of Enite's horse and saddle (and on several occasions) Hartmann opts for rhetoric, and that the full treatment of 'sloth' has Erec's completely unmanly behaviour as its consequence:

> sîn site er wandeln began.
> als er nie würde der man,
> alsô vertreip er den tac. (2934-6)[10]

Erec's scrambles to get from bed to the dining-table (where he authorizes his knights to keep their engagements: 'ich lobe an im den selben site', 2965) – and to Mass, preserve only tenuous links with his kind and with his obligations. His reaction when corrected is also all too human rather than chivalric, from wounded pride. But in time his true *manheit* (manliness and knightly courage) reasserts itself, and, God so willing, the fortune (*sælde*) which was Erec's from the cradle (see below, II) prevails. In the end he may, to a late twelfth-century audience, have appeared to deserve his final success, despite the unnecessary trials to which he subjected Enite. More important is the fact that his individual fortune survived his period of complete unworthiness. Sentimentally we may, with Hartmann, wish to attribute his timely recovery to Enite's patience and loyalty. Arthur's court (Hartmann is narrator) was more perceptive: it attributed Erec's success to Dame Fortune (*vrou Sælde*), see below, II.

As for the complete Boethian hierarchy of historical forces, man and fortune are clearly active in *Erec*, but what has happened to divine providence and fate? (Providence is timeless; its projection in the created world of time is fate.) The answer has, I think, to be that providence was not available, and that fate was not needed.[11] I argue as follows. We have reached the point where we must (at last!) distinguish between history-writing proper and story-telling, between the imperial historian Otto of Freising (or for that matter the policy-maker Reinald of Dassel and the propagandist Archpoet) making claims concerning the divinely inspired (providential) mission of Frederick Barbarossa, and Hartmann entertaining his public with the 'romantic' exploits of Erec. It would surely have been the height of impiety seriously to suggest a divine purpose manifesting itself through the career of Erec or any other of Arthur's knights. As for fate, the concept itself was in Hartmann's day still indispensable in a completely systematic moral philosophy – in the always contemporary *De Consolatione Philosophiae*, for instance, and in Alan of Lille's *Anticlaudianus*.[12] The whole chain of causation could indeed be referred to as *ordo*, *lex*, or *series fatalis*.[13] But Augustine's strong deprecation of the use of the term was evidently remembered; *fatum* could on etymological grounds be held to mean the word spoken by God (thus Augustine and Isidore), but one should always refer to the will of God, not to fate.[14] This was theologically correct; it was equally a welcome solution for writers and speakers of all kinds, whether for deliberate statements involving religious conviction or for even the most casual expression of Christian 'fatalism', as in the modern ultimate reduction of *deo volente* to 'd.v.'[15] That leaves little room for either the term 'fate' or the discrete idea. Even so, expression had occasionally to be found for the lot to which an individual is content to resign himself, see below, II.

From the foregoing remarks it is evident that in chivalric romance the expression 'the will of God' will rarely be a direct reference to the God of Christian faith and dogma. That is indeed the case in *Erec*. Even at his devotions in church the hero prays for no more than the favour (*genâde*) of God, the bestower of success in combat. Much more regularly reference to God's will serves as the proper (or merely formal) preface to a more carefully worded attribution of cause to fortune (*sælde*) or chance (*geschiht*), both of which are manifestations of God's will. The former remains, as it had been in antiquity (classical and Germanic) and still is, an idea of some complexity. It is an outside force governing the course and outcome of human affairs, particularly change (*wehsel*); it is also a 'charismatic' quality of leaders of men and of individual heroes – they 'have' fortune. Chance, as the unforeseen coincidence of courses of action undertaken independently, determines the circumstances in which fortune (in either sense) comes into play. For all these basic ideas – God's will, fortune, chance – there are, of course, in medieval Latin (the language of the poets' schooling) and in the vernaculars, more or less synonymous expressions and a range of grammatical possibilities which ideally one would wish to distribute and define. I have no such ambitions.

With that observation I conclude my argument that

Hartmann's Erec is as Boethian as the genre and the identity of the hero allow. It remains to adduce the textual evidence. As for the manner of presenting it, I have discarded a synopsis with annotated quotations, in favour of a review of Hartmann's use of the various 'fortunistic' terms *sælde, heil, gelücke* etc., which I refer, individually or jointly with others, to important narrative contexts. I have reduced my complementary observations on 'Minne' and 'Minnedienst' as other motivating forces to a few asides or footnotes. My hope is that the essay as a whole will provide an alternative introduction for colleagues who wish to re-read *Erec* in an unmarked copy.

II

VROU SÆLDE, SÆLDE, SÆLEKEIT

The unanimous verdict of Arthur's court on Erec's crowning adventure – his triumph of *Joie de la curt* and his signal efforts on behalf of the eighty widows whom he had rescued from their enforced sojourn at Castle Brandigân – is that this could not have happened had *vrou Sælde* (Dame Fortune) not assisted his nurse when he lay in the cradle:

> wan daz vrou Sælde ir stiure
> gap sîner ammen diu sîn phlac
> dô er in der wagen lac,
> sô enmöhtez nimmer sîn geschehen. (9899–902)

Does Hartmann's treatment of Erec's *sælde* in the story up to that point make this somewhat emotional acclaim (the sudden appearance of eighty widows was a sensation, 'ein vremdiu sache', 9903f.) also his own verdict? The following outline account of Hartmann's development of the theme suggests strongly that it is.

The first reference to Erec's *sælde* comes, it must be admitted, bewilderingly early. Hartmann introduces Erec as 'fil de roi Lac,/der vrümekeit und sælden phlac' (ll. 2f.). This is, I think, merely a formula meaning that 'things have gone well for Erec so far; here he is, equerry to Arthur's queen, his story now starts'.[16] Erec's story starts in fact with a humiliating encounter with a dwarf, a *leit* that will be avenged in the defeat of the dwarf's master Îdêrs at Tulmein in the sparrow-hawk contest. With what hopes does Erec approach this, his first real test? He hopes that God may give him increase of *heil* (139, cf. 496). He is wished *gelücke* (657) by Duke Îmâîn. 'Luckily' (see 751) he was also wished *heil* (753) by the onlookers before the contest. [Note: *heil* is not *sælde* but may contribute to it, see below.] Erec then fights with borrowed and antiquated arms, not expertly, for he is still inexperienced, but 'sam er wuote' (859), until, having caught a glimpse of Enite, he feels the strength of two men (939). He is victor. He himself attributes his victory to *sælde* (973), but it is interesting that Hartmann is satisfied with 'Êreck sô wol gelanc' (1296), and that Arthur's court rejoices only at his *gelücke* (1302); the queen was 'sîner âventiure vrô' (1528); all praised his *manheit* (1311). So far then, only Erec senses that *sælde* (clearly fortune) favours him.

Erec's next testing is not in *âventiure*, but at a regular tournament organized by Gawain, as his contribution to the festivities associated with the wedding of Erec and Enite at Arthur's court. It is to take place in three weeks' time. Erec approaches this engagement with great circumspection, aware of his inexperience ('wan er vor der stunde/turnierens nie begunde', 2252f.) and, no doubt, of his new armour. He does not presume to carouse (*giuden*) with other knights ('er enwolde sich niht gelîchen/einem guoten knehte', 2383f. in the context of 2378–90). This earns him a high opinion among the knights who pay their courtesy calls. Hartmann's comment is:

> in minnete allez daz in sach.
> er tete alsam der Sælden schol:
> man enspræche im anders niht sô wol. (2041-3)

Erec's behaviour, namely his self-restraint as a test under approved auspices approaches, is 'such as Fortune requires' of a prospective favourite. When early the following (Sunday!) morning his competitors are still in their quarters attending to spit-and-polish (2407–10), Erec is out doing trial runs with two other early risers. He does well – why?

> zwô genâde vuocten im daz:
> sælde und grôze werdekeit,
> die hâte got an in geleit. (2437–9)

Hartmann has now committed himself: *gratia Dei* Erec has *fortuna* and *virtus*. Erec also excels at the *vespereide*, the fuller practice session on the eve of the tournament (2452–75). Surely, one would think from these indications, Erec's quite outstanding prowess in the actual tournament must earn him open acclaim in terms of his *sælde*. That is not the case. King Arthur, hearing on the morning of the contest that Erec has been out for fifteen spear-casts (he has also been to chapel, but Arthur is not aware of this), rebukes his knights for their sluggishness and says 'good luck to him! it's his for the asking' ('got gebe im heil swenne er sîn gert', 2531), and indeed Erec performs, according to Hartmann, 'on that one day even better than Gawain' (the gist of 2720–63). But there is no direct reference to Erec's *sælde* from any quarter. Instead, quite extravagant – and at first sight irrelevant – praise is showered on Erec by all who have seen him on and off the field:

> .. .man begunde gelîchen
> sîn wîsheit Salomône,
> sîn schœne Absolône,
> an sterke Samsônes genôz (2815–8)

– not to mention Alexander, with whom Erec is compared for his *milte*. But *are* the comparisons irrelevant? Though I doubt whether Hartmann did better than to stumble on it,[17] he found in the clichés 'wise as Solomon' etc. a means both of describing Erec at a moment when everything seemed to be going in his favour, *and* of foreshadowing a calamitous fall from grace. The fall from grace is a concealed *tertium comparationis* in the likening of Erec to Solomon, Absalom, Samson, and Alexander, for Hartmann knows that after the tournament Erec will repair with Enite to Destregâles – and to bed! (Hartmann remembers Absalom as a prototype when he deals more explicitly with the fall of Lord Henry in *Der arme Heinrich*, ll. 82–9.) The comparison is, in the event, belied by Erec's career, for his *sælde* survives, or at any rate chance brings him back to the path – 'der Sælden wec'.

The true path to *sælde* (fortune) is what Erec claims to have been seeking all along – not mere *âventiure*, which is *unmâze* (7012–23). He chances upon it after taking what to his companion and friend King Guivreiz was the wrong route at a fork in the road (7811–906). This leads to the final testing of Erec at the *âventiure* (still *âventiure*!) of *Joie de la curt*. Despite all advice Erec argues his decision to accept the challenge as follows:

> 'ich weste wol, der Sælden wec
> gienge in der werlde eteswâ,
> rehte enweste ich aber wâ,
> wan daz ich in suochende reit
> in grôzer ungewisheit,
> unz daz ich in nû vunden hân.
> got hât wol ze mir getân
> daz er mich hât gewîset her
> dâ ich nâch mînes herzen ger
> vinde gar ein wunschspil
> dâ ich lützel wider vil
> mit einem wurfe wâgen mac.' (8521–32)

In his assurance that he has found *der Sælden wec* Erec is alone. Hartmann uses every means further to isolate his hero by enlarging on the alarm of Enite and the fears of well-wishers. He suggests even an element of arrogance and vainglory in Erec's behaviour. The latter's words 'got hât wol ze mir getân' border on presumption; he assures Enite as he takes leave of her that his victory is certain ('swenne mich der muot iuwer mant,/ sôst sigesælic mîn hant', 8868f.). For a reliable interpretation of Erec's words and behaviour at this juncture one should probably recall Hartmann's earlier remark: 'er tete alsam der

Sælden schol'. He has made his decision to risk 'lützel wider vil' in the gambler's throw. The rest follows: the words expressing confidence and resolve, and the composure and restraint required by one who puts his fortune to the test. With the words 'herre, alsô got wil' to his host, Erec retires for the night (8589f.). The following morning he attends Mass and prays earnestly that he may survive (8636–40), breakfasts frugally, drinks 'sant Jôhannes segen' at leave-taking (8651f.)[18] and arms himself for combat with the Red Knight. He is victorious. I think we may take it that Hartmann endorses the verdict of Arthur's court which was our opening quotation, above, p. 116. Wolfram von Eschenbach was less reticent. Of his hero Parzival he affirms: '. . .den ich hân brâht/dar sîn doch sælde het erdâht' (827, 17f.).

A few further points remain to be made about *Sælde, sælde* and *sælic,* before we consider *sælekeit.* The successful pursuit of fortune is necessarily the prerogative of the hero of any given story: Erec has *sælde,* and in due course brings it to fulfilment. And Enite? She triumphed *sæleclîche* (1381) at the beauty-contest (part of the sparrow-hawk adventure), and she no doubt shared Erec's fortune (and fall from grace) until the estrangement. But when Erec has so cruelly made her his groom and accumulated eight horses, Hartmann attributes her ability to bear the hardship to Dame Fortune and God's courtesy:

> wan daz vrou Sælde ir was bereit
> und daz diu gotes hövescheit
> ob mîner vrouwen swebete,. . .
> sô wære kumberlîch ir vart:
> des wart diu vrouwe wol bewart. (3460–7)

In her trials and near-despair Enite can only think of herself as *unsælic* or *sældenlôs* (3357, 5992, 6006, 6038), indeed, she was born to be unlucky: 'unheiles wart ich geborn' (5940). With the reconciliation comes a renewal of *sælekeit* of the married state. Incidentally, nobody argues more urgently that fortune favours Enite than the completely deluded Count Oringles. The *wehsel* (a marked change of fortune) that will follow marriage to him (6251–61, 6270, 6486f., 6499) should be sufficient proof, he thinks, of her *sælde*.

Arthur's court knows *sælde*, it will be recalled, as an almost permanent state of being – as such it is probably *felicitas*. It is occasionally threatened by intruders, but always assured and even augmented by the exploits of Arthur's knights. For the duration of Erec's story there are, however, after the awkwardness with the dwarf, no real threats. Hartmann, who knows and says often enough that *sælde* (fortune) is God-given, seems to have no difficulty in accepting the convention of romance that, in addition to being *sælic* itself, Arthur's court recognizes *sælde* and accords due praise and honour to those blessed with it. In that sense it 'bestows' *sælde*. With that goes the corollary that merely to be admitted to Arthur's court is a measure of good fortune. We noted above the fortunate case of Erec when he was still a newcomer: he later offers the following words of encouragement to Cadoc, who on his way to Arthur's court was waylaid and mercilessly scourged by giants:

> swer ez dâ gevürdern kan,
> der wirt schiere ein sælic man. (5686f.)

Sælde is of course cordially wished, e.g. at leave-takings (3598, 5709). A final point: Hartmann waggishly says of an otherwise unimportant wedding-guest (Gimoers of Avalôn): 'des sælde enwas niht kleine/wan er minnete ein feine' (1932f.) – a case not envisaged by the moral philosophers!

Sælekeit is occasionally interchangeable with *sælde* (4242, 6130, 6713f., 9591); it is generally 'happiness'. When 'wished', it carries, expressed or understood (5709, 9670), the qualification 'lasting'. It is then the equivalent of *fortuna manens* or (earthly) *beatitudo*, the latter being the highest good according to *De Consolatione*, Book III. An important passage enlarges as follows on the parting wishes of the *spilliute* at the wedding of Erec and Enite:

> Êrecke und vrouwen Ênîten
> wunschten si aller sælekeit.

> diu was in doch nû bereit
> lange unde manec jâr.
> ir wunsch wart volleclîche wâr,
> wan zwei gelieber wurden nie
> unz ez der tôt undervie,
> der allez liep leidet
> sô er liep von liebe scheidet. (2203–11)

The happiness will last 'lange unde manec jâr', but end with death. This is in accordance with the teaching of *De Consolatione*: even lasting happiness is impermanent.[19] Consideration of this instructive passage gives, however, little guidance to the interpretation of Hartmann's first description of Enite (323–41) – her 'beauty' and her *sælekeit* (Hatto knows the passage well):

> ir lîp schein durch ir salwe wât
> alsam diu lilje, dâ si stât
> under swarzen dornen wîz.
> ich wæne got sînen vlîz
> an sî hâte geleit
> von schœne und von sælekeit. (336–41)

God's favour manifests itself in Enite's beauty and, I think, 'grace' (or Enite is 'well-favoured').[20]

FATE

On the limited need for this concept, see above, pp. 114f. In *Erec* I find no word which in itself means 'fate'. The only character who both resigns himself to his fate and finds words to express his sentiments is Koralus, Enite's father. The victim of predatory attacks by enemies and now living in dire poverty, he says:

> nû hât got über mich
> verhenget swes er wolde. . .
> daz wil ich von gote hân. (535–9, cf. 601)

He continues, echoing the words of Hannah's prayer (Canticle of Hannah in I Sam. 2.7):[21]

> des gewaltes ist alsô vil,
> er mac den rîchen swenne er wil

> dem armen gelîchen
> und den armen gerîchen. (540-3)

These words suit the patriarchal figure whom Hartmann describes (275-80). He has none the less kept his arms by him, and lends them to Erec.

One may wish to read fatalism into the words of the accident-prone knight Keiîn ('nû enmac doch daz nieman bewarn/daz im geschehen sol', 4801f.), or more certainly those of Enite in her overlong lament at Erec's 'death'.[22]

> dâ vür enhœret dehein list,
> man enmüeze im (*sc.* God) sînen willen lân.
> der muoz ouch an mir ergân:
> ich muoz et unsælic sîn. (5989-92)

Misfortune is the lot 'dealt' (*verteilet*) to her, she thinks (see 5985-6007 and compare 6037-41). There is, of course, in romance no room for fate as 'doom', or for a fate which has to be defied.

HEIL, GELÜCKE, (WOL) GELINGEN

These seem in *Erec* to be almost interchangeable expressions. I see no gaps for the insertion of the lexicographer's wedge, or in the case of *gelücke/gelingen* of the etymologist's. By contrast with *sælde* they seem to refer primarily to success on a single occasion; they may indicate that the hero has *sælde*. There are no 'sacral' overtones to *heil*, and only in the context of prayers may we assume that hopes of 'salvation' are expressed. Its general meaning is 'safety', 'safe outcome'. Of the hero, and of any other worthy, it may be predicated that he has *heil* or *gelücke*, or that 'im gelanc' or 'geschach wol'. In this con-nection Erec's encounter with Guivreiz le pitîz, king of Ireland, is instructive. In Hartmann's long account (4277-610) there is no express reference to the hero's *sælde*. (He has known *sælde* and will later chance upon *der Sælden wec*. Erec's victory over Guivreiz is a turning-point.) Guivreiz, though a dwarf, is a highly reputable and doughty fighter, and has hitherto had *gelücke* (4305) in many a combat.

> dar umbe man noch von im seit
> daz im an sîner manheit
> unz an den tac nie misselanc. (4308-10)

He is able to engage Erec only after provoking him. The outcome will be *heil* (4343), he says: 'as God wills', favourable to the one or the other. Since neither combatant was a coward, says Hartmann, strength (Erec is already wounded) and *heil* will decide the issue. The term in Hartmann's use must cover the *gelücke* of Guivreiz and the at least potential *sælde* of Erec, see 4382-7. As for Erec's victory: 'dô Êrecke alsô gelanc' (Hartmann 4463), 'dâ ist iu wol gelungen an' (Guivreiz 4519). Guivreiz refers in his words specifically to Erec's success in making him his 'man', and if his vanquisher is 'ein edel man', Guivreiz will not deem himself unsuccessful (4528-34).

A prefaced reference to God's will does not materially affect the meaning of *heil* (139, 2531, 4343, 6126) or *gelingen* (140, 1265).

TIME, CHANCE, OPPORTUNITY

These ideas are of course interlinked and cannot be separately (or fully) illustrated. Towards the end of the romance, Hartmann – and his hero, Erec – seem increasingly to be concerned with time (*zît*), both the appropriate time (for weeping, rejoicing etc.)[23] and time in relation to chance circumstances and opportunity, let us say 'kairos': the recognition of the favourable moment. The key passage (8521ff.) was quoted above under *sælde*; see also the continuation of the passage (to 8538), below, under 'the gambler's throw'.

As for time in relation to freely undertaken commitments, Erec – unlike Iwein – has no difficulty in keeping appointments. His promise to return within three days from his pursuit of the dwarf (in the event, from the sparrow-hawk contest) – 'failing sickness' ('ob ich vor siechtuome mac', 143) – requires no final dash to Arthur's court. Tension results rather from the author's manipulation of the unplanned movements of hero and heroine (they travel *wîselôs*, 'without a guide'), and of various assailants who have no particular reason to be abroad at the time, particularly in the tale of Enite's trials. The possibilities are comically or tragi-comically exploited. There is the timely escape from the inn to dupe the amorous count (3644–4100), and then in the episode of Enite's attempted suicide, the entirely fortuitous arrival, willed by God, of Oringles. Hartmann stays Enite's hand to give her time to curse the sword (responsible for Erec's 'death'), and to allow Oringles to take in the scene on which he has chanced – and to misread all the signs. He believes himself favoured and acts on the strength of this *wân*. Everything is in fact under control: 'got hete den gewalt und er den wân' (6351).

As for chance (*geschiht*) itself, it is so fixed in Hartmann's mind that chance is willed by God that he can be specific in a prayer: 'nû müeze got gesenden/disen ellenden/. . .ros dâ sî ûfe rîten' (6698–700). God restores to Erec his own horse which a *garzûn*, unaware of the need of the moment, has brought out to water and hands over without comment. This, says Hartmann, proved Erec's *sælekeit* (6713f.).

THE GAMBLER'S THROW

Insufficient attention has been paid, I think, to the gambler's throw as a simultaneous challenge to all the forces which may govern a man's destiny – God, fate, and fortune – to side with him. Erec rejects all 'wise' advice to forego the adventure of *Joie de la curt*. He ignores it as he also ignores omens ('ern was dehein wetersorgære', 8128; 'er enphlac deheiner spæhe', 8135). He puts his trust in God (8147f.) and in his own conviction that his decision is right (8119–23); he was consequently 'sorgen vrî' when he put his fortune to the test. (I have referred elsewhere[24] to the disaster which Gregorius brought upon himself when he put his case to a similar test. This was inevitable because he had earlier, in a mood of anger and frustration at the abbot's advice, made a wilfully wrong decision.) We pick up the previous quotation (8521ff.) at the 'throw' itself. Note the emphasis on God's will and the favourable time and circumstances – 'genædeclîchiu dinc':

> got hât wol ze mir getân. . .
> ich vinde gar ein wunschspil
> dâ ich lützel wider vil
> mit einem wurfe wâgen mac.
> ich suochtez unz an disen tac:
> gote lop, nû hân ichz vunden
> dâ ich wider tûsent phunden
> wâge einen phenninc.
> diz sint genædeclîchiu dinc,
> daz ich hie vinde solh spil. (8527–38)

Erec goes on to explain his reasoning to his host at Brandigân: great honour will be the prize. His host accepts the validity of his argument, whereupon they 'call it a day': 'nû gân wir slâfen, des ist zît' (8579).

As for the fight, and the inspiration which sustains the contestants, these are properly treated under more conventional headings – chivalry, honour, love etc.

III

There are a few remarks that I should like to add in the light of my re-reading of Hartmann's source, the *Erec* of Chrétien de Troyes,[25] and of a selection of chapters in which Hartmann's work is considered both in its own right and as an adaptation. I found it useful to expand a footnote here and there, and necessary to say a little more about Hartmann's 'courtly God'. To avoid misunderstanding I also expanded my title to include Hartmann's name.

To take the latter point first: the emphasis on Erec's *fortune* is Hartmann's! I now think it rather strange that this should not have been recognized long ago, for the comparison of the two texts has so often been made, and has provided the evidence for dozens of statements about Hartmann's techniques and his preoccupations. I shall, I hope, not be misunderstood if I quote the example of Jean Fourquet's useful comparative edition[26] designed specifically to illustrate the extent and the nature of Hartmann's 'remaniment' of *Erec* (and *Le chevalier au lion*). One will find no reference to *sælde* in either introduction or notes. There is nevertheless a glossary entry ('*sælde*: chance, faveur de la fortune') which shows that Fourquet could have been quite specific about Hartmann's more 'reflective' approach to Erec's story. But on balance he may have been justified, for there is so little in Chrétien with which 'Hartmann on *sælde*' could readily be compared.

Does this then mean that Chrétien is not interested in Erec's fortune, and that his romance is not Boethian in conception? It *is* Boethian, if only because it is an Arthurian romance, but I must confess to relief at finding the fortune motif adequately attested: it is merely not used thematically throughout. Chrétien is in fact, like the majority of medieval historians, more concerned to tell his story vividly than to philosophize about it. Even so, the references to fortune are not mere rhetorical embellishments. The first occurs in Enide's lament at the unhappiness which has befallen her: 'mout estoie buene eüree' (2605). This is followed by.

> . . .a si grant joie
> m'avoit Deus mise et essauciee,
> or m'a an po d'ore abeissiee.
> Fortune, qui m'avoit atreite,
> tost a a li sa main retreite. (2782–6)

The count who promised Enide a better future, claims: 'N'est pas fortune anvers vos chiche' (4800). Finally, Erec's triumph is thus acclaimed:

> Deus saut le plus buen eüré
> que Deus a feire et anduré. (6377ff.)

God had 'exalted' Enide, Fortune withdrawn her hand from her, God has made Erec the most 'fortunate' (*buen eüré*) of men. Hartmann's use of the corresponding Middle High German terms is more systematic.

Among treatments of Hartmann's *Erec* I single out Kurt Ruh's in *Höfische Epik des deutschen Mittelalters*,[27] since I see that he had already pointed to Erec's words claiming to have found at last *der Sælden wec*, as the key to Hartmann's understanding of the story. He writes, however, not of emphasis on fortune, but of a 'religiöse Akzentuierung' as being, by comparison with Chrétien, 'Hartmanns Eigentum' (p. 135). I have had to think hard whether this amounts to a serious difference of interpretation. The simplest solution would be to say that it does, but there is a formula on which a measure of agreement could be reached (and after all, ten years ago neither *Höfische Epik* nor *Augustinus oder Boethius*, Part I, was in print).

For that to be possible, Erec's long speech on *der Sælden wec* must be taken as a whole. That means: Erec acclaims as 'genædeclîchiu dinc', attributable to God's guidance and favour, his discovery 'here and now' of Fortune's path and the contingent 'chance of a lifetime' (*wunschspil*), calling for the gambler's throw ('der große Wurf', Ruh p. 133, but not p. 135). There can be no doubt, I agree, that Erec speaks as one who has 'seen the way'. He is filled with a high and noble ambition. But can one speak of his 'religiöse Ergriffenheit' (Ruh, p. 135)? That is the point at which, despite all that I have written on fortune in the context of Christian thinking, I hesitate; and if I am to agree, it will be by disregarding Erec's throwing of the dice, for a moment, and turning to Hartmann at his own game of dominoes!

Virtually the only God known to the Arthurian world of Hartmann's *Erec* is the 'courtly' God who looks after knights in their perilous exploits and governs their chance encounters. It is the same God to whom private prayers are offered in 'church'. There are, it is true, passages where Hartmann remembers that the Church is 'spiritual':

> mit dirre rede si kâmen
> dâ si messe vernâmen
> von dem heiligen geiste:
> des phlegent si aller meiste

128

> die ze ritterschefte sinnent
> und turnieren minnent. (662–7)

(cf. 'mit vrouwen Êniten er kam/dâ er messe vernam/ in des heilegen geistes êre,/und vlêhete got vil sêre/daz er im behielte den lîp', 8636–40.) Of the 'messe' as such, we hear once that Erec did not leave until after the blessing (2501), no more. As for officiating and supporting clergy, if one excludes a bishop 'von Cantwarje ûz Engellant' at the wedding of Erec and Enite (2125), they are at best 'diu phafheit' (9751), at worst 'such bishops, abbots and priests as could be got' (or 'rustled up'?: 'swaz man der mohte berîten', 6342–5). The God and the church of the Arthurian world in Chrétien's *Erec* are to nothing like the same extent disestablished. Chrétien has, it is true, no patience with clerics at festive gatherings; but when he deals with the Mass, he remembers not only the Holy Spirit but also procession, altar and the crucifix before which Erec kneels (700–5 and 2374–8). In short, if one allows Hartmann's opening lead that God is 'courtly', all the rest follows, and Erec's faith in his God-given fortune was not misplaced. I prefer the more strictly Boethian interpretation. Erec's real concern is his fortune. His religious observance is 'courtly'.

8. HISTORICAL THOUGHT AND MORAL CODES IN MEDIEVAL EPIC

For several years now I have been invoking the names Augustine and Boethius in an endeavour to draw more accurately the frontier between medieval narrative works written in conformity with a scheme of history going back to the Fathers, Eusebius and St Augustine himself – Christian 'Heilsgeschichte', and others which take their historical doctrine, still Christian but secular, from Boethius's *De Consolatione Philosophiae*. I expounded this historiographical thesis at considerable length in 1967 in the first volume of an independent study.[1] If reviews are anything to go by I seem to have persuaded some theologians and historians, and indeed some literary historians that I have drawn the dividing line correctly, in such a way for instance as to make Wolfram von Eschenbach's *Parzival* a 'Boethian' work.[2] Volume II of the same study presents a chronological documentation of the orginal thesis, and direct textual evidence, some of which I shall quote from or allude to in this essay.[3] I want none the less to concentrate here on some problems which still require consideration even when the principle of discrimination 'according to Augustine' or 'according to Boethius' has been accepted. There are for instance, almost obviously one might think, important medieval works written according to *neither* of the masters, for though there are in my opinion no other masters than Augustine and Boethius, there is a mistress – history itself, 'Geschichte schlechthin'. That is my present argument in a nutshell. I now proceed more slowly and methodically. In doing so I seek to take account of the 'moral codes' which have more generally been recognized as a preoccupation of medieval narrators.

As modern readers and interpreters we should, I think, occasionally consider in a simpler and more primitive way than is usual in academic studies, the problems of literary composition involved when 'given story' is retold in a medieval narrative work. By what devices is it made to conform to, or why must it ignore, established patterns of history ('Geschichtsbilder'?) Further, though I myself think that a secondary consideration: what control does the medieval re-narrator gain over his story by interpreting the deeds of his hero (and the hero's antagonists) in the light of an ideal moral code? To take this second point first, it is surely a commonplace of our experience that no major narrative (by that I exclude the *exemplum*) illustrates a *code* of values, for instance the chivalric code, perfectly, and one cannot interpret medieval stories satisfactorily in terms of an assumed consistent 'characterization' invoking those values. There are all-important actions of the hero (let us keep to heroes!), essential to his story, which conflict with the code or his 'character'. There are also grave dangers in the so-called 'werkimmanent' interpretations now in fashion,[4] for no medieval writer is to that extent master of the story he tells. It is the hero with his story who is master ('der âventiure herre'), and the author is his spokesman merely, commending according to his lights the right decisions of his hero and glossing over his wrong decisions as he makes them, or offering little or no comment. He may be an unsatisfactory interpreter of the *deeds* of his hero.[5] It is not a purely rhetorical question when the narrator asks: 'What will he *do* now?'

The reason for the frequent non-coincidence of heroic action and moral code, whether the latter is thought of as contemporary with the hero or with the author, is that history itself (which literature must mirror) is not moral in origin, and its course and outcome are not determined by merits. That has always been the teaching of history, which literature cannot flatly deny: that the righteous man or the good cause will not necessarily prosper here on earth. (*Virtus* and *fortuna* are not causally connected.) It is an occasion for rejoicing (or boasting) when they seem to, for public grief when they patently do not. And so, rationally, evident deserts may have to await their reward in an afterlife. On the whole we vastly prefer for our 'entertainment' stories which encourage us in the belief that virtue and the good life have their reward and a 'happy ending', which may be success, with the prospect of further activity, or the beatitude of a career or life well completed.

To put all this another way, historians and narrators prefer to deal with merits and qualities systematically in an ethical 'code', and as a matter of major concern only in *digressions* from narrative, in a prologue or epilogue, or when taking formal leave of some character, see below an example from Regino of Prüm's *Chronicle*. Or the author may change genres to write a didactic work, a mirror of knighthood for instance. In terms of story, only a carefully staged and self-contained episode such as that of Job or of Jonah (episodes in God's own story) can illustrate a moral principle or a truism of faith. A life lived strictly according to a code or creed must be a martyrdom. I shall exclude martyrdoms (whether sacred or profane) from my further remarks, and, despite the reference just made to Job and Jonah, I exclude Biblical story, for by the Middle Ages (say the twelfth century) some five-or-more hundred years of theological exegesis had made all books of the Bible serve the one theology. The exegetes brought Christian story, doctrine and ethic into one register by means no longer available today.

But let us press on! Literature concerned with man as a historical being, and literature setting forth ideal conceptions of man, have little more than language in common. They make different statements. Man's first preoccupation is his destiny. This he understands first and best when it is represented to him in the form of story, in the indicative, not as a list of prescriptions in the imperative. The *sensus historialis* is the first and always the most important sense in which words are used at all. No elevated doctrine, for example of love, and no spiritualizing gloss can annul the facts of 'given story', the fact, for instance, that Tristan is a bed-hopper from first to last. That is his story which no power on earth or in heaven or hell can alter. Being not Biblical – it is not the story of David the adulterer, Solomon the womanizer or Samson the frequenter of brothels – it is

beyond redemption by even the most elastically-minded ex-
positor. Tristan and his Isolde remain memorable adulterers,
tricksters, Tristan is to the end 'der listenrîche', the evader of
codes, several of them in succession if one takes all the versions
of his story into account. These observations may preface the
general remark that the more memorable a piece of history or
story, the less likely it is that we shall find it illustrative of any
ideal scheme – of history or of morality.

Let us keep to works of literature in the conventional sense
(I shall want to consider historians, below), say *Hildebrandslied*,
Nibelungenlied, the French *Chanson de Roland* and Icelandic
sagas. These live and have their being as *story* first, com-
memorating in whatever refraction 'real history': these things
happened in a more or less remote past. Theoderic's army came
to Italy at the bidding of 'Hunneo truhtin' (or his antecedent),
the Burgundian kingdom on the Rhine was wiped out, Charlemagne's campaign against the heathen Saracen ended with the
destruction of his rearguard but Christianity was vindicated,
douce France (according to the German Konrad, the Empire)
survived; Iceland was successfully settled. I will refer to these
works again.

At the other end of the scale in respect of factual and 'real'
history is the *Anticlaudianus* (c. 1181–4) of Alan of Lille, a
purely intellectual construct with, for all that, a notable 'plot'
of considerable relevance for anyone seeking the theoretical
connection, if any, between ethical codes and history or story.
The *Anticlaudianus* is an allegorical epic in which all the
characters except one – the hero to be – are personifications of
philosophical (or theological) concepts, Natura, Ratio (Fides
etc.), or are Virtues or Vices. All are present in a virtually
encyclopaedic muster. Concerning the hero in whose interest a
momentous enterprise is here set in motion, nothing is more
certain than that he, the ideally conceived 'new man' to replace
in Nature's world the fallen man of an earlier dispensation, is
destined to have a *history* – whether he likes it or not, and
whether his sponsors want it or not. Ratio is obsessed with the

idea of what 'should be possible', Prudencia or Philosophia is slow to assent at all to the project of starting all over again! The Parcae (that is Alan's 'antique' name for Providence) have so decreed, and they determine in higher regions what 'Fate' shall bring to pass in the world of time. So the new man, having been endowed by God with a soul, must, according to this story, on his descent to earth pass through Fortune's kingdom.[6] – Alan, it should perhaps be noted, had only recently invoked the Holy Spirit as his Muse, to enable him to treat God's assignment of a soul to the new man. He now reverts to his initial Muse, Apollo, and continues his narrative in a purely Boethian vein: the new man must now be prepared for his future. This can only be done, one notes, with considerable co-operation from Dame Fortune – whose 'realm' Alan describes at quite inordinate length. Alan's fiction is that to avoid the imputation of graceless envy, Fortune will make a special concession: she will for the new man's sake 'endeavour to be less arbitrary' and 'restrain herself'. That is her contribution. (The Virtues have already undertaken to endow him lavishly with their qualities.) He must obviously also be of noble birth. Noble birth is in Fortune's gift through her daughter Nobilitas. What next? It only remains for the new man to *act*. This he does first in alliance with *all* the Virtues against all the Vices in a rather long and tedious *psychomachia*. The Vices and Discord herself are of course routed. Fortune's own waverings and desertion of this 'good cause' cannot affect the outcome. What happens after *that* cannot be told within the framework of this allegory. Clearly the new man has nothing more to do until there is a new real world, somehow re-populated, in which he can make use of the qualities bestowed on him. This will require his *decision* to act, and – as the irrational principle governing the outcome of all action – Fortune will be back in business, attending to the new man's *history*. There appears, therefore, to be no such thing as man without a history, and history of some kind he will make in the exercise of his free will.[7] Before he acts on his own account he has (the *Anticlaudianus* shows) potentially all the virtues. Thereafter there is history, and there are historians, to record it or not, and to interpret it as they may.

Ranged between the ultimately historical *Nibelungenlied* and the patently pre-historical *Anticlaudianus* we may see the scores of medieval tales which enjoyed the authority of more or less established tradition. These we must for the purpose of this essay consider as being 'just as true' as chronicled real history. Parzival, for instance, must win the Grail Kingship after a failed first attempt, for that is his story, the story is 'given'. No scheme of values by which the hero's actions should be judged is in the same sense 'given'. Any re-narrator of the story is free to impute motives for Parzival's actions (and his failures to act) according to his personal prejudices, his social class (etc.). In another context Iwein *must* pour the water on the slab, give pursuit to the Lord of the Castle and slay him. In a desperate attempt to gain some kind of 'moral' control of this unfortunate sequence of events Hartmann von Aue will offer as a personal contribution that Iwein did not remember self-discipline ('zuht') when in hot pursuit. That was 'wrong' of him, we gather. And so on! Hartmann's Lord Henry has apparently all the qualities, including rather strangely an aptitude at Minnesang, required of the perfect knight or lord. But in respect of the structure of this tale, these qualities belong to Lord Henry's untold career; they are prehistorical. It is merely the narrator's historical postulate[8] that he was afflicted with leprosy as punishment for a moral defect, his arrogance or his neglect of God. Remoter from any kind of historicity are then such works of fantasy as Chrétien's *Cligès*, *Moritz von Craun* or – much earlier – the *Ruodlieb* romance, the hero of which is from start to finish Fortune's child.[9] Ruodlieb owes his virtues to the accident of good birth and native genius (according to some writers genius is in Fortune's gift), and acquires his experience *ambulando*, through chance encounters and through a somewhat enigmatic 'set' of gnomic precepts, trustingly followed.

So much for literary works in the accepted sense. I myself should like for a moment to extend the list of works to be considered to medieval historians and chroniclers, who are so much more rewarding for the general-purposes medievalist than at any rate the minor poets. They range from more or less 'objective' chroniclers of events like Gregory of Tours *via* speculative historians like Bede on the one hand, Regino of Prüm (see below) on the other, to speculators on history, Otto of Freising, for instance, who drifts irresponsibly from edited history into fantastic prognosis in a work conceived on Augustinian lines, the *De Duabus Civitatibus* (c. 1143–46). Then there are exploiters or wilful falsifiers of real history for the purposes of dynastic and political propaganda (Widukind of Corvey and the Archpoet) and vulgarizers of historical fictions of greater or lesser magnitude and complexity: the poet of the *Annolied*, or the slightly later 'Kollektiv' of Regensburg clerics responsible for the *Kaiserchronik*. About some of these I shall have a further word to say.

And so I return to my starting-point to ask whether the various medieval authors to whom I have alluded so far, see history and story in terms of Augustinian 'Heilsgeschichte' or of Boethian secular history: or whether they see history as history pure and simple. I refer now to a number of works in a logical but not chronological order, and as a word of guidance I may mention that the Augustinian scheme of history was known to the Middle Ages from the days of Orosius (c. 400). Its complexities were reduced to memorable form by Isidore of Seville (seventh century), and this was transmitted in uninterrupted clerical teaching and preaching. *De Civitate Dei* itself, however, Augustine's own work, was rarely cited or even properly read. Charles the Great certainly did no more than stare at and brood over the few sentences about the *rex justus* and *pacificus* indicated to him by Alcuin's forefinger. (Alcuin pressed his teaching particularly in his correspondence with Charles.) Boethius's *De Consolatione Philosophiae* on the other hand was from the time of its completion (c. 525) to about the time of the same Alcuin not known; it was apparently lost to view. Isidore did not know it. Otfrid of Weissenburg (c. 860) on the other hand did, of that I am convinced, but cannot stop to elaborate the point. The first medieval historian to show a full and complete grasp of Boethius' scheme of history with no Augustinian reservations, no illusions about Charlemagne and the Franks, or the *translatio imperii*, was Regino of Prüm, c. 900. Regino accepts and *uses* the Boethian philosophy of history at exactly the time when King Alfred of England was *translating* the tract. (This was after Alfred had translated Gregory the Great's *Cura pastoralis* and 'Orosius', seeking in all cases guidance on the office of Christian kingship.) Let us bear the date in mind: from about A.D. 900 at the latest Western Europe knew *De Consolatione*. It must have come as a revelation to theologian-advisers of kings, makers of policy and writers of history. It was a Christian scheme of history which had the inestimable advantage of according a function to Fortune as the dispenser (with man) of 'history as we know it'. It afforded respite from the incubus of Augustinian 'Heilsgeschichte'. Western Europe, to the extent that it speculates philosophically on history at all, is still indebted to Boethius.[10]

Now prior to both Augustine and Boethius in respect of the interpretation of history are, remarkably, the *Nibelungenlied* and the Icelandic sagas. These late-twelfth to thirteenth-century works recognize no pattern of history other than that inherent in the events they treat. The poet of the *Nibelungenlied* seeks no doubt the 'meaning' to him in his day of the destruction of the Burgundian kingdom. It has clearly nothing to do with the Fall of Man, the Six Ages or with God's divine dispensation. It is not Augustinian. More important to the poet are the events themselves and the famous men and women who perished. Their fate is the history he narrates, not any theodicy – reducing as he may the tempo of events, retarding the catastrophe which he has nevertheless foretold in his opening stanzas. But History itself duly negates the poet's efforts at retardation. It will not let Giselher grow old with the passage of years, and it destroys the poet's most modern hero Rüdeger, and the thousands of warriors introduced to delay the final act in what remains a family or dynastic feud of (vaguely) the Merovingian age. As for moral codes, that of the *Nibelungenlied* is similarly Merovingian, with a few late chivalric embellishments associated with self-cancelling cadenzas of action. No City (*civitas*) of this world or the next arises from the devastation, there is no promise of a better future. Equally the past glories of Worms are not to be restored, and Etzel's court is in ashes. There is cause, after the events, for lament ('Klage') only, melancholy reflection on the sorrow which must follow happiness. This is not the Christian cry of *vanitas*, or illustration of any doctrine of the rise and fall of earthly kingdoms. In other words: the history of the Migrations, elsewhere a story of triumph in battle, conquest and settlement, is in the case of the Burgundians a story of the decline, fall and destruction of one people. That is final. The settlement of Iceland on the other hand does not end with the destruction of a people, save perhaps here and there of a clan or family. Saga history ends with a present in which a 'civitas' of this world *is* established, requiring no remorse, no act of penance from its inheritors. The sagas reflect a conception of history in which a fall, original sin or guilt, redemption and salvation play no role. And so, despite all idealization of man in situations of heroic conflict, despite all accommodation to traditional narrative schemes, what *Nibelungenlied* and the sagas commemorate is memorable history. In that history, Christian institutions may be mentioned. An important encounter may take place before a minster (Worms) or in a stave-church (in Iceland or Norway), and the Christian faith may offer comfort to some characters, or alarm others. It is perhaps significant that in these works Christianity is represented *inter alia* as sustaining swimmers in fjords or saving a parson thrown into the Danube. Christianity is, in these late works, still the new religion which, as in sixth-century Europe and Britain, some important people were giving a trial, little more. There can be no question of an Augustinian view of history. As for the Boethian conception of history as the work of God's Providence, Fate, man's Fortune and his free will – that is equally absent. In *Nibelungenlied* and the sagas Fate is still spoken of in pre-Christian and Germanic, not in Boethian terms.

And now to Regino of Prüm, some passages in whose *Chronicle of the Franks* (c. 900) are, I think, almost as important for students of medieval literature as Walther von der Vogelweide's *Sprüche* in the 'Reichston'. It was indeed an essay by Heinz Löwe[11] on Regino's historical thinking on the Carolingians, on the Empire, on Divine Providence, Fate and Fortune, that prompted me to foresake the conventional paths of 'Germanistik' a decade ago – to declare my Boethian thesis; for to be reminded by Regino, as Löwe was, of Dante and the historical speculations of the writers of the early Renaissance, is no doubt aesthetically satisfying – but it is historically topsy-turvy! Regino's philosophy of history is (like Dante's) purely Boethian. Furthermore – as Löwe recognized – it involves an abandonment of all ideas of a divine mission of the Franks or any other people. It involves abandonment of the doctrine of a *translatio imperii*. In Regino's day this was surely a phenomenal feat of independent historical thinking; he was at least two-hundred years ahead of his time. This the historians have so far only partially recognized. Otto of Freising, who 250 years later exploited Regino's *Chronicle* for its facts, was conceivably converted by it.[12]

I submit now (in Latin and in translation) a passage from Regino's *Chronicle* which exemplifies the Boethian mode of history-writing. It is my hope that it will continue to engage the attention of medievalists for many years to come. In the context of discussion of 'codes' it is also instructive, namely in that in a first self-contained section it treats the 'character' of King Karlmann, of whom the historian takes his leave (see above):

(a) [880 A.D.] Anno dominicae incarnationis DCCCLXXX. Carlomannus rex paralisi dissolutus diem clausit extremum VII. Non. Apr. sepultusque est cum debito honore in Baioariam in loco, qui dicitur Hodingas. Fuit vero iste precellentissimus rex litteris eruditis, christianae religioni deditus, iustus, pacificus et omni morum honestate decoratus; pulchritudo eius corporis insignis, vires quoque in homine admirabiles fuere; nec inferior animi magnitudine. Plurima quippe bella cum patre, pluriora sine patre in regnis Sclavorum gessit semperque victoriae triumphum reportavit; terminos imperii sui ampliando ferro dilatavit; suis mitis, hostibus terribilis apparuit; alloquio blandus, humilitate ornatus, in ordinandis regni negotiis singulari sollertia preditus, prorsus, ut nihil ei deesse regiae maiestatis competens videretur.

[In the year 880 of the divine Incarnation King Karlmann died on the 22nd March, a paralysis of the limbs heralding his collapse. He was buried with due honours in Bavaria at a place there called Ötting. This most excellent king was a man of learning, a devout Christian, just, peace-loving and in every way of distinguished bearing. He was a most hand-some man of admirable physique; he was equally high-minded. He con-ducted many wars in the kingdoms of the Slavs, at first in the following of his father, thereafter still further wars against them alone. He always returned a victor. He extended the confines of his kingdom with the sword. To his enemies he was a man to be feared, to his (friends and allies) he was a lenient lord. In his conversation he was affable but modest; he was extremely efficient and conscientious in the conduct of state business. In short he seemed to lack no quality required of the bearer of the royal title.]

[Having taken his formal leave of Karlmann, Regino turns to his successor, his natural son Arnolf, and reflects on the rise, pre-eminence, decline and fall of the Carolingian line:]

(*b*) Huic ex legitimo matrimonio non est nata soboles propter infecundi-tatem coniugis, sed ex quadam nobili femina filium elegantissimae speciei suscepit, quem Arnolfum nominari iussit ob recordationem reverentissimi Arnolfi, Metensis ecclesiae episcopi, de cuius sancto germine sua aliorumque regum Francorum prosapia pullulaverat; quod non casu accidisse, sed quodam presagio portentoque futur-orum actitatum videtur. Siquidem ab illo genealogia regum *caelitus provisa* per intervalla temporum secundis incrementorum successibus coepit exuberare, quousque in magno Carolo summum imperii fastigium non solum Francorum, verum etiam diversarum gentium regnorumque obtineret. Post cuius decessum *variante fortuna* rerum gloria, quae supra vota fluxerat, eodem, quo accesserat, modo cepit paulatim diffluere, donec deficientibus non modo regnis, sed etiam ipsa regia stirpe partim inmatura aetate pereunte partim sterilitate coniugum marcescente hic solus de tam numerosa regum posteritate idoneus inveniretur, qui imperii Francorum sceptra susciperet: quod in subsequentibus suo in loco lucidius apparebit.

[He had no descendant from his official marriage, his wife being barren, but by a woman of noble birth he had a son of most excellent presence whom he caused to be named Arnolf in memory of the most venerable Arnolf, Bishop of Metz – of whose sacred line his family and the families of other Frankish kings were descended. This seems not to have been a matter of chance, but, as it were, a portent and foreshadowing of things to come. For with Arnolf the royal house began in accordance with *Divine Providence* to ascend by a succession of stages to that eminence which had its final culmination, under Charles the Great, in empire not only over the Franks but over various peoples and kingdoms. After his [Charles's] death *through a change of fortune*, the glory of the empire which had excelled all aspirations began to ebb in the same way as it had once risen, until not only the kingdoms fell away, but the royal line itself was lost through the premature deaths of young princes, the barrenness of wives, and finally there was left only Arnolf worthy to receive the sceptre: this will be shown more clearly in due course, below.][13]

From this passage and others in Regino's *Chronicle* one can show (that is, Heinz Löwe has shown) that he saw the Imperium itself as subject to Fortune's law, i.e. as a purely historical phenomenon.

[But to repeat,[14] Regino was at least two-hundred years ahead of his time, and when Otto of Freising exploited the passage on Karlmann (in his *De duabus civitatibus* – an 'Augustinian' work) he edited out the reference to a 'change of fortune', and later dismissed the Wheel of Fortune as 'an idea of the philosophers', see above p. 110. We return now to the poets, and their more traditional view of Charles.]

From Regino of Prüm on the Carolingians I turn now to a brief consideration of the O. Fr. *Chanson de Roland* (c. 1100) and its German adaptation by Pfaffe Konrad (at the latest c. 1170), a delicate task for an English writer, and for nothing do I hold my teacher in Breslau, Friedrich Ranke, in greater esteem than for his treatment of this traditional compare-and-contrast exercise. Having spent some two hours characterizing Konrad's 'clerical' adaptation, Ranke put it firmly in its place, reminding his German audience of the primacy in every respect of the French national epic: in historical conception, in characterization, in poetry. The *Chanson de Roland* is one of the great achievements of Western European literature. What I myself would also stress is the *Chanson's* treatment of Charles as a Christian emperor and his campaigns as those of Christendom against the paynim – indeed also his treatment of Roland as a martyr. One must also bear in mind the vast amplification of the Roland tradition in the lands of Romance language. The Oxford *Roland* is selected for literary study on aesthetic grounds and for convenience. It is but one representative of a rich tradition. It is a gross simplification of German scholarship to say, as is now so fashionable, of Konrad's adaptation: 'der Stoff ist in das augustinische Weltbild eingeordnet', as though an 'Augustinian' revision were in itself a meritorious achievement, an advance on the all too modern and national *Chanson*!

I do not wish to belittle Konrad's poem. It is a work in its own right, not merely a testimony to the 'influence' or the popularity ('Wirkungsgeschichte') of the *Chanson*. Given that 'douce France' was an idea which a German poet could not sustain, the picture of Charles had to be brought into line with German ideas of Charles, German ideas of a *translatio imperii* to the Carolingians and their historical successors, i.e. with the picture in the *Kaiserchronik*. Charles had to be represented as God's Regent here on earth. This Konrad does most remarkably in his opening passage. Where the *Chanson* says that Charles, having heard matins, conferred with his barons in an orchard, Konrad shows Charles prostrate in a night-long vigil in the presence of God, seeking guidance as to the Divine Will with him. This is the Charles who was to be canonized, albeit by the wrong Pope, and under strong political pressure. Thereafter Konrad sees the campaign against the Saracen in terms of a swift crusade, the paladins positively hastening to their martyrdom. But this is all the bread-and-butter story of the handbooks.

What I wish to stress is rather that – not for the first time (that was in the *Kaiserchronik*, as I shall mention in a moment) – a historical formula is used by Konrad which persists down to Milton and the poets of the German Baroque: The heathen (or the devilish adversary of the Christian faith), the would-be frustrator of God's purpose, is credited not merely with a ridiculous belief in 'Mahmet' or the like, but with a foolish philosophy of history, a belief in 'fortune' (*sælde* or *wîlsælde*), and, *as summum bonum*, a 'beatitudo' to be found on earth. Germanists will recall that in the *Kaiserchronik* there is a long disquisition on *wîlsælde*, extremely difficult to follow, which clearly taxed to the limit the intelligence of the clerical compilers – who, as Friedrich Ohly has shown, had 'lifted' the text bodily from the so-called Clementine *Recognitions*.[15] They were learning from it as they rendered it into German. They were only able to disparage this intellectually demanding *Kairos* doctrine with the help of further liftings. So too, but in much simpler terms, in Konrad's adaptation of the *Chanson* the heathens have a worldly doctrine of *sælde*. It is therefore not merely the bravery in battle and the soldierly code of the heathens, and their decorum in parleys, to which Western writers accord esteem. In any well-organized work of Augustinian conception, the philosophy attributed to the heathen may be based on the *best secular* philosophy available, in Boethius,[16] of which Milton says in *Paradise Lost*, without mentioning Boethius by name, of course, that it affords but 'vain consolation' to the routed hosts of Satan. This becomes, as I have hinted, a commonplace clerical formula. But the German *Rolandslied* is, for all the careful thought which has gone into it, not always a temperate and controlled work of adaptation. The author is occasionally carried away by his fervour for the cause of the holy Empire established by Charles, and the martyrdom of his own personal nominees for canonisation. It has often been remarked that Konrad allows his most Christian heroes – knights – to slay the heathen like dogs, 'sam die hunte', or like cattle, 'sam daz vihe', ll. 5421–3. This will have sounded to Konrad's audiences like a reference to procedures in the medieval slaughterhouse – and that was no doubt the intention of the author too, but the idea itself is of course old, and in origin – strange as this may seem – liturgical. The enemies of Christendom, particularly those who beset the just man, the Man of Sorrows in his affliction and Agony, are *canes, vituli, tauri pingues* in the words of the 21st (A.V. 22nd) Psalm, the Good Friday Psalm. As such, according to Konrad, they must be slain. The clerical propagandist forgets in other words his training at this point. He risks a misuse of O.T. prophecy, knowing he will not be contradicted. He also shows himself a somewhat crude pragmatist when he allows the most Christian emperor Charles to proceed to the execution of his hostages after the singing of a *Te Deum*. It is at times difficult to associate the deeds attributed to the heroes in medieval epic, with moral codes.

For all that one may not forget that Western man in his perplexities has always sought comfort in *ideal* schemes and norms. He has reflected on history, 'given story', and on man as he is in his imperfection, to derive some lesson. In my concluding remarks I will now suggest that though modern literary historians may have identified the literary genres for the portrayal of various ideals of life and career, *Vita* and legend for the saint of course, *chanson de geste* for the feudal baron and *âventiure* for the knight, they have been slow to recognize the basic philosophy of history of these latter two secular genres. It is clearly *not* 'Heilsgeschichte', nor any modification of 'Heilsgeschichte'. It is, I think, also essential, to assert that it has equally little to do with moral codes, which are concerned with character or behaviour but not with action and story itself. The philosophy of history hitherto lacking in our armoury is that of the Christian philosopher Boethius which makes the decisions of mortal men taken in the exercise of their free-will the mainspring of *action*, action followed by consequences, an *eventus* which is the work of fortune (*sælde*). About that I have written often and talked, perhaps *ad nauseam*. The point I stress now in final reinforcement of the argument is the medieval narrator's concern to deal with mortal man's decisions in their *time context*: the *moment* of time.[17] Man should make his decisions at the right time and in the right frame of mind. He rarely does. He is rarely given the *chance* to act wisely. It remains for us medievalists, in short, to recognize more readily the medieval counterpart of the *Kairos* doctrine of Antiquity. It is not enough to make 'witty' remarks about Iwein's failure to keep his appointments, or the efforts he has to make to catch up with his obligations. Failure to recognize time as a central problem in historical thinking and in narrative technique in the Middle Ages is responsible – for instance – for hopeless confusion concerning the 'guilt' of Hartmann's Gregorius. Gregorius decides to leave the monastery in a fit of youthful rage. He says so himself: he makes his decision in *tumpheit* and *erbolgenheit*.[18] He says he is determined to 'give chase to fortune' (he will *sælde erjagen*) and so invites disaster, and has the *metanoia* which must follow from a wilful refusal to accept advice. He follows the call of the blood. His pride is wounded. He seeks fame and glory, honour and esteem. *These* are his values in the moment of decision. His decision in the exercise of free will is wrong, irrational, made at the wrong time. This must be stated before one can begin to consider the role of *coincidence* in his future career. Gregorius may spend seventeen years alone on the rock, but the fatal decision was the work of a moment, and Hartmann's skill as a time-keeper, stop-watch in hand, at a later point, saves Gregorius from a final blasphemy when he demands a miracle of God (see p. 108). What he demands as a miracle is however already fact – his tablets have not been destroyed – and the emissaries from Rome who have come to lead him to Peter's throne deem that 'fortunate', not an act of grace.[19] I will however spare readers the ardours of yet another 'Nacherzählung' of *Gregorius*. As for Hartmann's treatment of chivalry and chivalric values in this story, he has no option but to represent them as something of which the hero has prior knowledge by virtue of his princely birth. Hartmann knows that such knowledge is incredible. He therefore makes it the subject of a completely frivolous passage in which Gregorius claims not only to know chivalry and horsemanship but also of the German Knighthood League-Table, Division I.[20] This is my last example of the priority of story over morality, and on that note I will abruptly end.

9. THE WESTERN IMAGE OF BYZANTIUM IN THE MIDDLE AGES[1]

With its converse ('the Byzantine view of Western Europe', etc.), this subject has occupied me increasingly in recent years.[2] What I have to offer in this essay, however, does not so much treat the topic in the light of my present reading as suggest a framework for future discussions, preferably by historians and literary historians in collaboration. This may well involve the revision of some accepted ideas, not least, I think, by literary historians.

Even after such a preliminary observation, representatives of traditional 'Germanistik' will no doubt still be startled to note the modest place to which I have finally assigned our *König Rother* – the first work to leap to mind if I mention my preoccupations to colleagues. It is after all, a medieval German tale of daring-do in the world of Byzantium. All the more reason therefore, for a *captatio benevolentiae*, which also suits my purposes. I quote first from a work of Old High German literature (or scholarship) by Notker of St Gall.[3]

Introducing in a German *prologus* his adaptation of Boethius's *De Consolatione Philosophiae*, Notker says of the Ostrogothic king, Theodericus (ultimately the slayer of Boethius): 'The Emperor Zeno invited him thither, to famous Constantinople, and kept him there for a long time and heaped honours upon him.'[4] A comparison with the probable Latin source suggests that Notker contributed the epithet 'famous'. I have never felt that I could comment with assurance on this passage. What did Constantinople mean to our monk of St Gall about A.D. 1000, and, equally important, why are our handbooks so reticent on this and several other references to Greece in medieval literary texts, for instance (again) in the *Rother*, in the *Ludus de Antichristo*, or indeed in Geoffrey of Monmouth, Wace and Chrétien de Troyes?

I have long felt that nothing is to be gained here by conventional further research. We have rather, I think, to reflect first in simpler terms on the political scene in the Middle Ages: it was one of East–West confrontation – in many ways like today's. We should therefore anticipate evidence in Western texts not so much of knowledge, as of wilful ignorance concerning Byzantium, drawing on the clichés of anti-Byzantine propaganda. We should equally expect some reflection of factual knowledge of those who had 'been there' (in Constantinople) as emissaries or traders – stereotyped references to splendid 'but threadbare' ceremonies and rituals, with due exaggeration of the humiliations offered to Western visitors at the Byzantine court. As for imaginative narrative, such attitudes could not help but generate adventures stories: of Western heroes liberating some languishing princess of the royal blood, etc. So far one can get by a rapid piecing together of evidence in the 'Spielmannsepen', or in Wolfram's *Parzival* (if we think with Burdach that the Grail ceremonies reflect some knowledge of Byzantine court ritual and Eastern liturgical forms).

From my own reading, however, which for some years now has been concentrated rather on medieval historians and chroniclers than the poets, I am coming to take more seriously a charge one will hear from committed Byzantinists, namely that our ancestors were not so much – despite the confrontation – curious about the East and fascinated by it, as obsessed by their own sense of guilt, or fear, not dispelled by evident political successes of the Carolingians, the Ottonian emperors and Barbarossa, that the Western world's claims to legitimacy might in the end be as dubious as they were in the beginning. This fear seems to me to account for much that is characteristic of the Western view of Byzantium as this is revealed in medieval works, histories first no doubt, but also in other kinds of writing including imaginative literature. That is, however, at this point, merely a general indication of the course this statement will take. (*Nota bene*, it is not part of my enquiry to ask to what extent Western defiance was provoked by the sheer arrogance of

Byzantine spokesmen. It would equally involve a total change of subject, were I, in the interest of a more 'balanced' account, to recall those many, and ultimately more important areas of agreement between East and West: their shared delight in exotic goods, in prestigious feats of skill – tales, lore, 'Kultur-güter' of all kinds.)

How shall we then describe and evaluate such evidence as there is of a Western interest in, or attitude towards Byzantium? What shall be the norm by which we decide that a Western picture is biased, ill-informed, or simply irresponsible? I have no ready answer to propose. I shall therefore present the subject for discussion tentatively, in anthology form under three head-ings, only the third of which is devoted to a selection of medieval *literary* works. That is preceded by a section (2) in which I invite attention to two outspoken expressions of views by distinguished Byzantinists: their opinions of the medieval Western world, its aspirations and its claims, and their inter-pretation of the role of Byzantium. Before this, in section 1, I offer some observations of my own. They may seem in the event to mediate between extreme statements, the Eastern and the Western orthodoxies of *history*.[5]

1. No matter what our own medieval writers say about Greece and Byzantium, we may in our critical assessments not forget, I think, the realities of the Middle Ages (see above): the division of Europe into two camps and the confrontation (officially from 1054) of two political ideologies, two worlds. This is the reality which the writers of the period treat in some way, or ignore.

It is for instance possible to assert, as indeed I do, that the ideals of kingship, government, knighthood, religion, portrayed notably in Wolfram von Eschenbach's *Parzival* are almost en-tirely 'romantic'. In the Western world there could, since earliest medieval centuries, never be priest-kings: the idea is politically impossible; it is in fact more or less Byzantine! – Further, Wolfram carries the idealization of knighthood (the Knights Templar, guardians of the Grail) to the point where the Church as an institution no longer exists: the world of Parzival does not include Rome or the Pope, or the possibility of an interdict or an excommunication. It is a world of romantic dreams.

Next, chronology! – European knighthood, as we know, never matched the standards set by the narrative poets in the romances of the 'Blütezeit' and the years 1200–4 lead, according to one's standpoint, to one of two climaxes: Parzival's accession to Grail Kingship, the fulfilment of the romantic dream, *or* they are the years culminating in the sacking of Constantinople by the knighthood of Western Europe. Villehardouin, expert adviser of the military leaders conducting the Fourth Crusade, reports in Chapter XIII of his *Conquest of Constantinople* (ca. 1210):

> The Marquis of Montferrat, commander-in-chief of the occupation forces, designated 'on behalf of the barons and the Doge of Venice, in a general order to the troops, *three churches*…for the reception of the spoil, and certain of the most notably trustworthy men among the French and the Venetians were posted in each to act as guards' (April 1204). (What had been found missing was the contents of two palaces and countless churches.)[6]

By comparison with such reality, the chivalric behaviour of Arthurian knights, of Parzival himself and of Willehalm (elsewhere) is a noble but a sentimental fiction – as sentimental as anything in Goethe's *Wilhelm Meister* or in *Iphigenie*.

To these sentimental fictions we in the West none the less accord willing homage. The noble 'humanity' of Wolfram satisfies us, we are not ashamed of our Middle Ages. Other views are possible. We rarely hear them. We do not read the Byzantinists on the subject of the years 1200–4. We shut our minds to such history, for we cannot 'confess' it. Instead, the West has for a decade or more been zealously re-confessing Charles the Great (the Aachen exhibition of 1965),[7] the Ottonians and Barbarossa.

For the Middle Ages I think we have to postulate a similarly motivated rejection of the Byzantine world, compounded of (*a*) a wilful ignoring of the political opponent and mockery of his claims; (*b*) the incompletely exorcised malaise of Western man: *his* rulers (Emperors, Kings, Popes) might be the usurpers of a power and authority rightly belonging after all to Constantine's direct successors. So much for my own preliminary observations.

2. I now invite consideration of statements by two Byzantinists on the right and on the wrong interpretations of history, including 'Heilsgeschichte'.[8] The Byzantinist interrupts the Western narrative of history where it first refers to St Augustine's *De Civitate Dei*. Whereas Momigliano, surely a neutral, may declare it to be 'the most famous of all philosophic meditations on history', sealing the triumph of Christian historiography over that of pagan Rome, Eastern and Western, the Byzantinist will call a halt: that is a story 'wrongly told'. This protest of the Orthodox world was first raised in the early Middle Ages, and it had become a cliché of imperial propaganda by the time Constantinople was having to cope with Charles the Great.

(*a*) I quote first from Ernst Benz, *Geist der Ostkirche* 1957, 2nd edition 1972, from a chapter 'Political Ideas of the Orthodox World', pp. 140–3. It is worth noting that Benz is writing specifically for Western readers. The Byzantine charge is, rather strangely, not that we in the West have got our *facts* wrong, but that we have got hold of the wrong *fiction*, namely Augustinian 'Heilsgeschichte'! I quote, translating:

'The structural difference between the Roman Catholic Church and Eastern orthodoxy can best be made clear by comparing the two great theologians, Eusebius of Caesarea and Augustine.' 'Eusebius in his writings, his speeches and in his *Church History* determined for centuries the orthodox world's sense of history ("Geschichtsbewußtsein") and its view of Church and State. For Eusebius Empire and Church are closely linked. The central figure is not the spiritual head of the Church but the Christian emperor. By founding Constantinople – the foundation was solemnized on 11th November 330 – Constantine had made evident his own conception of his role within empire and church. Constantinople was to cast off the demonic powers of the pagan past and be the metropolis of the Empire and the Imperial Church. Eusebius in turn made this the cardinal idea in his "political theology", centred on the Christian emperor modelled on Constantine. He, Constantine, is the protector of the Church,...its champion, its intercessor. Constantine is a second Moses.'[9]

'Even at Mass the Emperor had a special position as the only layman who may be present behind the *iconostasis*.'[10] The grace of God ("Gottesgnadentum") by which the Emperor rules makes him the equal of the ordained priesthood.'

And now the same author on St Augustine, under the heading: 'Die Schuldfrage beim Zusammenbruch des heidnischen Imperiums' (pp. 143–6).

'Augustine set down his ideas on the Church as the City of God[11] in the years 412–426. They are Augustine's answer to "die schmerzlichste Schuldfrage dieses Jahrhunderts". In his refutation of the charge levelled against the Christians – namely that they were responsible for the sacking of Rome – Augustine does not use the one argument staring him in the face (..."das damals zu erwarten gewesen wäre"). Augustine ignores the most obvious political idea available in his day, namely the "myth of Byzantium as the new Rome" completely.'[12]

'For Augustine the Christian empire of his own day seems not to exist. In the few allusions there are to the Roman *imperium*, they refer to the pre-Christian Roman empire which is assigned to the City of the Devil. The question why Augustine ignores the "new Rome" has scarcely been touched on.'

Benz next sketches the emergence of the Papacy from the bishopric of Rome; this 'fills the political vacuum of the West'. He treats the Donation of Constantine as (not a forgery, but) an attempt to construct an ideal prehistory of the Papacy. 'It is a myth which later ousts the myth of Byzantium as the new Rome.' These things having been stated, Benz can in his next chapter raise such issues as the 'defection of Rome', its refusal of Caesar's tribute and the conspiratorial alliances of renegade bishops with usurping Frankish kings. The special Western doctrine of a *translatio imperii* is to Benz of course a fiction.

(*b*) My second Byzantinist is Werner Ohnsorge, whom I quote from the penultimate essay in the volume *Konstantinopel und der Okzident*, 1966, dealing with 'the significance of the

Byzantine Empire for European history'. First, however, two introductory remarks. (i) In contrast with Benz, Ohnsorge never mentions Augustine's *De Civitate Dei*;[13] (ii) in most of his essays Ohnsorge is concerned in some way with problems of authenticity and legitimacy. (He offers most detailed accounts of the versions of the Donation of Constantine and speculates on the intentions revealed by any individual reading.) In the much more general essay which interests us here, he addresses a wider audience, and outlines the sequence of history up to about A.D. 1200 with particular reference to Byzantium. I single out what we need for our guidance:

'In the East Roman Empire of the Middle Ages (which we customarily call the Byzantine Empire) there were united: a *Roman* conception of the state, the *Greek* cultural inheritance and (orthodox) *Christianity*.'

There are three periods:

(i) from A.D. 330 to the end of the sixth century: Early Byzantine,
(ii) seventh to eleventh centuries: the Middle Period,
(iii) eleventh to fifteenth centuries: the Late Byzantine Empire.

Of the Middle Period, which interests us most, he says:

'The Empire is now less extensive territorially after the loss of Egypt, Syria, – and of the West in consequence of the [Barbarian] migrations; and because of the expansion of Islam'. But: 'opposing this latter threat, Byzantium is culturally and economically the leading European power'.
'Within Europe, to the end of the tenth century, the centres of European civilisation and power are in the East. There is a falling-away towards the West.'[14] Constantinople had over half-a-million inhabitants. In Western Europe there were "Kleinstädte" of a mere 3000 inhabitants, at a time when cattle were grazed within the confines of Rome.'[15] 'In respect of administrative efficiency and an ordered structure of society Byzantium was far ahead of the West.'

Of the late period:

'This is the epoch of the feudalistic state, a period of disintegration in which the holdings of the cashiered soldiery disappear and corruption is rife in the civil service. There is increasing reliance on mercenaries (etc.), and there are successive losses of territory.' Next, in foreign affairs:
'This is a period of conflict with the Seljüks – later the Serbs and

152

Turks. It is the period of massive aggression from the *Romano–Germanic West* in three powerful thrusts from the eleventh century onwards: by the Normans ("Eroberungsdrang"), the Crusaders ("Glaubenseifer") and the Italian city-republics, particularly Venice ("Handelsgeist"). To these in succession and in combination, in 1204 during the Fourth Crusade, Constantinople, plagued by internal disunity, falls a victim.' (op. cit., pp. 289ff.). 'As for the rise of the so-called "Latin East": it is a blow from which Byzantium only temporarily recovered before finally, after a further century-and-a-half of disintegration, collapsing in 1453.'

Of Byzantium's role within European history Ohnsorge states:

'Byzantium links and at the same time divides Europe and Asia. Its history is more intricately interwoven with that of the major powers to the East; Persians, Arabs, Seljüks, Osmans, Turks, than with the Western powers. That must be stated clearly! *Asia Minor* proves time and again to be the real territorial centre of the Roman Empire.' 'And yet', he continues, 'Byzantium was firmly rooted in European tradition and fulfilled its historical destiny as the protagonist of Europe.'[16]

'The main cultural achievement of Byzantium was the preservation and fostering of Hellenic culture and literature, throughout the Middle Ages and down to the age of the Humanists, when the West, encouraged and instructed by emigrés from Byzantium, was itself able to take over the custodianship.' As for Eastern Europe, Byzantium's task was to hold the Slavs and the Hungarians in check. The 'geistige Substanz' of Byzantium lived on in Russian imperialism, and Moscow is the Third Rome.

Ohnsorge asks, as indeed one may, in conclusion: 'How could it come about that the West so completely lost sight of the thousand-year Empire, that it is now left to the Byzantinists of the twentieth century to recall it?'

There is, without doubt, a strongly polemical edge to the passages quoted from Benz and Ohnsorge, and one may wonder whether there is room for purely objective scholarly statements in these areas. There is, but that is very recent. But what in the end is achieved by the endeavours of twentieth-century (Western) Byzantinists? Nothing they do now or henceforth can reverse the course of past history and deny Western Europe its political and cultural successes. What does it matter today if an eighth-century 'donation' was a forgery, and so many things happened otherwise than as the Western world thought, believed, wrote and *taught* until after 1900? What does it matter if the more important acclamation of Charles was suspect, and if there was a certain amount of improvisation about the coronation ceremony, and if the *patricius* title meant one thing to the bestower, another to the recipient? Conscious of Western successes in the Renaissance, the Enlightenment and since, the Western historian can be magnanimous and make his retrospective concessions. Meanwhile the Byzantinist derives a certain *academic* satisfaction from proving, with evidence, major and minor sins of omission and commission of our Western ancestors. But in the Middle Ages? According to Karl Bertau the 'blutige Unwahrheit' of the Western myth of history oppressed the soul of the boy-emperor Otto III.[17] We are no longer so guilt-laden.

3. And now a selection of texts and authors of varying dates, to the extent that I have been able to call them to mind and re-read them, or have been reminded of them by colleagues.[18] First, Isidore of Seville – why not!

The historian Arno Borst has contrived to extract from the seventh-century Spanish bishop's encyclopedia (the *Etymologies*) a 'world-picture' and a scheme of history, and in so doing to define Isidore's attitude towards Byzantium.[19] I doubt, however, whether the medieval user of Isidore's reference book had such a guide, and so what follows is thankfully taken from Borst for our own information. (For easier reading I make one continuous quotation of dozens of excerpted statements):

Constantinople is, according to Isidore: *et nunc Romani imperii sedes* and the head of the whole East, just as Rome is the head of the West. But this formulation in itself excludes the possibility of an imperial rule shared by East and West. Why there is no emperor in Rome (and for how long this has been the case) is a matter of indifference to the Spanish bishop. Isidore makes only casual reference to the emperor's ruling from Byzantium.

Constantine was a law-giver and the founder of Constantinople, but Isidore attributes to the emperor (whom he never calls 'the Great') merely the summoning and the protection of the Council of Nicaea.

There is not a word of Constantine's endeavours to further the christianization of his empire; there is nothing of his vision of the Cross or of his mother Helena's invention of the Cross. *Justinian* too is named, but there is nothing about his re-conquest of Italy and Spain (which affected Isidore's own family); equally there is nothing about Justinian's contribution to Roman law, otherwise highly esteemed by Isidore. – Is one to explain this by saying that Isidore lacked information, or by assuming that these matters did not interest him? – Borst again suggests 'indifference'. Of the seats of *patriarchs* of the Christian Church, Isidore names Rome, Antioch and Alexandria – not Constantinople. He *does* say quite clearly that Byzantium inclines more and more to heresy. – The final event of profane history which Isidore mentions is a victory of the Sassanids over Byzantium, A.D. 621.

This is perhaps the point at which to re-consider Bishop Liudprand of Cremona's remarkable report on his experiences as an emissary to the Byzantine court. It was written about 970 and is some thirty pages of print in a modern edition. Liudprand deals with the unsuccessful negotiations he conducted on behalf of Otto I in Constantinople with the Greek emperor Nicephorus Phocas II.[20] (They were to have led to an alliance and to the betrothal of Otto II with a Byzantine princess.) The report is generally classed by historians as a piece of memoir-writing, or it is 'ein geistreiches Pamphlet von unschätzbarem kultur-historischem Wert' (Rau, citing Ostrogorsky); or it is 'a re-markable and exceedingly original piece of writing' (Henderson). For the purposes of our present enquiry I would claim that the report, however self-exculpatory, 'witty' and 'original' it may be, should stand substitute for that fuller account of Byzantium which we otherwise lack as a norm, for, firstly, Liudprand had an escort of some twenty-five persons as witnesses of his endeavours. Secondly, the recipients of his report were Otto I, Otto II, and the Empress Adelheid, that is to say Ottonian court circles, who, at the time when they were making most energetic claims to legitimacy, received through Liudprand the full text of the Byzantine rejection of precisely such pretensions. His rhetorical embellishments, meant to excuse his failure, can only have served further to scandalize his hearers:

this was worse than a routine rehearsal of the Byzantine claims. The report also contains passages of a more anecdotal nature which must surely have gone the rounds. I therefore consider it unimportant that our knowledge of the report is derived from a single and incomplete manuscript. As for history itself, as early as 972 Archbishop Gero of Cologne accompanied the Byzantine Princess Theophanou to Italy. She was betrothed in the same year to Otto II, at that time seventeen years old. The event may have led to attempts to suppress the written record of recent failure, witness the sole manuscript.

Liudprand does not describe Constantinople. He had been there before, as had his father; he knows his way about. (He had adequate Greek. Other works show him to be phenomenally well read, and even to have looked at works of the Byzantine court historiographers.) It would, I think we may assume, have been superfluous by 970 to describe Constantinople to anyone of any knowledge and position. Liudprand complains of bad, unheated quarters, poor food, wines spoilt by the addition of resin: no doubt commonplaces, see above, p. 147. He complains of being left to wait in antechambers, of not knowing when to appear at table. He protests energetically at finding himself, Otto's representative, less favourably placed than a Bulgarian emissary.

One can quickly identify what were the really disputatious matters at that time, the use of titles, for instance. Liudprand naturally refers to his own master (Otto) as 'Caesar', and knows how to extricate himself when the Greeks explode. But the situation is much more serious when papal legates address Nicephorus as 'imperator Graecorum'. According to Liudprand this nearly costs them their lives. He soothed the Greeks, he tells Otto, by referring to the general ineptitude of (roughly) 'these people'.[21] But clearly there were repeated East–West confrontations in which each side belaboured the other with its own theories of state and church, and of past history. One notes that Liudprand refers to the Western variant of the Donation of Constantine, and to the doctrine of a 'translatio imperii'. It is therefore understandable if he more than once had to return to his unheated quarters without an escort.

Liudprand, a sophisticated Italian prelate representing a Saxon emperor, had indeed a difficult task and role. Imagine him defending his master in the context of Church history in Saxony! Had there been any important synods there recently? ('We had Nicaea!') 'At any rate we have no heretics!', he retorted.[22] It was harder to claim equality in respect of parks and wild-ass enclosures. The altercations were of course most bitter when the Greek emperor complained of Otto's Italian policy. (The Greeks regarded Benevento and Capua as provinces of the Eastern empire: Otto had seized Apulia and besieged Bari.) Liudprand claims to have defended Otto. He was no doubt briefed to do so.

Interesting in context is the military intelligence and strategic information which the Italian bishop seeks to convey to his master. We do not need the details, but may usefully note that the Greek emperor and his advisers evidently discussed strategy (in relation to the Muslims) in the light of the prophecies of Daniel. Liudprand carries their arguments further in a malicious parody of imperial prognostication, likening Nicephorus to the 'wild ass' which will be destroyed by 'the lion and his whelp' (Ottos I and II).[23]

Next, the *Pèlerinage de Charlemagne*. The date of this work is problematic. Anything between 1060 and ninety years later! It is, or it is not, the earliest *chanson de geste*. I doubt whether the historians have yet paid much attention to it, and my own acquaintance with it is recent. Scope: about nine-hundred twelve-syllable lines.[24]

The theme of the work is a fictitious journey of Charles the Great and his paladins to Jerusalem, where they acquire precious relics. On the return journey they resolve to see Constantinople and meet the famous Greek king – Hugo le Fort! They encounter him out in the fields ploughing with plough and oxen. This does *not* seem to surprise them. Charlemagne introduces himself and his nephew Roland. Hugo says that for seven years he has waited to meet Charles, of whom one hears so much. He promises the Franks gold, silver and cattle, and then mounts his mule and proposes to lead the Franks back to the town. This *does* surprise the Franks! Namely, that he proposes to leave the precious plough, gold-covered, in the open field. But Hugo says that 'in [his] empire, which includes Persia, there are no thieves'.

This requires a word of commentary. In Hugo le Fort, the king who does his own ploughing, the Franks apparently see, as we would now say, a semi-mythical regal figure. If he, on the other hand, says that in his vast kingdom there are no thieves, we may conclude that Byzantium as a well-governed and policed state was a familiar idea to Western audiences: it could be alluded to in the context of a fictitious tale. We note that Charles is ashamed of his own, by comparison, modest wealth. Hugo has meantime instructed his wife (*sa moillier*) to dress festively and prepare for guests.

There follows a description of a splendid room in the palace of King Hugo. – This seems to remind some French editors of the 'golden room' (*Chrysotriclinium*) in one of the palaces in Constantinople. ('*Charles vit le palais e la richece grant*', etc.).[25] – The tables were of fine gold, seats and stools also, the pillars were of marble, decorated with motifs in *cloisonné*, the walls of the room were decorated with mosaics; there was a domed roof, and so on. What causes the amazement and later the terror of the Franks are the concealed organ pipes, drums, bells, which according to the wind and weather outdoors give forth concerts of birds in song or the roar of storms or tempest. This description is derived at least to some extent from medieval works on Alexander the Great, but note: In the midst of all this splendour and magnificence the Franks possibly feel themselves to be indeed *rustici* (in context, however, *ruiste* = 'doughty'). There is a banquet, with music. In their quarters the Franks are observed by a concealed spy of King Hugo, and they spend the night characteristically boasting of what they will do tomorrow.

From the point of view of literary history, the boastings are the main contents of this part of the *Chanson*: this is a comic epic. We need not go into the details of the boasts, which involve strength, cunning, military and acrobatic skill. On the next day the Franks are required by Hugo to make good their boastings, which they succeed in doing with God's help. Then, richly rewarded, they return to their home.

Shall we be able to use the *Pèlerinage* as evidence of Western attitudes to the Byzantine world? Does it not reveal Western man as being conscious of his own inferiority in power, wealth? He knows himself to be a provincial; he compensates for this inferiority by cunning, as a practical joker – an early Eulenspiegel or Münchhausen(?) Whatever one may think of that suggestion, it was at any rate an easier task for the poet as a public entertainer (particularly as a narrator, as we shall see again when we return to the case of Chrétien de Troyes) – than for the counsellors of emperors and kings (Saxon, Hohenstaufen), or for their official historiographers, to deal with Byzantium. The entertainer could dismiss the problems of East and West by making fun of all Easterners. And that is why at this point, *rallentando*, I bring in a further *historical* document, to show how in reality (at any rate, reality as recorded) all the resources of partisan rhetoric had to be drawn upon to body forth what was still a transparent fiction as the historical truth, to be defiantly declared.

Recording the events of the year 1155 in the later of his two histories (*Gesta Frederici*), Otto of Freising states that Frederick Barbarossa had on one occasion to address the Roman Senate in person. This he did, says Otto, 'without any particular preparation, and in intricately composed periods in the Italianate style'.[26] It is difficult to conceive of anything *less* spontaneous, as even the brief extract (about one-fifth of the whole speech), below, will adequately illustrate. What interests us here primarily is the historical logic of the political argument itself:

'We have heard a great deal of the wisdom (*sapientia*) of the Romans and of their fortitude – a good deal more, however, about their wisdom. . . .And you yourself have just praised to the stars the *nobility* of the divine republic.'
'I know, I know (*agnosco, agnosco*), and I will use the words of your author [Cicero]: There was, there was once virtue (*virtus*) in this

republic. Once there was, I say. Would that we could say just as truthfully: there is now. But your Rome, rather should we say *our* Rome, has suffered vicissitudes (*vicissitudines rerum*); it was as unable as anything else to escape the eternal law which the Creator of all things had destined for those living beneath the lunar orb. What shall I say! It is well-known how the power of your nobility (*robur nobilitatis tue*) was first transferred from this our town here to the royal town of the East [Constantinople], and how then for many years the languishing Greek (*Greculus esuriens*) sucked at the breasts of thy glory (*ubera deliciarum tuarum*). Then came the Frank (*venit Francus*)!'

'In name and in fact (*nomine et re*) *nobilis*, he, the Frank, wrested from you what residue of nobility there was. If you would know what was the former glory of Rome, the dignity of the senatorial estate, the correct disposition of commanders and armies in the field, the efficiency and discipline of the equestrian order (*equestris ordinis virtutem et disciplinam*), its undaunted courage in moving to the attack, observe *our* state (*rem publicam*)! All these things you will find with us! They passed to us together with the imperial rule (*ad nos simul omnia hec cum imperio demanarunt*). . . .'In your *misfortunes* you called upon the fortunate one, in your *weakness* you called upon the strong one, in your *impotence* upon the *powerful* one, in your *peril* upon him who stands secure (*implorasti misera felicem, debilis fortem, invalida validum, anxia securum*)'.

A tirade of Barbarossa's then, directed against the Romans in Italy: in the Italian style, mentioning *en passant* the miserable Greek, the parasite on the breasts of 'Rome', and representing the Hohenstaufen themselves, successors of the Franks, as the saviours of Rome! Is this not a desperate perversion of history, and the ruthless exploitation of a myth at a moment of political and military 'Konjunktur'? Whatever we may think of this document, we may not ignore it, or reserve indignation for Reinald of Dassel and the relatively innocent Archpoet. (In the latter's so-called *Kaiserhymnus* there is disparaging reference to the Greek emperor as 'Constantine!'. He is seen as raising his hand in impotence and told not to do so.)

I shall find it convenient if I may at this point merely recall the *Ludus de Antichristo*. (There is not the space to rehearse the complicated 'plot' and comment on it.) I prefer instead to direct attention to those shifting patterns of basic historiography of which Karl Bertau has wisely reminded us in his recent study of literature in the Middle Ages.[27] Towards the end of the Middle Ages history was being made not only by kings and emperors, but by powerful magnates, spiritual and lay. Since the days of the Investiture Contest emperors and kings had been divested of their 'sacral' dignity, and the emperor was a secular ruler like any other (Bertau I, 231f.). And so it is that Abbot Suger of St Denis can take the initiative as historian, and propound in a moment of inspiration a new variant of Western history whereby it is now the *French* king who is the main recipient of the sanctity transmitted by 'Charlemagne'. (And of course Otto of Freising himself believed that the migration of power and wisdom from East to West had in his day passed through Germany and reached the Atlantic.)

After these introductory remarks we can at last turn to Chrétien de Troyes, and our subject in the remainder of this survey is the 'fantastic' history purveyed by entertainers, see above. Among the entertainers we may assume included: Geoffrey of Monmouth and Wace.

At the beginning of his *Cligès*, Chretien writes in considerable detail about Alexander, father of the hero Cligès. We note that Alexander, despite all the representations of *his* father, forsook Greece, where he could have had a perfectly respectable and praiseworthy career, in order to become a knight at the court of King Arthur in Britain. What are we to say of this?

Chrétien had already told his audience: 'our books relate that pre-eminence in knighthood (*chevalerie*) and in scholarship (*clergie*) once belonged to Greece. Then *chevalerie* migrated to Rome, learning to France. Of Greeks and of Romans one no longer hears anything; their fame is passed' (lines 1–44).

About Greece and the Greeks – and others! – Chrétien then has a good deal more to say, to tease both his own audience and us today. In the course of the complicated story of *Cligès*, for instance, the emperors of both empires, Greek *and German* have roles to play. These are amusingly reminiscent of recent real history (see below). As rulers they remain, none the less,

contemporaries of King Arthur of Britain. But Arthur's kingdom now includes Southampton, Winchester, Wallingford,
Windsor and Oxford. Cologne and Regensburg represent
Germany, Constantinople and Athens indicate Greece. Nothing
in the romance, however, recalls the 'theocratic' role of the
Greek emperor, and instead of the theory of a 'translatio
imperii' to the Germans, Chrétien asserted, as we saw, the pre-
eminence of (presumably) the cathedral schools of France. It is,
therefore, surely worth mentioning in this fantastic context that
the heroine, Fénice, apparently dead, is entombed in a church in
the Greek capital dedicated to St Peter. Was this a political joke
(St Peter's, Constantinople)? Or was it a topical allusion to
St Peter's, Beauvais, in the treasury of which Chrétien claimed
to have found the source of his romance?

The allusions to contemporary history are clearly not to be
taken any more seriously than the author's conclusion, namely,
that after all these scandalous happenings (it will be remembered
that the *Cligès* can be interpreted as an anti-*Tristan*) the Greek
emperor introduced the institution of the harem. A sorry end to
the glory that was Greece (see above).

Finally, the observation of our colleagues in Romance
philology that Chrétien's allusions to contemporary history
(betrothals, personal unions and so on, of the imperial houses of
Greece and of Germany, and the difficulties both sides had with
a Saxon duke), are a simple reversal of well-known facts, so that
for instance a Greek prince petitions the hand of a German
princess – invites comparison with the findings of Germanists
on the subject of *Eraclius* and the *König Rother*. Eberhard
Nellmann speaks of the 'unreflektiertes Verhältnis zur
Geschichte' of these two works. Of the *Rother*, for instance, he
writes:

'In the *Rother* the hero resides in Bari, he receives the crown in Rome,
he is emperor, he appears in the role of judge in the land of the Franks
and he gives the sword of knighthood to his son Pippin (the father of
Charles the Great)! Thus Rother gradually falls into the role of a German
emperor, although the original Rother is Roger II of Sicily, who was
reputed to be one of the enemies of the emperor.'[28]

But enough of the entertainers. I have mentioned in passing, but still said nothing in detail about the more familiar attitude towards history (and Greece and Rome) of Geoffrey of Monmouth and Wace, and nothing at all about the *Kaiserchronik*. These raise too many problems of literary history (written sources, etc.) for discussion in this experimental framework.

10. ECONOMIES OF HISTORY.
WHAT IS FICTION?

A German review of 1967 opened with an expression of mild shock that Roy Pascal should begin his reflections on the nature of autobiography by considering his own case. From the remainder of the review I recognized that Pascal's problems were uncomfortably like those which had preoccupied me for many years, and there seemed indeed to be a risk that if I read him, my own ideas might not survive to be worked out in writing. I should say at once in partial justification of my behaviour (delaying my reading of Pascal) that my immediate problem is not autobiography, but general questions concerning narrative and history-writing, particularly in the Middle Ages, but also subsequently; and that in the course of a good deal of hard thinking, some writing and much debate I have also been driven to reflect on my own case, as the only one to which I find any reliable access. More specifically, to ask what it is that happens when I myself write, and to what extent this activity is covered (or obscured) by the conventional phraseology in which we customarily take note of such activity. Encouraged by Pascal's example I propose to talk freely of my thinking on this subject, offering only a perfunctory apology for doing so, because I think my own case may be typical enough. A further convention which I must ignore is that of attempting a definition of the terms I shall use, for frankly I do not know what history is or what fiction is, either in the medieval or the modern world, and I cannot find anyone to tell me. As for examples of the one or the other – and criteria, they seem to beg the questions I want to ask, and to be evidence only of accepted notions.

Carefully avoiding the term 'example', therefore, let us try to break into the subject. We do not hesitate, I think, to find Goethe's *Wilhelm Meister* a work of fiction with no claims to be considered as history, despite undoubtedly autobiographical elements (authenticity), and many pertinent reflections on the contemporary scene. And whatever the professional historians may think of Toynbee's twelve-volume *Study of History* and its fiction of successive 'societies' (without which the story he has to tell could not have been made intelligible), it is not a work of fiction as that term is commonly understood. Next, the *Chanson de Roland* or the *Nibelungenlied* (epics) and Wolfram's *Parzival* (a romance): to the extent that these reflect 'real history' in memorable idealization, or transmit an almost *authoritative* tradition concerning the quest of the Grail, they are far from being pure fictions. The 'veracity' of these various works is, however, clearly different again in kind from that of St Augustine's *City of God*. Conventionally we would say that this work, literally epoch-making, operates with two truths – that of 'real history' (Rome had fallen before Barbarian attack, and that is the initial subject), and the revealed truth of the scriptures of the Christian faith. In correlating these St Augustine propounds a prognostic economy of history, of which the vehicle is the *fiction* of the 'two cities'. This fiction came for all that to be confessed as the higher *historical* truth by which the medieval Western world lived, and on which it acted, generating in the process more real politics and history than any half-dozen treaties which the professional historians care to name. On balance, however, literary historians will class the *City of God* as a theological work. An official economy of history need not, of course, be Christian, but it must draw its authority (or some of it) from scripture of some kind – Marxist–Leninist, for instance.

So one could go on endlessly, arguing about the nature of history, and of historical fictions and fictitious history, but generally we prefer to settle for working principles. Despite all this the Muses remain as in Antiquity some nine in number, of whom Clio (history-writing) is but one; and like the rest of them she refuses to be finally institutionalized, or to work alone, or to inspire only professional historians. When we try to determine what Charles the Great *did*, Einhard's *Vita Caroli Magni*, though patterned on Suetonius and in large measure a literary exercise, will accordingly appear to us to have been written with rather more help from Clio than were, for instance, the *Gesta Caroli* or the *Chanson de Roland*. We judge that to be the order of approximation to our conceptions of what history-writing should do, and what genres of history-writing there are. We then find it expedient to remit the unsolved problems of discrimination and definition to a special branch of literary or philosophical studies, namely the theory of history (*Geschichtsphilosophie*) which has its own masters.

In my speculations on history-writing and the writing of fiction, and in my search for a reliable basis for assertions about any works of mainly narrative content, I have been driven, as I have already indicated, to ask what it is I do when I myself write: what it is I *make* out of 'my material' (works, and records of past events, which interest me), in relation to the genres of writing accessible to me more or less now.

That I should want to turn past events into plots for a novel, or visualize them as well-ordered conflicts (drama), or that I should choose verse as my medium is as unlikely now as ever it was. It is equally predictable now (it was not always) that I shall continue to *make* something in writing of what I read, whether what I read is a source or so-called secondary material. It is also predictable that I shall give considerable attention to matters of literary form, but in *intenti*on my work will be some kind of history-writing – the narration, based on the scrutiny of evidence, of certain kinds of events in the Middle Ages. An important point to be made at this juncture is that without some previous success in endeavours of this kind, I should by now probably be incapable of such intentions. This amounts *inter alia* to an assertion that my contemporaries have, by their previous verdicts and present interest, become in part responsible for this future likelihood. Similar predications, suitably modified, could probably be made of most works in any genre, from those as humble as my own to the greatest. My next point is that such history-writing as I have myself already undertaken, was, for all its humility formulas, a *temeritas*, a risk taken.

Let us disregard the bold front which any new piece of writing appears to present. I think here rather of the appalling *ignorance* from the midst of which most works of scholarship and interpretation (creative writing also) are wrested, whether this is an ignorance of inexperience (youth), novicehood (first book) or of incomplete information or curtailed enquiry. *I presume* to tell contemporaries this and that about artists and writers in the Middle Ages – as it happens, particularly about the medieval artist's choice and his treatment of themes from literature in the light of tradition and of dogma; even about the properties of the treatment of these subjects in certain periods. But on reflection I am even more alarmed when – as the result of such presumption – I am said here and there to have broken new ground or to have shed new light on these matters; or when colleagues consult me, or explicitly assure me that they 'take my word for it'. Perhaps I should recall our present subject: the difference between *history*-writing and the writing of *fiction* or *fictions*, which latter, in the areas where I work, might be a fairly bold thesis to explain otherwise enigmatic events, or a formula which allows us to see parallels and relationships between literature and art, perhaps even models and adaptations. Where in these circumstances does the imaginative interpretation of evidence cease and the creation of fiction(s) begin? We may, any of us, at any time fail in our intention to keep to the historical facts. At that point we must cut short this line of argument.

And now the 'ignorance' itself. I do not say that my ignorance of the Middle Ages is greater than, or merely different in kind from that of other medievalists. It is, however, an ignorance personal to me, and has contours determined by many distressingly negative factors, such as inability to grasp certain kinds of evidence, or impatience with certain patterns of argument. There are ways of looking at things that I ignore, or am glad to leave to others. These deficiencies I find it difficult to distinguish objectively from *lacking curiosity*. The result is that my ignorance extends into some areas where knowledge is assumed to be general. In reflecting on this situation I derive little comfort from knowing where the information which I do not use can be found. Conventionally one would say that I am interested in certain things, not in others, while in practice my ignorance is something with which I daily come to terms – skimping, skimming, or temporizing with (alas) completely ineffectual marginal *nota benes*. While conceding that *all* this *might* be attributable to a schooled sense of the relevant (flair), it involves me in procedures perilously near to dilettantism, a charge to which I should probably react with aggressive (self-defensive) questions about the organization of bibliographies and card-indexes, and *their* principles of inclusion and exclusion. At the same time I have to admit that I no longer read with what would be called a full and proper responsibility toward the subject which officially I profess. I continue with my considera-tion of the circumstances in which, and the manner in which we may come to terms with our ignorance and *dare* to say what 'we find'.

Let us put down as a provisional answer that we each work with a personal conception of obligations (to our subject as we see it), possibilities, feasibilities; and in such circumstances, when we have something important to say, we act – we write. We may be satisfied or dissatisfied with our work and our workmanship: the work is indeed often something very different from what we set out to make of our material. We may also be gratified or disappointed by the outcome in terms of success or failure: we may fail to persuade and convince others. Whatever the circumstances in which a work is produced, it remains to be read properly, noticed merely or ignored by others, to be influential or to make little or no impact. It may be found untenable in its principal thesis and faulty in detail – by others who have an equally personal conception of what is relevant, their own economy of history, their *kind* of history. I find it difficult to believe that the generality of works, whether they are works which we class as being of pure scholarship, or treatises or tracts intended to sway or persuade, or freer creations of the imagination meant to delight and entertain, are produced in conditions fundamentally different from those I have indicated. We accept the fact that we cannot know everything; we are satisfied with enough; we know when we can do no more. I also find it difficult to distinguish between the historian's criteria of relevance and adequacy when he approves or disapproves of a work purporting to be historical, and the critic's appraisal of, say, Schiller's *Jungfrau von Orléans* or Goethe's *Tasso*. Common to both situations is the question as to what could or should have been *made* of this material in this *genre of writing*. How good is the *work*? Put another way: for all their uniqueness, all works produced under the guidance of whatever Muse have certain features in common, of which none is more important than the decision of their makers to declare them, or allow them to be declared, finished (generally published). All *scripta* become *acta* of their own kind – or the kind to which opinion assigns them, from the moment they are made public; and on them there will be passed the never quite final verdict which Antiquity called a *fama* (or *infamia*). Works take their *chance*, once they are published; they succeed or fail, or have their vicissitudes in much the same way as their makers. Like ventures of any kind, written works of all kinds are essays which 'come off' or do not. That works of scholarship and history-writing may 'date' in a way in which works of the imagination need not, may be asserted. It is, however, a distinction which can only be made and sustained if several important questions are begged. These we need not go into. The verdict of history determines who were the great historians, who were the great poets, and *they* set the relevant patterns and standards in their works. History is in the final resort the works of those whose *fama* is to have been historians, and by the same token literature and scholarship are the works which are reputed to be 'of literature' and 'of scholarship'. The criterion seems to be success.

Carried a stage further, the personal admissions I have been making concerning ignorance (and ways of coming to terms with it) mean that nowadays I myself tend to read, though not exclusively, mainly with reference to my 'interests'. At the same time I may entertain thoughts of what I (or others) might make of what I read. I may suggest to others what they should do. Previous experience enables me to envisage what it would be feasible for me still to make of my material, and to exclude thoughts of anything for which I should not have the time, the organization or the opportunity. I can find few fundamental differences between this mode of operation and that of a historian, poet or novelist considering subjects or themes which he might treat, except those differences I have already indicated – the available (accessible) genres, and the nature of the *intention*. ('Inspiration' is not limited to the poets.) Allowing for the historian's conceptions of 'subject', the narrative writer's inevitable interest in historical figures or periods, and mine in themes and their treatment by notable and less notable authors in the past, the gaps become mere dividing lines between crafts. But where does one draw the lines, or rather, what writers and what works have drawn them in the past, providing the models and setting the standards?

At this point I slacken the pace somewhat, to be certain of formulating a crucial question correctly, concerning intention. We can fairly clearly dissociate the historian from the poet or novelist, insofar as we shall not generally impute to the historian an intention to create a fanciful story, or anything designed mainly to entertain, or to occupy our leisure. That is not the historian's office. The intention of any kind of historian must be to tell an honest story, verifiable by reference to evidence of things said and done 'in fact'. I myself can, I hope, by now be relied upon not to intend fictions. But it is already admitted that through deficient curiosity, and by working with inevitably incomplete evidence I may produce fictions, even interrelated fictions, which, until discredited or superseded, are to all intents and purposes history.

We move on now to consider briefly whether 'what happened' is history, whether the account of it has been given or not (that history is written 'lest men forget' is a *topos* of official historiography), and, further, whether conjecture and surmise are fictions when these *have* been committed to writing by historians. Again I have to come back to my own case to get my bearings for a renewed attack on the problem of history-writing and the writing of fiction. Are the historian's conjectures and surmises fictions? Evidently not in intention. That consideration alone will, however, not make them into history. A further word now on intention – and on ignorance.

One works as a scholar, presumably also as an author of whatever kind, in constant awareness of threats to one's intentions: namely the wishes and intentions of others. There is a conflict between what one wants to 'get done' and what others 'want done' – the modern equivalent of keeping patrons satisfied. There is for instance, as I write this essay, a possibility that I might be requested to contribute a footnote to the history of German Minnesang, in the form of a review of a substantial monograph on the canon of the genuine lyrics of Reinmar von Hagenau. This threatens my other intentions. It is a work fiendishly set as a decoy to tempt me – to seize the opportunity to return to a neglected field of study. I have, however, meantime come to terms with my present ignorance; I have skimmed the work, underlined key statements and picked out what I need in any case. But suppose I were in fact asked to review the book. Should I refuse? And if I accepted and did the necessary checking of versification schemes and reflected on the author's methods, his findings (already underlined, see above), what should I write? I spare readers my surmises. What I wanted to lead up to was the 'what would happen if?' question which precedes deliberate action of all kinds including writing, history no less than fiction.

If historians protest that they do not spend overmuch time asking 'what would happen?' or more particularly 'what would have happened if?' (Charles the Great had not accepted the

crown, or Hitler's headquarters had not been a light temporary
building), they are equally concerned not to hear the reproach
that they did not even consider the policies or strategies which,
in a given situation, were recommended but not carried out.
They therefore offer their surmises and conjectures. This brings
them nearer to the writers of fiction. Much nearer than is
commonly allowed, for it is – conversely – quite fallacious to
believe that the so-called 'omniscient author' of the world of
fiction has any knowledge of those actions of his characters
which he did not narrate: they are *non acta* – just as certainly as
the episodes he cancelled during the final revision of his story.
That he would know what his characters would have done in
given situations is a theoretician's fiction.

By now I must seem to be wasting the time of my readers:
'we all know the difference between history-writing and the
writing of fictions'. I will now concede that we are fairly certain
that we can distinguish between the two activities in the modern
world, even when history-writing is encountered at its most
popular. For the Middle Ages discrimination is ultimately
possible, but by no means simple. We have for instance the
problem of the traditional story which cannot be varied in any
essentials. Think of the main stories only. With some of
these the greatest authors struggled in vain: Gottfried von
Strassburg failed with *Tristan*, Wolfram von Eschenbach with
his *Willehalm*. They did not finish their stories; they could not
have finished them. They had sought to impose on them an
interpretation which the stories themselves, having greater
authority than any individual author, would not bear. We have
the paradox that whereas medieval writers could struggle for a
decade to produce the true story of Tristan or the true story of
Willehalm and fail, their contemporaries could (also with a
struggle) tell the story of the Western Empire and Papacy with
scarcely a reference to Constantinople and the Byzantine world,
propagating in the process a fiction (the Donation of Constantine) – and succeeding in this. The official national historians
meanwhile derived their nations from a mythical Francus, or

Brutus or some other of the worthies who left Troy in the following of Aeneas. This was the endeavour of the Western world to legitimate its existence, its success, by the glorification of its past deeds, its true history. Such history is confessed autobiography; it becomes belief. Once successfully confessed, such true history could not be refuted in its own area. Elsewhere (for instance in the Byzantine world) it was a fabrication, a transparent fiction, a lie.

Could it then be that history is that narrative of past events which has been successfully told? – and that what we call the consensus of historical opinion is a form of group confession? Or is history the statement in which we agree collectively to come to terms with our ignorance? Is it the facts and the relevance of the facts we know? In either case 'As you Like It' equals 'Wie es recht eigentlich geschah'. And should these questions be further pursued at Tintagel or at Aachen, or in Rome, or elsewhere – perhaps somewhere where all Western Europeans are infidels and Franks?

I conclude with brief reflections on two recent 'historical' occasions (occasions when some kind of history was in process of being fashioned). They have contributed – with many others – to the difficulties I experience in distinguishing between the making (fashioning) of history and the making of a work of fiction.

In Göttingen in the early years after the War huge university audiences heard a distinguished historian [Percy E. Schramm] review the recent past, and ask at the end: 'who was responsible?' His account – as the work of a professional – was no doubt 'wissenschaftlich', which to a German audience would in context be synonymous with 'historical'. The British University Officer of the day duly consulted his superiors but there was nothing to be done. German respect for 'Wissenschaft' would in the circumstances not have risen to the task of considering any other reading of history, least of all from an inevitably prejudiced British or American historian. I do not suggest that all Göttingen or anyone in Göttingen would still consider the lecture to have been scholarly and objective; it may indeed have failed in its purpose both then and now. It was an attempt at any rate so to 'make' history that it could be confessed by some, and not easily unmade by others.

Twenty years later the Carolingian Age was celebrated on a scale and in a way which will soon seem immodest and perhaps even unscholarly. There were some critical voices raised at the time, and suggestions that the picture presented of the Age of Charlemagne was at least incidentally a 'message for Eùrope', or – to revert to some of the terms we have been using here – a chapter of European autobiography. Hundreds of thousands may by their presence at the Exhibition in Aachen have seemed ready to confess such a reading of the Carolingian Age. As for the monumental volumes of essays appearing in the wake of the Exhibition catalogue, to lend permanence to the occasion, they testified to a phase of historical thinking: they were also, in a manner of speaking, votive offerings. Collingwood said with, I think, unconscious ambiguity, that history is 'self-revelatory'. In fact it can be uncommonly like our better fictions.

III
SYLLABUS STUDIES

11. ON COMING TO TERMS WITH CURTIUS

It is thirty years since E. R. Curtius's *Europäische Literatur und lateinisches Mittelalter* appeared (1948, English translation by W. R. Trask in 1953). It seems by now clear that it will not 'revolutionize' our studies of literature, as was at first thought possible by some reviewers. There is indeed a risk that, like so many monumental works devoted to the expounding of a central thesis (Burdach's *Vom Mittelalter zur Reformation* for instance) it will be prematurely set aside with a perfunctory general acknowledgment: in this case the addition of 'any *topoi?*' to the schedule of questions we customarily ask of medieval literary works. I find the position more complicated. One has to come to terms with Curtius. In its aim to discredit the various medieval philologies and suggest in their stead a scheme of 'European studies' his monograph is in part success-ful, and adjustments will have to be made. A knowledge of Curtius should, I think, henceforward inform our teaching and our interpretation of texts. In the working formula of the *topos*, as propounded by Curtius, however, I find a simplification of important issues. In the space available I can unfortunately do no more than illustrate this final negative statement.

I

There are several objections to the simple acceptance of the term *topos*, particularly, I think, in an age when the use of multipurpose tools for precision work is likely to be frowned on. Curtius uses *topos*, according to Professor Edgar Mertner,[1] in a sense which the equivalent *locus* and *locus communis* of the manuals of rhetoric did not acquire until the eighteenth century – of a commonplace *statement* or *cliché*. He also brings together as *topoi* not only statements, but any recurrent pattern of argument, and traditional metaphors and similes. All these things we need, I think, to be able to identify and name individually; their common denominator is highly complex and cannot be expressed in any such simple term. A minor objection is that Curtius gives prominence to a number of *topoi* which he has himself investigated or had investigated [...]

But we need a term, it may be advanced in Curtius's support, which in literally one word will tell the uninitiated reader of medieval works not to imagine that a catalogue of kings whose realms are gone (of the great lovers of the past, of famous men befooled by women) is 'original' – so why not *topos* or *topical* (Curtius)? Why are these themes 'topical' rather than simply 'typical'? *Topos* suggests elaboration as it was practised in the schools. It is apt enough if we are dealing with *ubi sunt qui ante nos*. If the theme, however, is *de contemptu mundi* or *vanitas vanitatum*, the ages of the world, the fifteen portents of the Day of Judgment, or if the sentiment is *erat dolor sicut meus* or *pereat dies in qua natus sum*, it would surely seem more appropriate to relate it to Christianity's *own* stock of themes, *its* diction, formulae, figures, which the rhetorics do not include in their purview. The older nineteenth-century method of illustrating the typical elements in a passage was to quote plentiful parallels; it was slow but sound, and was based on the study of texts, not of manuals. It did not always insist sufficiently on continuity from long before to long after the passage annotated. It occasionally failed completely, and postulated 'influence'; our handbooks still carry forward the suggestion that Otfrid must have known the *Muspilli* because he too describes Heaven as a 'life without death and light without darkness' (I, 18, 9).

Traditional formulae, recurrent themes and patterns of exposition, arrays of proof-texts, *loci communes* as hitherto understood (as schemata of 'headings under which' a subject had to be, or could be treated) are indeed a large part of the substance and of the form, the stock-in-trade, of medieval literature. For that very reason we should be wise not to label, frank and expedite the lot, without differentiation, as *topoi*. Nor can we have them attributed to an overwhelming influence of a merely rhetorical, mainly secular tradition. Schwietering is surely right to insist that we continue to call his *Demutsformel* a *Demutsformel*, however much it may, in its verbal organization, exploit the rhetorician's 'protestation of incompetence'.[2] [...]

II

The main lines of enquiry in our medieval studies were worked out, according to Curtius, by scholars who paid little heed to the Latin literature of the earlier Middle Ages. Our various medieval philologies are therefore insecurely founded; our picture of the Middle Ages is incomplete. This we may readily concede, at the same time noting that Curtius's main conclusions after *his* excursions into Medieval Latin fall far short of providing all that is lacking: it is not enough merely to insist on an unbroken rhetorical tradition reaching back to Antiquity (evidence of which can be established by the asking of the new question 'any *topoi?*'). How then are we to complete our picture of the Middle Ages and at the same time detach ourselves from those special lines of enquiry which seem, in fact, on all the evidence to have limited our vision?

If we look critically at our present equipment of knowledge I should say that about the persistence of a pre-Christian, Germanic and heroic tradition (*its* conventions and its rhetoric) we know more than enough, and have something to discard; about the *matière de Bretagne* and the chivalrous convention with which it became associated, for the time being enough. The study of the medieval inheritance from Antiquity meantime proceeds apace. There remains the further, by comparison neglected, component of Western tradition: the Christian. Here Curtius suggests that we should read more widely in the Fathers 'as literature'. We should address to them not the theologian's stock questions (God, Trinity, Christology, Grace, etc.), nor accept his word for what is interesting and important; we should, says Curtius, read the Fathers – for their *topoi*![3] I would agree with this if we may firstly italicize *their*, carry forward instead of *topos* a more detailed schedule of typical features, and add to the list of things to be observed as we read: their genres, their literary conventions and – before all else – simply their 'lore'. Of the importance of their lore Curtius is aware. He says we should cease merely consulting Isidore, and read him. This is given, however, rather as an instruction, for the Fathers have not contributed significantly to Curtius's picture of the Middle Ages. Jerome, Augustine and Cassiodorus are introduced to us as his more recent acquaintance and comparative strangers.

If we were all more generally conversant with medieval Christian lore, our equipment of knowledge and experience would be more like that of at any rate the *secular* authors we read. At present we share with them 'common human experience' and a few annexes of special knowledge – heroic, classical and Arthurian (which we in addition see in depth and in historical perspective). We lag behind them particularly in Christian lore; we have little conception of its range, stratification and chronology. Is there not something improper in our expecting relative newcomers to medieval studies to be familiar with the conventions of stylized chivalric behaviour (*sicherheit*, for instance), whilst ourselves continuing to be surprised that it was the Trinity which performed the Works of Creation? Like latter-day Gurnemanzes we could even place *sicherheit* in a code, and gloss it with examples; but should we not stumble over the proof-texts of the Trinity, and probably get the division of labour wrong? We can expatiate on Kyot but are (generally) unaware of the medieval significance of Melchisedech. We are better able to explain the origin of the name Nibelungen than say where Lucifer came from.

These pieces of Christian lore have, it is true, been brought to our attention in suitable footnotes, as required. But we receive them as supplementary information; they are not secure knowledge, and we miss passing allusions to them. We are tutored to respond to *Ruomoldes rât* and to *sich verligen*; we do not forget them, because they are peculiarly ours. We do not respond so promptly to 'Procla's advice' or *verwâzen wart. . . der tac, da sîn geburt ane lac.* We recall the pun *amur-ameir*, but find *homo–humus* and *Eva–Ave* tedious clerical conceits. Lack of familiarity is part of our malaise, and malaise explains the excessive care with which editors annotate such allusions as they do identify. The general fault is in consequence often a more or less serious over-shooting of the mark, and the quotation of authority far beyond the competence of the author annotated. (The *Heliand* poet and even Otfrid, not to speak of Wolfram, would be staggered to know what learned doctors have been invoked to provide parallels to what they themselves wrote.) We gloss general knowledge by reference to learned authority.

But to leave such minor points, where footnotes perhaps provide what is needed for the moment, and turn to larger issues. How do we justify our pretence that Hartmann's *Armer Heinrich* and *Gregorius* are in some way less important and meritorious than *Erec* and *Iwein*? Is a reluctance to admit that the Middle Ages were Christian part of the explanation? Why, as a rider to that question, do we find Konrad von Fussesbrunnen's *Kindheit Jesu* mainly notable for being written in a courtly diction (see our histories of literature)? One would have thought the fact that a *layman* wanted to versify *Pseudo-Matthew* more central than his craftsmanship. Or, to return to Hartmann, should his interim verdict on Arthurian fictions (in the prologue to *Gregorius*) not make us modify our approach more drastically, when we deal with his non-Arthurian works? At any rate to the extent of admitting that Lord Henry is a model of knighthood only in the 'till ready' passage (lines 1–74), not during his main story, and certainly not at the end; and Gregorius only during a disastrous interlude? These works surely merit interpretation within the conventions of the genres to which their author assigned them. *Der arme Heinrich* and *Gregorius* were not written to extol chivalry; their portraits of knighthood are set pieces, in which an element of irony, appropriate to the author's main purpose, may rightly be detected.

If we wish to become more fully aware of the complete range of medieval literature, and see our authors in a juster perspective, we must be prepared to read more generously what was written by clerics as clerics, and by medieval thinkers. Possibly in the hope that we shall find something to illuminate our own studies, but preferably on the look-out for nothing in particular. An impartial reading is more likely both to make us aware of what is in its own context significant, and to give our minds a chance to indulge in some possibly useful associative thinking about significant things. An *aperçu* may then be worth more than an index; it is better to kick oneself for having been blind, than to find one has built a house of cards.

III

It is, I think, not a stable ingredient of our teaching – Curtius certainly does not teach it, and I cannot find any hint of it in what he writes – that the Christian Middle Ages recognized a hierarchy of genres governed by subject matter. This is a large topic, only one aspect of which I feel prepared to touch on at present. It used to be stated quite openly that although Boethius had written in his *De Consolatione* a work entirely Christian in spirit, he could not have been a Christian, since he never refers to God and Christ; he had therefore not written the treatises *De Fide Catholica* and *De Trinitate* which were attributed to him. The position has now changed in Boethius scholarship.[4] He wrote all these things. But we are still far from a general conviction that medieval writers indeed distinguished so rigorously between philosophy and theology. (Perhaps we have insisted too much that the Middle Ages made philosophy the handmaid of theology.) The economy within which Boethius can represent himself as taunted by Fortune but instructed and consoled by Philosophy, knows – and evidently can know – no higher instance than God's Providence, which restrains the arbitrary operation of Fortune.[5] Christ and the Trinity belong to a different order, and are beyond the limits of the genre in which the moral philosopher's abstractions or personifications can be treated. On the other hand, Philosophy and Fortune do not appear in the same writer's theological treatises: the scope of a *Summa* cannot be extended to include them. This seems to cause us less surprise.

The strict proprieties observed by Boethius in his treatises (which were after all standard works) may help us in some of our interpretations. Perhaps to define the degree of licence permitted at each stage, as we move away from the exact treatise (theological or philosophical) to Christian allegory (the *Psychomachia* for instance), and – *via* hymns and sermons – to moral tales, written by clerics, or written by laymen. What, for instance, is the hierarchy of 'instances' when a secular writer as a devout exercise tells the story of a worldling punished by God for his lack of Christian humility? The degree of licence in Hartmann's *Armer Heinrich* is, in fact, slight. First, Lord Henry is described as a paragon of gentlemanly distinction. He has *êre* and *guot* – in Boethius's terms: *honores* and *opes*. There is a break at line 75; the story proper begins when Lord Henry is forsaken by *Sælde*. With reference to what has gone before, his *Sælde* is his Fortune; with forward reference – [only the poet knows what course Lord Henry's story is to take] – it is his hope of salvation – now lost, until he merits it, the poet suggests. He is smitten with leprosy; not for his foolish philosophy (he should of course have distrusted Fortune), but for his lack of Christian humility, and for his failure to recognize that in a Christian (not Stoic) sense, all is vanity: *media vita in morte sumus*. If in his Fortune he had been a 'mirror' to his fellows, he is, when judged on other terms, found lacking in patience by comparison with the prototype of sufferers – Job.[6] Hartmann thus steps in his commentary on the story across what in exact genres would have been a barrier. He does this with ease, and crosses backwards and forwards, so that on the grounds of a somewhat perfunctorily motivated conversion the hero may be reprieved and miraculously restored to happiness. The strict properties of the treatise will also help us to appreciate what vast problems of organization Hartmann set himself when he chose to write next of Gregorius. Here was no merely thoughtless worldling, but a man destined by Fate *and* the machinations of the Devil ('instances', that is, belonging to different orders) to be in succession the offspring of an incestuous marriage, a *betrogen klosterman*, a self-styled knight, a fabulous sinner, a legendary martyr and a fictitious Pope! Need we wonder that we find it difficult to choose amongst the philosopher's and the theologian's *standard* terms in translating crucial passages in *Gregorius*? It is with good reason that we puzzle over *zwîfel, hilfe, gnâde* (3546, 3753), *trôst* (3614), *hulde* (3142, 3967). Even more complicated, as we well know, is the situation with Wolfram, who introduces a quasi-Church (the Grail community) to mediate between man and the Kingdom of God. Again one may ask whether we shall ever find a true coincidence between the terms Wolfram uses, and the terms in any passage in the *Patrologia Latina*.

If we turn away for the moment from edifying tales to more abstract statements; will it not, if the assumptions we have been making concerning genres and subject matter are correct, always be fruitless to look either to thinkers or to theologians for the source of Walther's prayer, that in a pacified *Reich* prosperity and honour may be 'brought together in one shrine with the grace of God, more precious than either'? Prosperity and honour (*opes* and *honores*) are, we noted from Boethius, the gifts of Fortune (and the Middle Ages still believed in a *fortuna cæsarea*, in the Interregnum evidently lost). According to Boethius the grace of God cannot be mentioned in the same book, let alone in the same breath, as prosperity and honour. A good deal of the controversy there has been about the source of Walther's 'drei Wertgebiete' – including Curtius's suggestion that no more is involved than a mnemonic formula of three – was therefore probably nugatory. Not in the writing of theologians and philosophers, but possibly only in the special prayers or the sermons of a court chaplain, or in the words of another secular writer – should one expect to find an allusion to such a consummation as Walther wished for. In saying this I do not, of course, seek to judge in detail the contributions which have been made on the subject of the poem; merely to suggest that we should be mindful of the genres (or 'orders') involved, when we look at authors and their works. Let us test one last example, applying the same criteria to a medieval Christian poet's adaptation of a tale from Antiquity.

Hugh Sacker [in 1957] analysed the role of the gods of the ancient world in Heinrich von Veldeke's *Eneit*.[7] No attempt is made to get rid of them. They clearly have the function of directing the hero's Fortune. They seem to Dr Sacker, simply from a study of functions, to personify Providence. This is in keeping with what has been said above on the basis of Boethius's *De Consolatione*: Fortune (as chance or as personal fortune) *is* governed by Providence. Heinrich would, of course, know what tales from Antiquity were recommended for the full *interpretatio christiana*, and how they were to be treated if so interpreted: *inter alia* not in their original form and at their full length! To seek to interest the Christian God in all the exploits of a non-Christian hero – even when these led to the founding of Rome – would have been an indefensible solecism. Not, however, in any way to suggest a Christian interest in the origins of Rome would have been a lost opportunity, and at the end Heinrich does indeed establish the link with Christian history. A convenient middle term for relating the course of pre-Christian history to universal history as the fulfilment of God's will, was Providence; and for Providence the gods stand substitute in the *Eneit*. The fact still remains that before Sacker's essay the *Eneit* had been studied only for its versification and language (the technical excellence which impressed Gottfried), or for the treatment of the one love story which was not already prejudged, that of Lavinia. It is treated as a case of 'amour courtois'. *This* made no impression on Gottfried, but *we* need it for our history of a particular convention; it is one of our 'lines'. We have hitherto seen little else in the *Eneit* to interest us, or indeed that could have interested Heinrich's contemporaries. Had we been more aware of the author's intention with the 'gods', we might have added other oddments (Mediterranean lore generally, the picture of the pagan underworld) and found something to talk and write about other than mere craftsmanship, in the nine-tenths of the tale. There is now the possibility, which Sacker has so fully realized, of interpreting the work as a whole.

IV

There may have been other equally important considerations determining and restricting the medieval writer's exercise of his craft, of which we are still unaware. Our secular poets were clearly mainly otherwise engaged than in the actual writing of the works by which we remember them. Nor were they always reading the works of their rivals! They also read and listened to other kinds of literature. We may perhaps profitably think of them as particularly attentive readers in the genres lying slightly beyond the range of their own competence, and observant of the skills, devices and conceits proper to those genres. There is at any rate in the works we read plenty of evidence of the application of skills learnt elsewhere.

After what I have said of Curtius's *topos* I naturally hesitate to recommend a new term, but I think there may be room in our studies for the discreet use of 'accommodation'. On first encountering the phenomenon in patristic literature one might be tempted to say that 'accommodation' lies midway between plagiarism and parody; but the intention is clearly reverent. As one becomes more familiar with the convention and notes the many occasions and circumstances in which 'accommodation' was practised, it will seem to fit, according to the author's intention, into the series: imitation, accommodation, parody, blasphemy. In dealing with secular authors we may be able to use it, at least analogically, when we feel that parody and blasphemy are too condemnatory. 'Accommodation' is the conscious but reverent transference of sacred or sacrosanct words, similes, metaphors, symbols, or whole mosaics of quotation to a

186

new context; or it may manifest itself as sustained allusion: for instance the use (or echoing) of the words of Job, or of *Lamentations*, or even of Christ's Agony in Gethsemane in the context of private prayer. By remembering the existence of this convention, we may be able (and may wish) to screen Gottfried of Strassburg from the full charge of irreverence and blasphemy: by speaking of an accommodation of Bernardine phraseology, when he extols the love of Tristan and Isolde; of an accommodation of a known pattern of symbolism, when he allegorizes the architecture of the 'Minnegrotte'. Boldest of all would then be his accommodation of liturgical formulae and ritual in the 'offices' and the 'hours' of his devout lovers. Where as an agnostic I should in this last case myself incline to the verdict of blasphemy, others, more reverent, may wish to settle for parody.[8] Let us, however, try the term further. It may be possible to represent Gottfried as an 'accommodator' when he so consciously and blatantly juxtaposes Tristan the bed-hopper and Tristan the exemplary martyr of love. (The details are well known, but German critics do not as a rule admit that Gottfried tells the 'juicier' parts of his story with relish and conviction.) It is useful to recall that the Middle Ages were familiar with similar juxtapositions: of unseemly or frankly sinful behaviour, and real sanctity. From the frequency with which the subject is treated by the exegetes, we may surmise that it was a regular instruction to clerics in training to 'account for the two Davids' or the 'two Samsons'. David on the one hand feigning madness and fouling his beard, slaying the bringer of bad tidings, David the adulterer; and the other David, the progenitor of Christ, the royal minstrel and author of the Psalms. Samson the frequenter of brothels, and Samson the type of Christ storming the gates of Hell. Gottfried must have been familiar with the method of reconciling the crude events of Old Testament *historia* and the David and Samson of the Christian faith. He could not openly apply the *method* in dealing with Tristan and Isolde, but he could 'accommodate' the known pattern of contrasting images. Tristan and Isolde on the one hand re-enacting the escapades recorded in the *mære* (as *historia*); Tristan and Isolde (or Gottfried as their exegete) expounding *der âventiure meine* (*interpretatio*). He clinched the matter in the culminating idyll of the 'Minnegrotte' by banishing from it *expressis verbis* all trace of the original *historia* (the hunting for food). Before using 'accommodation', however, we must be convinced of a reasonably reverent intention; we should need evidence from Gottfried's contemporaries to decide.[9]

Hartmann's intention is certainly reverent when, in narrating the infancy of Gregorius, he accommodates a pattern of incident from the life of Christ according to *Pseudo-Matthew* (*Gregorius*, lines 1235–1305): the child is by his very perfection a source of annoyance to neighbours and becomes the innocent cause of tale-bearing and dissension. It is, I admit, an indifferent example. His utilization, on the other hand, of a patristic commonplace to describe the appearance of Gregorius when he is released from his seventeen years' penance on the rock is a devout and reverent exercise, a convincing example.[10] The commonplace in question is 'the two figures of Christ'. Time and again one encounters this 'set piece' of Biblical interpretation: the systematic comparing and contrasting of Christ as he appeared transfigured to the disciples, and the Christ of the Passion story – each supported by Old Testament prophecy, for which the all-important texts are *speciosus forma prae filiis hominum* (Psalm 44. 3, A.V. 45. 2) and *videmus eum...Non est species ei, neque decor* (Isaiah 53.2). Hartmann offers, it will be remembered, first a hyperbolical and realistically detailed description of the handsome nobleman whom the emissaries from Rome did *not* find; then an equally rhetorical and detailed description of the emaciated martyr whom they found (lines 3371–3465). If anyone should doubt that this was indeed Hartmann's intention, I would refer to the concluding lines of the description: Gregorius's skin was 'stretched over his bones like a linen sheet over a thorn bush; one might have counted all his bones through his skin'. The latter half of this is an accommodation of the words *dinumer-*

averunt omnia ossa mea (Psalm 21. 18, A.V. 22. 17), to the importance of which as a source of the Gothic crucifixion I have drawn attention elsewhere;[11] the first part alludes to one or more of a cluster of similes for the body of Christ stretched on the Cross (the ram caught in a thicket from the story of Abraham and Isaac, and the altar-cloth stretched on the altar of sacrifice).

If these affinities, and possibilities of allusive practice are *not* recognized we may find ourselves misjudging our medieval poets, as critics before Rosamund Tuve misjudged George Herbert.[12] We have, in fact, forgotten collectively since the Reformation and the Renaissance much of what was a common store of Christian knowledge. If therefore we need to read the Fathers, as Curtius says, 'as literature', it must be first to recover their stock of lore (notions, images, concatenations of ideas, patterns of argument), and not merely to seek examples in what they wrote, of 'topoi' belonging to other orders of literature.

V

Having stated the case against an uncritical adoption of the term *topos*, and against much of what it was intended to mean in respect of method, we may safely allow that, of course, Curtius differentiates between the mere occurrence of *topoi* and the use successive authors made of them. But that is not enough. They must, I think, be given back to the writers, so that we may see them in their true setting and gauge the purpose they serve. Of the 'pleasance' (*locus amoenus*) Curtius gave a preliminary account in his Chapter 10, Section 6. With it one may profitably compare Rainer Gruenter's article analysing the description of Paradise in the *Wiener Genesis*;[13] he accepts the label *locus amoenus* as a mere 'common denominator', locating the theme amongst possible themes. His characterization of the individual variation on the traditional theme involves fine discriminations which in the end make one doubt the real existence of the so-called *topos* itself. By concentrating on recurrent elements Curtius has probably helped us all to look more closely at our texts. At my last reading of *Der arme Heinrich* I was struck as never before by the intrusive *und sanc vil wol von minnen* in the portrait of the knight (which made Hans Naumann ask whether there was not here a possible allusion to another Henry – the Minnesinger Kaiser Heinrich); and by the fine propriety with which Hartmann adapts the metaphor of the Heavenly Bridegroom (his cellars and vineyards) to the experience and imaginative capacity of the child heroine of his tale. The possible justice of my old Professor, C. E. Gough's observation on the text of *Meier Helmbrecht* has also come home to me for similar reasons: it is indeed noteworthy that in so slight an elaboration of the theme 'all God's creatures' the poet should have singled out wolf and eagle (line 459) to represent all beasts and birds: it will be remembered that it is partly on this evidence that Professor Gough thought that Wernher der Gartenære might have been a Franciscan.[14]

But finally, if *topoi* are as important and pervasive as Curtius would have us believe, and so essentially linked with a classical tradition handed down through the *artes* in the schools, we shall evidently find little to concern us in the *Nibelungenlied* and Wolfram. If it is to be *topoi* or these – *owê, der mich dâ welen hieze!*

12. UNIVERSITY GERMAN AND THE SYLLABUS OF STUDIES[1]

The traditional 'language and literature' syllabus of the past few decades seems to reflect an assumption that linguistic ability and aptitude in literary studies go together; or that the two can be fostered and developed in parallel; or again, that by some higher ordinance the decision to study a language implies the study of the literature accessible through it. There are few who make the first assumption nowadays. (Real aptitude for literary studies normally leads to the study of English.) The second is correct; it worked in my own case and in hundreds of others. The third is wrong, I should have thought, if the first is. The actual situation is often much simpler and not satisfactory. Namely, that anyone who was good at German at school may 'find himself' doing German literature, and perhaps German philology as well, at the university.

Let us consider the latter case first, for here the difficulties prompt some of the re-thinking, both about language teaching methods and about syllabuses, that is now going on. Would such a student not be happier learning other kinds of German to supplement a reasonable command of the German of literature, and making an approach to 'Germany and the Germans' through some other *study*, where the German contribution has been and still is significant, or in which, more simply, 'the German material' needs to be considered, but often isn't? The student might be both happier, and better at deciding whether a text makes sense and is correct, than whether it is beautiful, or typical of this or that phase of literary history. German might then lead into fields where tabulations and graphs are the final stage of discourse and language is more or less discarded. But if this is the sense of our advice, we must have suitable university courses ready.

Here and there programmes of study are already in being for

the student whose interest beyond language lies in the social sciences: that is, courses for combination with 'straight' History, or with Economics, Politics or Sociology, all taken in the appropriate Departments. (Such courses involve a certain amount of retraining for some of the members of our present German staffs.) This does not mean that German is thereby reduced to the status of a tool, or that a second subject is being provided with students different merely in their ability to read 'the German material in the original'. (Much of what has been recognized as the German material is available in English translation.) The German half of such combined courses need not in fact be markedly different from what many students compose for themselves when they make their selection of options in a still conventional course, choosing perhaps 'history and institutions' or 'thinkers' rather than philology, or the poetry of the Baroque or the twentieth-century novel.[2]

Whatever the German syllabus we work to, it will determine the kind of German at which we shall endeavour to become more or less expert. It will condition our understanding and our use of German. There is, however, no reason at all why it should dictate, as it at present tends to, the range of our efficient reading – our proficiency as readers of German. That sounds a reasonable, even a simple remark to make. It will, however, take me some time to make clear what I mean by all this, and I fear that my next paragraph may cause some offence, both to university teachers and students of German, and to teachers and students in other institutions.

Generally under provocation or as a challenge the university attitude is sometimes stated in the extreme form: 'we are not here to teach (you) German'. The wording is crude and drastic, but correct. It sticks in the mind of any student who hears it, whether he has provoked it himself or not. The good student will always have the sense to relate this blunt disclaimer to the obvious efforts which *are* made to teach him German during his university years. How are these things reconciled? The basic fact is that the mere acquisition of a foreign language is not an academic discipline, and can never become one. This is a bitter truth for many a student to accept, for that is often exactly what he thought himself good at, just German. There is a danger that, as the truth dawns, he will become depressed and start to slack. (He has 'come to the wrong place'.) Only a fellow student can jolly him out of this and persuade him (if it is true) that he is capable of and wants more from his studies.

The difference between studying a language for its own sake and an academic study of the same language is not obvious to everyone. (To be doing something for its own sake sounds very academic, and academics use the expression.) It is, however, impossible to study a language with no motive at all, so 'for its own sake' would presumably mean 'for any reasonable purpose'. That is, though laudable, not an academic undertaking. Language learning in a university must be associated with the study of *works* of some kind or other. Works are the product of man's rational and less rational faculties, fashioned in and through language. Command of language gives authors access to us, and gives us access to them and their works. Whether this ever becomes an effective exchange is, to put it in contemporary jargon, a matter of communication. This depends only secondarily on our ability as linguists. Primarily we must be interested in works as works, whether these are poems, dramas, novels, or a philosophy, a record of events, documents. The language involved may happen to be German, not necessarily modern German. This – the German – is initially an obstacle, for the surmounting of which we acquired a basic equipment at school. Our willingness, and indeed our ability to develop that equipment in an appropriate manner at the university is determined by the kind of curiosity – interest – aroused in us by works. Here then is the difficulty, that it is rare for a boy or girl who is good at languages to know what kinds of works he or she will want to *study*. The built-in weakness of the school German curriculum is that it leads almost at once to stories, and so inevitably on towards the study of literature (in the form of set books) – a study for which the pupil may hitherto have shown little aptitude. Let us concede that this may be the saving of him. He finds the way to a profitable study of literature. He may, on the other hand, never become a reader and be 'stuck with German' for the rest of his life. Let us take the more favourable case, namely, that in respect of literature he is a 'late developer'. A very complex process now begins in the university student's learning of German as a language.

There will of course always be a good deal of straightforward learning and testing of German in practical classes – the weekly 'prose comp', the conversation class, and during the term or year abroad. For the rest there is an interplay in seminars (discussion groups, etc.) of language learning, and critical discussion of works as these come up in an ordered programme of studies. The student reads in German – phrases, lines, stanzas, outbursts of longing and passion, reflections on man's destiny, and in a narrower context vituperative attacks of sixteenth-century or eighteenth-century sectarians. It is a matter of complete indifference that the German in which the ideas and ideals of past generations are expressed is archaic, regional – from a twentieth-century point of view 'useless'. In other words the student reads works, rather than examples of German, and also reads works about works. The native speaker of German has an initial advantage over an English student of German in all these activities, but will lose it just as soon as the works are beyond him. He may fail in the *subject* German. And then the student writes, sometimes in German, what he thinks about all these things. The essay in German provides us with a regular reminder of the often mixed success with which students and their supervisors have laboured. All too often the result is platitudes or nonsense in correct German, or sensible ideas and a thoughtful argument in impossible German.

Let us now try to compare the endeavours of the non-academic expert at languages. The expert masters, say, a research report on fuel-injectors or semiconductors, or on the geology of the Teutoburg Forest. His understanding of these reports arises from the full use he makes of the techniques of the translator.

These include asking people who know the subjects (and the objects) involved for guidance and explanations. As a motor engineer, however, he has no knowledge, and electrical theory (or geology) is something he understands as sense, not as science. His topics may change almost daily, or at any rate several times a year. Our topics in a university study of German may be ephemeral only in the hours we set aside specifically for practical work, but even then we do not practise outside a generously measured subject range. To take an extreme example, I should hesitate to take an hour of my students time to translate with them an article dealing (even in homely terms) with the mechanics and hydraulics of a new spin-drier. But in my history-of-the-language lectures I might cite its neologisms, Anglo-American loans and perhaps its sentence structure.

Having made this reservation, I proceed now to a crucial further distinction to be made under the heading 'learning German at the university'. One student, good at German (already on the Honours course) and learning German fast, proves to be after all incapable of reading the works we prescribe with the interest and profit we had expected; he has become a passenger and will get a poor degree. A second, showing great promise in the study of German writers, perhaps particularly the poets, hands in written work which calls for staff consultations: 'can we do anything about his German?' Generally we can if we still have the best part of two years to rectify matters, and if we can persuade or require him to cultivate the approach which he has clearly been neglecting. He needs to have a set of books and magazines to work on for the language only.[3] His German essay in Finals will then probably not fall short of minimum requirements in respect of grammatical correctness; it may be good enough for the examiners to give full credit for his essay as an essay. It may be almost as good as his theoretical papers.

The burden of all this is that in learning German as part of a programme of studies we have to train ourselves to observe and imitate good German – accurately and at will, *and* to read literature as literature (or history as history, economics as economics, if we combine our German with a social science). Now we must continue the argument. We can scarcely stop at a point where we seem on the one hand to have suggested that language learning is high-grade mimicry, whereas on the other hand no imitation, but only independent critical thought is involved in the study of subjects such as literature (history, etc.). How do we proceed?

The best thing is to consider first the situation of those who are nearer than the university student to the extreme ends of the line linking all learners and users of foreign languages. Take first the 'ace' interpreter, who, after due preparation, translates semi-automatically, almost in a trance. His critical faculties are suspended for the duration of his 'simultaneous' translation: it is a somewhat disquieting performance. His faculties are under a tight rein too, when, with only occasional discreet improvements, he translates his source 'immediately'. At the other end of the line is the distinguished scholar (in Classics, History or a science) reading a German article on his own subject. Thumb in dictionary, he is fully extended, just able to follow the sense and most of the grammar, because he knows what his source ought to be (and probably is) saying. Or he may be skimming the latest *Forschungsbericht* to make certain there is nothing in it for him. From the point of view of his subject studies he knows where he is and what he is doing. If he is enjoying his reading, that will be related to the very modesty of his claims as a linguist.

The university student of German is expected to be able to operate at different points along this same line, according to the time-table of his classes – and examinations. So are his teachers. The extremes of the line we have in mind do not come into play in an academic study of German. The special ability of the 'ace' translator would (with respect) result mainly in 'gush' and platitudes. The limited linguistic ability of the scholar we were just now considering is, of course, simply not adequate. (It could be made adequate if the scholar would drop his Classics or his science for a number of years. But why should he? He is not interested.)

Concentration on distinctions has led us into some exaggerations, both in stressing the element of mere mimicry in the performance of the linguist and in suggesting that there is no imitation in subject study. There is an important element of imitation even in apparently detached and critical study. Let us keep to literature. Imitation may range from learning by heart – a poem, a speech, or a notable or a preposterous formulation – for use on an appropriate occasion (the quotation), *via* grateful noting of the opinions of writers who should know. It extends all the way to by no means entirely reprehensible exercises in *pastiche*, parody or 'take-off' of authors and critics. All these forms of imitation can be worked by the individual student into a steadily evolving pattern of recall, sensitive response and informed comment, and so contribute to the schooling of his taste and the establishment of criteria and standards. Meantime a solid hard-factual foundation of subject knowledge is being laid. This knowledge may remain cool and detached. It may, however, be used polemically or to gain adherents for a 'school'. Younger colleagues will not necessarily endorse this account of the approach to literature. This is, however, scarcely the place to argue for and against a simpler untutored study of literature with appeals to the student's experience. A matter for concern is rather the narrowness of the frontier separating the one kind of imitation (in learning a foreign language) from the other (forming opinions), and the danger of slipping or drifting from the one into the other, for the imitation of correct usage may encourage thinking and writing in ready-made formulae. Many an elegant piece of writing may, under *critical* scrutiny, be revealed as useful only on its own terms. They may be terms which the student is delighted to learn but not qualified to use. They express generalizations which he is not equipped to make. He would use other terms if only he could think of the German for them. The temptation to think and talk about German literature in German terms is, however, in undergraduate days almost irresistible, and it is better to indulge it for a time in the interests of a general fluency: with the intention of snapping out of it as soon as possible, for there is nothing more frustrating for a supervisor to read than half-digested or half-translated second-hand criticism – an inept and often inaccurate display of mimicry. There are nowadays plenty of patterns to help the student to formulate his views on German literature in English. They do not and cannot exact the same degree of intellectual subservience as the common currency of German handbooks. This is *not* an attack on German criticism and literary history as such. On the contrary, it is an exhortation to understand it properly, not merely to echo it.[4] This is possible only by dint of a more aggressive approach to it.

An aggressive approach to German must, however, also be made on a broader front if it is to be well-founded. The study of literature and literary criticism is not enough. At the same time as we endeavour to become expert at the German of literary studies, we must try to become efficient readers in other areas; that is, to read intelligently and critically, reflecting on what we read and looking things up, not only in dictionaries. A greater alertness is required when we are reading in areas where we have more or less everything to learn. More on this point, below.

Many colleagues and some whole Departments in our universities are now preoccupied with substitutes for prose composition as the main instrument of teaching modern German. But what kind of language work should this be? My own formula is 'text stripping' with translation into English. The final aim of all serious language study is after all translation – with *maximum* 'interference' from English. With those of my colleagues who want to cut back prose composition I agree that most of our language work should be focused on genuine German texts, not on pieces of English in our weekly German rendering.[5] I imagine, but I may be wrong in this, that my own approach differs from that of other 'substituters' in insisting that most exercises should be based on texts which present an intellectual challenge of some kind, so that students have some check on their reading of the German. If they cannot get a passage out, they must be able to infer that they have either misunderstood the German or not thought hard enough. They must sense that they cannot get by with their German only. They must learn to be judged by their capacity to think, to follow arguments, to fill gaps in their knowledge. At the end of each bout they should have a credit balance of words and of facts, information, insights. By text stripping I also mean giving a passage of German 'the full treatment'. There should be nothing in a passage so treated which has not been translated. (That there is no need to translate if one understands is the final absurdity of modern-language theory.) University students should be equipped to understand (or learn) through German whatever it is they would be expected to follow and learn in and through English. This can only benefit their reading of the more narrowly specialized German of literary studies, or any other study combined with German.

Finally, I come to one or two supplementary questions so often asked that they cannot forever be evaded. Why is the German one reads – German as it is written – in newspapers, magazines, articles, text-books, hand-books, so difficult; and (again) has it any right to be? What efforts can legitimately be expected of the foreign reader of German to follow at all? I do not want to provide us – university teachers and students – with any excuse for premature capitulation, for we should be the last of all to capitulate. Many highly qualified practitioners do in fact think that German as written is often unreasonably obscure and unnecessarily involved. Many responsible German writers agree with this view, but have grown tired of remonstrating. To explain why all this is so, would involve a history of German culture, with appropriate emphasis on the ideal of 'Bildung' and on the veneration for so long offered to scholars and scholarship ('Wissenschaft'). There is also the more familiar German respect for authority. These factors, together with Germany's undoubted successes in all branches of science and scholarship in the nineteenth and early twentieth centuries, have made it seem no virtue in German eyes to write briefly or simply, or to seek to convince by argument and evidence alone. A serious statement in German will therefore generally claim or suggest authority – entitlement to be heard. Unfortunately for us at the receiving end, one of the ways in which authority can at any time be shown is by sheer virtuosity in the handling of certain rhetorical conventions. These go back some three or four centuries. We recognize them today as the peculiarities of German sentence structure, word-order and word-formation. No matter what is said about the aesthetic merits of these conventions, they tend to diminish the efficiency of the German sentence as a means of communication. There is no doubt a great deal of elegantly structured prose in contemporary German literature, *belles lettres*, and even in the work of some scholars, but all too often this gives way to merely long and complex sentences, in which the reservations of the contro-versialist or the cautious scholar hang like a heavy wash on a flimsy line. Nothing can be done about it. German readers expect writers to show mastery of these rhetorical principles. They also appreciate it, if whatever contribution is being made to their *Bildung* is pitched at the highest level of diction and abstraction which they with their training can conveniently follow. I have laid it on fairly thick. I could now, and in fairness should, characterize the linguistic foundations of English one-upmanship, and the various tyrannies to which our pundits subject us, but there would be an important residue of differ-ence. We are in any case quicker to say we don't understand. We make (sometimes excessive) use of the deflating 'damn-fool question'. German readers and audiences are both too com-plaisant and too vulnerable. But then, curiously, they are far more vehement than we are, when conversation turns that way. To hear them talk about various kinds of preposterous German (*Professorendeutsch*, *Literatendeutsch*, *Beamtendeutsch*), one would imagine a serious revolt was brewing. It isn't. Nothing will be done in our time.

The thing that concerns us here is a practical one. German contributions to any of the current debates will generally be longer and more involved and abstruse, and therefore more difficult to follow, than anything we are accustomed to from the English or the French side. Before abandoning the attempt to follow the German statement we should, for that very reason, examine our conscience as university-trained specialists. Are we certain that we are not really interested in what this or that German writer has to say on a common problem, or on a problem which exercises him particularly? Or does it merely suit us not to make the extra effort which German writers are accustomed to expect? *Ich stelle es anheim*!

NOTES

The short title of each essay is followed immediately by a *prefatory Note*. This may refer the reader to essays not included in the selection. Serially numbered notes represent, with some revisions, the annotation of the essays in their original form. *New* notes are enclosed in square brackets. In addition, square brackets enclose rewordings of text requiring, I think, no further comment; they may signal my final abridgements [...].

I TEXTUAL STUDIES: ICONOGRAPHICAL APPROACHES

1. The Gothic Image of Christ. A translation of 'Das gotische Christusbild' etc., *Euphorion* 47 (1953), 16–37. The article was dedicated to the memory of Friedrich Ranke, my teacher in Breslau, 1930–2. A prefatory note recalled papers read in England and a German lecture; it also referred to a 'book in progress' which in fact ultimately became Chapter IV on the Crucifixion in *L. & A*. The article has been widely quoted in bibliographies, but is evidently too innovative to have influenced the presentation of Crucifixion iconography in recent art-historical handbooks. Its principal shortcoming is that it fails to point out the liturgical status of Old Testament prophetic texts, particularly Psalms 21 (A.V. 22) and 56 (A.V. 57): they are Good Friday and Easter Psalms respectively. I now make late acknowledgment of the guidance I received on this point from the first notice, by Eric Colledge in *The Life of the Spirit* 8 (October 1953), 'Extracts', pp. 190–2.

Excluded from this selection is a long supplementary essay of 1955: 'Christlicher Erzählstoff bei Otfrid und im *Heliand*', see *Publications* p. 227. It is of interest to readers of Old High German and Old Saxon, and is to be found in their principal journal, where I hope they will continue to read it. On the other hand its main findings, duly distributed, are incorporated (with some relevant Plates) in *L. & A*.

1 *Christi Leiden in einer Vision geschaut.* Translations and quotations from this work follow the edition of Robert Priebsch, Heidelberg 1936; references to my own edition (see *Publications*, p. 226) are added: here Priebsch p. 32f. [Pickering p. 65f.]. [See now also J. Marrow, *Christi Leiden* (etc.) in the Netherlands', *Ons geestelijk erf* 53 (1969), 337–80: this account includes an edition based on two M. Dutch versions.]

2 *Ein deutsches geistliches Liederbuch aus dem XV. Jhdt. nach einer Hs. des Stiftes Hohenfurt*, ed. W. Bäumker, Leipzig, 1895.

3 Thus in *Christi Leiden*, Priebsch, p. 38. lines 17–24 [Pickering p. 71, lines 19–25]; also in *Der Saelden Hort*, ed. H. Adrian, *DTM* xxvi, 1927, lines 9415–20 with editor's note.

4 Ed. J. Meadows Cowper, *EETS* 60, 1875, lines 610–14 and 629–33; also 662f.

5 *The Northern Passion (Supplement)*, ed. W. Heuser and F. A. Foster, *EETS* 183, 1930, lines 1524f.

6 *Historia Scholastica*, Migne, *PL* 198, col. 1628, = Jerome, *Comment. in Matth.*, *ibid.* vol. 26, col. 208.

7 *Etym.*, ed. W. M. Lindsay, 2 vols., Oxford 1911, Bk. V, xxvii, 34.

8 Compare essay no. 3 ('Exegesis and Imagination'), pp. 31-45.

9 *Hist. Schol. PL* 198, col. 1628; also *Glossa Ordinaria*, *PL* 114 col. 345. The source is presumably Jerome, *Ad Eustochium*, *PL* 22, col. 884.

10 [On Holy Places and Stations of the Cross, see *L. & A.*, pp. 228-30.]

11 A basic assumption in all standard works on Christian art, e.g. in Emile Mâle's *L'art religieux* (etc.), 4 vols. 5th ed. Paris, 1947.

12 In print, for instance, in R. Froning, *Drama des Mittelalters (DNL)* vol. 1, p. 276. [A statement of the problem of the ropes may almost be relied upon to induce this solution.]

13 The so-called 'Greek Recension B' of the *Gospel of Nicodemus (Acts of Pilate)* contains a notable elaboration of the Crossbearing and a Lament of Mary. Art historians have in the past been misled by this text. It is now believed to be late-medieval, and scarcely to be dated before 1250, see M. R. James, *The Apocryphal New Testament*, Oxford, 1924, p. 94f. and particularly 115f. Text in Tischendorf, *Evangelia Apocrypha*, 2nd ed. 1876 [repr. Hildesheim 1966], pp. 287-322, Engl. trans. in *Ante-Nicene Christian Library*, vol. 16 (1870), pp. 149-68.

14 [Isaac generally carries a 'bundle' of wood. The Widow of Zarephath (III *Reg.* = I Kings 17.12) carried, according to Jerome's rendering, 'duo ligna', and these she may be represented as holding in the shape of a cross, see *L. & A.* p. 258.]

15 [On *sicut-ita* and *ita-ut* comparisons ('description'), see *L. & A.*, p. 166.]

16 For instance Hans Multscher's 'Bearing of the Cross', reproduced in Alfred Rohde, *Passionsbild und Passionsbühne*, Furche-Kunstverlag, Berlin, 1926, pl. 22.

17 Theoretically more recent than the pulling with ropes is the motif of the 'holes bored too far apart' which I represented (above, in considering the *Northern Passion*) as being typical of the Crucifixion *jacente cruce*. [As will become evident from the discussion, below, of the *harp* as a symbol of the Crucifixion, I consider the holes in the Cross to be an inference from the harp image, see my fuller account in *L. & A.*, pp. 285-301.] The text of the Anselm-Dialogue printed in Migne (see above, p. 6) *lacks* the motif, but is based on two manuscripts only: some medieval editors may have found it distasteful. In a Rhenish translation of the Dialogue it is included: 'zo dem loch enkunden si niet gereichen, dar die nale inne soulden stechen': *Anselmus Boich*, ed. O. Schade, *Niederrhein. Gedichte des XIV. u. XV. Jhdts.*, Hanover, 1854, lines 835f.

18 See 'Brixener Passion...die jüngeren Teile', pp. 351-431 in: *Altdeutsche Passionsspiele aus Tyrol*, ed. J. E. Wackernell, Graz 1897, p. 409. Here also the holes had been bored too far apart, p. 406, line 2508. The motif is present *in nuce* in *Sterzinger Spiel*, *ibid.* p. 135, lines 2138-43 [in the context of 2102-57, *all* on the nailing].

19 Quoted from F. J. Mone, *Schauspiele des Mittelalters*, 2 vols., 1846, II, 357. The gesture of the *orans* is commonly referred to its immediate source (Christ on the Cross), e.g. Augustine on Psalm 72/73.5: '*in nomine tuo levabo manus meas*' – 'levavit pro nobis Dominus noster manus in cruce et extensae sunt manus ejus in cruce', Migne, *PL* 36, col. 755. Berthold carries the comparison further!

20 Jerome in *Praefatio* to, and *Commentarii* on, *Isaiah* (*PL* 28, col. 771 and 24, col. 18); Augustine in *Civ. Dei* XVIII, xxix. Similarly Isidore, *Etym.* Bk. VI, ii, 22.

21 This essay is not concerned primarily with the Flagellation [or with the use made of *Isaiah* in the Liturgy of Holy Week].

22 *Apologia ad Guillelmum*, *PL* 182, col. 902. Almost contemporary are the Early Middle High German lines: 'Adam der andir...er drat dî torculin altirseini' (*Summa Theologiae* in Waag, *Kleinere dt. Gedichte d. XI. u. XII. Jhdts.*, Altdt. Textbibl. 10, 1916, where, however, the subject of the sentence is also metaphorical.

23 *Unum ex quattuor*, *PL* 186, col. 537 (cf. 'venit hora' etc., John 16.32).

24 See for example Emile Mâle, *L'art religieux de la fin du moyen âge en France*, 5th ed. 1947, p. 119f. [Gertrud Schiller, *Iconography* etc., Engl. ed. II, p. 228f.]

25 *Lignum Vitae* in *Bonaventurae Opera Omnia* (Peltier, Paris 1868), vol. 12, col. 78b.

26 *In feria iv. hebdomadae sanctae sermo*, *PL* 183, col. 263f.

27 Cf. Note 31, below.

28 I have rarely made use of the indexes to the *Patrologia Latina*, but I acknowledge with gratitude the lead given to me at an early stage by the reference to Cassiodorus on the subject of *cithara*, see below.

29 Cassiodorus's commentary, *PL* 70, col. 117, Bruno's, *ibid.* 142, col. 44f. Jerome is believed to be the source of the tradition.

30 Notker the German incorporated Augustine's gloss in his translation (*c.* 1000) of the psalter. 'Fone démo óberen teîle scéllent seîten in psalterio, dannan châmen CHRISTI miracula. Aber in cythera scéllent siê fóne démo níderen teîle, dannan uuâren passiones CHRISTI. Psalterium scélle, sô irstânt mortui' [etc.]...Cythera scélle, daz Christus húnger unde durst lîde' [etc.] Quoted from P. Piper, *Die Schriften Notkers u. seiner Schule*, vol. 2, Freiburg–Tübingen, 1883, p. 216f. [cf. Sehrt-Starck, Altdt. Textbibl. 40–42 (1952–5): 42,369f.]

31 A. Hahn, *Bibliothek der Symbole*, 3rd. ed. 1897, p. 209f.: '...duabus duntaxat naturis, id est dietatis et carnis...nec imaginarium corpus aut phantasmatis alicujus in eo fuisse, sed solidum atque verum; hunc (credimus) et esuriisse et sitisse et doluisse et flevisse et omnes corporis injurias pertulisse, postremo a Judaeis crucifixum et sepultum...(First Council of Toledo, *c.* 400). Hahn quotes from vernacular credos in Germanic dialects from p. 86, among them some familiar from the syllabus of German studies.

32 *PL* 70, col. 404.

33 *Die Erlösung*, ed. Fr. Maurer, Dt. Lit. in Entw.-Reihen, Geistl. Dichtg. 6, 1934, lines 5618-49.

34 *Das alte Passional*, ed. K. A. Hahn, 1857, pp. 74, lines 38f. and 78, lines 82f. The passages are too long for full quotation here.

35 *Das Zerbster Prozessionsspiel*, ed. W. Reupke, Berlin, 1930, p. 27, lines 57-60.

36 *Liber de Benedictione Jacob*, PL 174, col. 1150.

37 [In *L. & A.*, pp. 301-7 there is a much fuller discussion of bow *and* *crossbow* as symbols of the Crucifixion, in the course of which I admitted (1970) that Gotfrid of Admont's interpretation was 'the one resolute attempt' of its kind that I had been able to find. I try to account for the 'failure' of the old archer's bow, and the success of the crossbow.]

38 *Von Gottes Zukunft*, ed. S. Singer, DTM VII, 1906, lines 2722ff. and 2791-4. [Christ's veins (*geeder*) are compared with the bow's sinew, possibly to avoid use of the identical word (*senewe*) in both cases.]

39 [On the *draco* in medieval representations of Moses, see *L. & A.* pp. 260-2 and illustr. 22 b, c, d.] The Isidore references are to *Etym.* Bk. XII, iv, 4 and Bk XVIII, iii.

40 *Ed. cit.* (note 34), p. 72, lines 7-9 and p. 78, lines 8-13.

41 The text of the *Lament*s from A. Schönbach, *Über die Marienklagen*, Graz, 1874. Schönbach also quotes (from Mone, *Lat. Hymnen* II, 137) the lines from the late Latin hymn (*Recordare*), here re-quoted.

42 Ed. W. Krogmann (Altdeutsche Quellen 3) Leipzig, 1937, lines 423f. The argument is not weakened by the inter-dependence of the texts adduced (*Passional, Laments, Osterspiel*). [Students of Middle High German will rightly surmise a word play 'überwinden'/'sich winden' when Christ fights with Death, cf. 'agony'.]

43 A. Hartmann (ed.), *Das Oberammergauer Passionsspiel in seiner ältesten Gestalt, 1. Das Augsburger Passionsspiel*, etc., Leipzig, 1880, lines 1516f.

44 This reference (Frauenlob, ed. L. Ettmüller, 1843, p. 20) I owe to the late Dr Helmuth Thomas of Hamburg. Frauenlob was [as I wrote in 1953] 'one of the countless authors whom I have not examined'.

45 [The missing canonical episodes are subsequently added in Netherlandish versions of *Christi Leiden*.]

46 The 'insight' to which reference was made on p. 4 was to come after long brooding over the word 'bret', and the manuscript variants of the word *fleine* in Priebsch's edition p. 46, line 23. [The full story will be found in *L. & A.*, p. 299, footnote.]

47 The *statera* here 'desymbolized' occurs in Job 6.2 'utinam appenderentur peccata mea...in statera' [see 'Exegesis' etc., p. 39 and notes for Rupert of Deutz on this symbol and its applicability to the Cross]. The text of Psalm 68/69.2 ('infixus sum in limo profundi') is 'historically' fulfilled in the narrative of *Christ Leiden*. The 'seal' may be taken from Cant. 8.6, 'pone me ut signaculum'.

48 [Twenty-five years have passed since this final sentence was written. I allow it to stand, but I have cancelled the two concluding footnotes

foreshadowing what further enquiries I might myself make along the same lines; see instead the Preface to this volume.]

2. *Exegesis and Imagination* (etc.) This is a translation and partial revision of the final section of the article 'Irrwege der mittelalterlichen Geschichtsschreibung: Rupert von Deutz, Joachim von Fiore', *ZfdA* 100 (1971), 270-96. In its present form it links the first and the fourth of the essays in this volume, and usefully fills a gap in the story of Gospel elaboration in the Middle Ages (briefly sketched in the first essay, more fully told in *L. & A.*, Chapter IV). As for the opening fifteen pages (approx. 270-85) of the original German article ('Irrwege' etc.), I do not myself regard them as cancelled or superseded. In other words I still regret the excessive attention paid in our studies to the 'spiritual interpretation' of Scripture in the Middle Ages.

1 In *L. & A.* p. 247, Note 1, I refer to Rupert of Deutz, but only to promise to treat him at a later date.

2 Fuller details of Peter Comestor's suppression of the words 'necesse est impleri...omnia de me' (Luke 24.44b), see *ZfdA* 100 (1971), p. 276f. By the end of the thirteenth century the *Historia Scholastica* had disappeared from the syllabus of studies, see Beryl Smalley, *op. cit.*, pp. 214f., 329. A late example of its pervasive influence is to be found in the *Holkham Bible Picture Book* (see Introduction and Notes to *ed. cit.*, p. 226).

3 *De Trinitate et operibus ejus*, Migne *PL* 167, cols. 197-1827.

4 *Geschichtsschreibung im Mittelalter. Gattungen, Epochen, Eigenart*, Kleine Vandenhoeck-Reihe 209-10, Göttingen, 1965, p. 74.

5 What follows may, in the light of 'spectaculum', fairly be called a 'scenario' for the battle of good and evil (*sapientia, stultitia*). Compare Rupert's use of 'spectaculum' in 'sanctae passionis spectaculum', *PL* 170, col. 509.

6 Despite all efforts I have not found the passage referred to. The meaning may be that there is no section of *De Trinitate* devoted to the Book of Job.

7 'Gaudemus ergo nunc eo ipso quod longe superius quodam loco condolebamus, scilicet quod cum futurae veritatis, id est Christi Filii Dei, venerandas imagines sive figuras in patriarchis, regibus et prophetis per ordinem contemplaremur, beatum Job exemplar patientiae praeterivimus, quem Patrum venerabilium auctoritas non tacuit in typum praecessisse ejusdem Domini Christi et Ecclesiae ejus. Hoc, inquam, nunc gaudemus; hic enim non parum habet locum commemoratio ejus', col. 1607.

8 To the contemporary devout this will probably have meant that the sufferings of Christ were more clearly depicted in the story of Job than in the accounts of the evangelists.

9 I indicate the scope of these developments in my first essay here, but more fully in *L. & A.* pp. 274-307. With particular reference to the Netherlands, see James Marrow, *op. cit.* (Preface, p. viii).

10 Rupert writes more than once about the *statera*, e.g. also *PL* 169, col. 188f., see Francis Wormald, 'The Crucifix and the Balance', *Journal of the Warburg Institute* 1 (1937-8), 276ff.

11 The narrative motif of the falling cross seems to occur only in *Christi Leiden in einer Vision geschaut*, [see above, pp. 29, 205] and in texts exploiting it. [My previous note 'auch sonst belegt', *ZfdA* 100, p. 292, Note 24, should be modified in this sense].

12 [For this revision of my original text I have examined Rupert's words more closely: '...ibi erat crux, statera Patris, habens disposita hinc in lance judicii peccata mundi, inde in lance misericordiae calamitatem generis humani. *Vicit pondere* calamitas in lance misericordiae, lancemque sustollens judicii, peccata decussit in profundum maris', col. 1612 (my italics).]

13 In Rupert's *De divinis officiis* (PL 170, cols. 9–332) one repeatedly encounters the expressions 'typum gerit', 'typum gessit', used of pre-figuring prophets and patriarchs, and of officiating clergy in the ceremony of the Mass. On the 'commemorative' interpretation of the Mass, see Adolf Franz, *Die Messe im deutschen Mittelalter*, Freiburg i. Br., 1902 (reprinted Darmstadt, 1963), pp. 416f.

14 *Studien über Joachim von Fiore*, Leipzig and Berlin, 1927, reprinted with Foreword, Darmstadt, 1966, p. 91. (Grundmann states that 'with minor corrections' Rupert's doctrine of the 'three ages' in *De Trinitate et operibus ejus* would closely approach Joachim's 'three phases' of world history.)

15 'Ralph of Flaix on Leviticus', *Recherches de théologie ancienne et médiévale* 35 (1968), 35–82. Radulphus Flaicensis (*c.* 1150) was the author of a much-used Leviticus commentary. 'The beauty of the spiritual interpreta-tion in the Middle Ages has been praised to the skies; its confusions have been underrated...Ralph shows...that the search for mysteries had an ugly side, when it was used for polemic against the Jews: it led him to waste of effort, complacency and insult', *ibid.*, p. 66.

Rupert of Deutz's hatred of the Jews leads him elsewhere to make state-ments which are perhaps not worse than comical, for instance when he states that he and his fellow-Christians are persecuted daily by the Jews ('Beati qui persecutionem patiuntur', PL 167, col. 1553); or when he finds Herod's neglect of 'Christian' prophecies inexcusable (*ibid.*, col. 1541). Perhaps it is merely medieval when he recommends a 'pia tortura' of the Jews (Psalm 58/59 does not allow them to be killed), so that they may repent their inherited guilt and make haste to have themselves baptized ('compellerentur ad fidem festinare', *ibid.*, col. 532).

16 PL 168, cols. 9–836, quotations from cols. 106–11.

17 *ibid.*, cols. 1307–1634, especially 1574f.

18 Beryl Smalley, *op. cit.* p. 288.

19 Despite the incompleteness of my enquiry, I believe that I have identified Rupert's main treatment of 'the drunkenness of the Jews'. Elsewhere (e.g. *De Trinitate*, PL 167, cols. 1276, 1295, 1297) the same charge is advanced without particular proof.

3. Trinitas Creator: word and image. Reprinted from *Reading Medieval Studies* 2 (1976), 77–90. There are some slight changes in the main text, an extended final Note, and an Addendum. Hugo Buchthal has meantime expressed approval of the revised interpretation of picture M9 (pp. 56f.). Otto Pächt thinks that whereas my reading of the Millstatt pictures is probably correct, there may have been a two-figure group, in the opening scene only, of an antecedent pictorial Genesis cycle. The meaning of such a representation would be less easily determined.

1 'Zu den Bildern der altdeutschen Genesis: Die Ikonographie der *trinitas creator*' (I and II), *ZfdPh*, 75 (1956), 23–34 and 83 (1964), 99–114. In revising these articles I have omitted my comparison of art-historical and 'philological' approaches to the question of 'meaning' – of images and words. Art historians stress the origins and the derivation of images, whereas textual criticism and philology recognize (after etymological preliminaries) 'usual' and 'occasional' (i.e. contextual) meanings, and are prepared to encounter 'neologisms' or even the *hapax legomenon* ('sole occurrence'). I have in the meantime written at length on such lines in *L. & A.*, Part II, Ch. I, 'Word, Image, Tradition,' etc.
2 The treatment of 'Physiologus' immediately after 'Genesis' is known from elsewhere to the art historians.
3 The editions are (a) *Die altdeutsche Genesis nach der Wiener Handschrift* (Altd. Textbibl. 31), ed. V. Dollmayr, Halle, 1932; (b) *Genesis und Exodus nach der Milstäter [sic] Handschrift*, ed. Jos. Diemer, 1862, reprint Sändig (Niederwalluf bei Wiesbaden), 1971.
4 Manuscript M has 32 drawings for the *Physiologus*.
5 There is, of course, no record of the correspondence of the 'litigants', or of certain retractions made verbally. I record a personal loss in the tragically early death of Dr Hella (Frühmorgen-) Voss of Munich.
6 At Buchthal's wish, *in extenso*, letter of 25 February 1964 from the Warburg Institute: 'I have postponed writing this letter until I could find the time to read your article with due care. This I have now done, and, for what it is worth, I am entirely convinced – though I admit it took some time until I came round to your point of view. This is really the only possible interpretation; and, as you say, we shall have to change our minds in some other instances as well if we accept it. Every art historian should be sincerely grateful to you – for solving this special problem as well as for raising these important matters of principle – which German art history, in particular, will probably take a long time to digest.'
   The late Otto Kurz wrote in May of the same year of 'an object-lesson in the methodical interpretation of illustrations'. Günter Bandmann and Dr Heidi Heimann endorsed specifically my reading, of M1 (W7) and M4 – and of W6 (as a Trinity, with Pächt, against Voss). I am naturally also grateful to a number of students of medieval German for their expressions of approval.
7 On the theme *trinitas creator* I received my first and some subsequent, more personal guidance from Dr Heidi Heimann of the Warburg Institute, cf. Adelheid Heimann, 'Trinitas creator mundi'. *Journal of the Warburg Institute*, 2 i, 1938–9, pp. 42–52, generously illustrated.

8 This is, of course, not to be confused with the *Wiener Genesis* of German literary studies, see note 3(a). For convenience see *The Vienna Genesis with an introduction and notes*, by Emmy Wellesz (Faber Library of Illuminated Manuscripts, ed. W. Oakeshott), London, 1960. This also 'introduces' the other cycles.

9 Pächt wrote (17 December, 1954): 'The only questionable point to my mind is whether the immediate model was a Middle-Byzantine Octateuch or a Western copy of an Eastern Genesis-cycle.'

10 See Réau, *Iconographie de l'art chrétien* (6 vols., Paris, 1955–9), vol. II, pp. 14ff., 21ff., etc. and Heimann *op. cit.*, illus. 6a and b (a winged and Janus-headed deity as *trinitas creator*, mid-fourteenth century).

11 There are, I think, other examples awaiting identification by the art historians. I leave that to them and concentrate on texts. In *L. & A.* p. 312ff., I drew attention to a Latin poem of some 900 hexameters, well known to art historians. It describes a picture-cycle in the Cathedral of Mainz; it was written by Ekkehard of St Gall for Bishop Aribo (before 1031); *Uersus ad picturas Domus domini Mogontine*. I interpreted *inter alia* the four lines devoted to the creation of Adam by the Trinity. I repeat those lines in note 18 where I seek support in interpreting the word 'al' in the *Altdeutsche Genesis*. Here I would find that they refer to a picture in which the Trinity was conceivably represented by two figures only. The picture-cycle was in all probability not executed, see *L. & A., loc. cit.*

12 The first of my 'passing references' to other interpretations of the Genesis cycle of manuscript M. The same applies to Voss 1962: for full titles, see the articles specified in note 1.

13 For all quotations in their original Early Middle High German form, see either the editions (note 3) or my articles (note 1).

14 Reproduced in Heimann, *loc. cit.*, illus. 4 and *L. & A.* pl. 16b. The rubrics are: (title) *Sancta Trinitas*; (above, left) *post angli casum fit de homine consilium*; (right) *trinus et unus dominus, trinus in personis, unus in substantia. Hoc una facies trium personarum demonstrat*; (scroll) *Faciamus hominem ad imaginem et similitudinem nostram et praesit cunctis animantibus terre.*

15 On the 'Throne of Grace' (God the Father holds before him the crucified Son; a dove as Holy Spirit above the head of the Son), see *L. & A.*, pp. 85 with note 1, 86, and pl. 17a.

16 Cf. Migne, *PL* 84, *De fide catholica*, cols. 449–538, the quotations cols. 455 and 453.

17 For the *text* of the *Altdeutsche Genesis* we customarily assume a common source *WM, see p. 46. From the pictures in M and the corresponding spaces in the W-text of *Genesis* and *Physiologus* it is clear that *WM was the source of the two pictorial cycles of M. Was it also the source of the *prefatory* pictures in W? – see my final remarks on 'fresh scrutiny', and the Addendum.

18 As in the verses 'ad picturas' for Bishop Aribo of Mainz, see note 11:
   Uiuit homo primus anima de complice limus
   Quem *pater et natus* creat et *ui compare flatus.*

Personis trinus, deitate perenniter unus,
Arbitri simile sibi plasmat et ratione.

In the second line grammar follows doctrine, singular verb 'creat' for 'pater et natus' and 'flatus', the latter being involved 'vi compare' ('compar' with the power of each? – or that of 'puer et natus'?).

At this point, and with reference to 'Son as Wisdom of the Father', the following snippet from Rupert of Deutz's voluminous *De Trinitate et operibus ejus* (*Commentariorum in Genesim Liber I, Caput III*) may be quoted: '[In principio creavit Deus, etc.]...Omnia in sapientia fecisti (=Ps. 103/104.24) quae videlicet sapientia non est alia quam Verbum Dei...itaque in principio, id est in Filio, in Verbo suo, in sapientia sua creavit Deus caelum et terram...'. [On man's 'likeness'] 'faciamus hominem, qui trinae operationis nostrae in semetipso habeat evidentiam'. Cf. *PL* 167, cols. 202 and 249. (Rupert died *c.* 1129).

19 Quoted from G. M. Dreves–Cl. Blume, *Ein Jahrtausend lateinischer Hymnendichtung*, vol. 1 (1909), p. 68 = *Analecta Hymnica* 50, p. 155:

Gloria, laudum pia plenitudo
Sit patri, proli, tibi, spiritusque
Sancte, qui trino vehis alma sceptra
Nomine solus.

The sceptre ('alma sceptra', poetic pl.), betokening the threefold (or triune) 'benign' rule of the Trinity, is clearly assigned to the Holy Spirit.

20 Otherwise the text! It proceeds methodically and at a smart pace, recounting first the creation of the angels, the defection of Lucifer (*lichtuaz*), his casting down into Hell, and then God's deliberation and statement of his 'other intention' (namely to create man in his own image); then the works of creation, day by day, in turn – 87 long lines, all *before* the rubric to picture M1. [That is to say there are no pictures to compare, for example, with the historiated Genesis *initials* in illustrated Bibles (where the Trinity often *presides over* the works of creation carried out by God).]

21 ...'in his (man's) likeness', German text and Genesis 2.18 (...*simile sibi*), cf. Genesis 2.20.

22 Cf. *PL* 198, 1074–5 (D–A).

[The evidence that poet and artist 'parted company' is clearer than I had hitherto realized. Picture M9 is on folio 12 recto. It is not until folio 15 verso that the poet offers his paraphrase of *Ecce Adam...quasi unus ex nobis* (Diemer 19, 20), i.e. long after his own 'homily', and in fact at a point midway between pictures M10 and M11.]

4. Justus Lipsius' DE CRUCE LIBRI TRES (etc.). Reprinted (with several editorial revisions) from *Festgabe für L. L. Hammerich*, Copenhagen 1962, pp. 199–214. Despite the sub-title and some of the content, the approach to the work discussed in this essay is mainly iconographical. (In *L. & A.*, pp. 248–53, the same subject is treated at an appropriate narrative pace with only passing reference to the text of *De Cruce*.) I felt an obligation to make my detailed analysis more easily available, for I know of no convenient modern edition or translation of what was once a widely-read work. [From my prefatory Note of 1962 I repeat the following bibliographical information:] I have looked at *De Cruce* in the following editions: Antwerp 1593 (British Library); *secunda editio correctior*, Antwerp 1595 (Warburg Institute); *ed. ultima, serio castigata*, Antwerp 1606 (kindly loaned to me by Prof. L. W. Forster), and in *Opera Omnia*, Wesel, 1675 (4 vols., 8°). The latter not always very convenient edition (inadequate pagination in vol. 1) is quoted for other works; it is probably the edition most widely held. My necessarily brief and limited encounter with Lipsius revealed little detailed preoccupation with *De Cruce* after the controversy about his orthodoxy had died down. I took what late guidance I could from L. van der Essen and H. F. Bouchery, *Waarom Justus Lipsius gevierd* (Meded. v. d. koninkl. Vlaamse Acad...van België, Kl. Letteren, XI, 8, Brussels, 1949); particularly from the copious critical bibliography. M. Ch. Nisard, *Le triumvirat littéraire au xvie siècle*, Paris n.d. [1852] (Lipsius pp. 1-148), was useful for general orientation, and as much anti-Jesuit bias as could amuse an agnostic. V. A. Nordman, *J.L. als Geschichtsforscher und Geschichtslehrer* (Ann. Acad. S. Fenn., Ser. B, xxviii, 2, Helsinki, 1932) discusses *De Cruce* on pp. 38-9 without, I should think, any conviction of its importance for the theme; p. 52f. offers a detailed analysis of the letter to N. de Hacqueville, but I had already made my own.

1 This is repeatedly implied by items in the *Fama Postuma*; more specifically in *J. Lipsi Principiatus Litterarius* by Gaugerius Rivius (*Op. Omn.*, vol. 1, separate pagination, p. 65).

2 The sources for L.'s career are his letter to Woverius (Epist. Cent. III, Misc., No. 87) and various Forewords to his works. These are used in the *Vita* contributed by Aubertus Miræus to the *Fama Postuma* of 1613 (*Op Omn.*, vol. 1). The articles in *ADB* and *Nouvelle Biogr. Gen.* exploit these and the correspondence more fully.

   On 'persuasion and official pressure' see the account in the *Vita* (*Op. Omn.*, vol. 1, p. 18): the often repeated story of the tempting offers of appointments 'at his own figure' (*stipendio et viatico quod ipse defineret*), which L. declined in order to return to Louvain.

3 The verdicts on the *Diva* tracts are amusingly divergent. Of more modern scholars Nisard speaks of an evident lapse into *imbécilité*; Catholics keep to the tradition of the *Fama Postuma* which permits them to be regarded as an 'aberration', *Op. Omn.* 1, *Assertio Lipsiani Donari*, p. 176. (See the *Diva Hallensis* for a version of the life of St Elizabeth of Hungary).

4 On an international scale. The attack of George Thomson of St Andrews, *Vindex Veritatis adversus J. Lipsium*, Alkmaar, 1606, is an essay in sustained vituperation of L.'s 'religion', his worship of wooden images etc. On *De Cruce*, see below, p. 74. The defence of L. in the *Fama Postuma* takes due cognizance of Thomson. L.'s embarrassing bequests are defended (with a full panoply of references to donations to shrines throughout the centuries) in the *Assertio Lipsiani Donari* (*Op. Omn.*, vol. 1). For a list of early writings *pro* and *contra* Lipsius, see v. d. Essen and Bouchery, *op. cit.*, p. 45 and Notes.

5 This is in Lernutus' *In obitum J. L. Elegia*; the other references are found in pieces in the *Fama Postuma* entitled *Pro Manibus J.L.* (etc.), directed against the anonymous broadsheet *Justi Lipsi Manes ad studiosam Iuventutem*, of which I owe the text again to L. W. Forster.

6 This 'wide reading' is simply asserted; similarly by L. in *De una religione* (*Op. Omn.* IV, p. 300), where he writes: *De Theologo: planissime non sum, fateor. Et patres tamen Græcos Latinosque legi*. A lot is made in the *Fama Postuma* of L.'s final apostrophe of the Crucifix (*haec est vera patientia*, i.e. not the Stoic philosophy) and of L.'s more formal confession.

7 See Note 5.

8 Nordman (see prefatory note, above) sees in this letter a considerable advance in L.'s view of historical studies since his Jena lectures. As *Justi Lipsi de ratione legendi historiam ad N. Hocqueville epistola* it was reproduced in *G. J. Vossii et aliorum de studiorum rationale* of 1651. Whether it owes anything to Jean Bodin (1530–96), *Methodus ad Facilem Historiarum Cognitionem* (see Nordman), I am not competent to judge.

9 1538–1607. His *Annales Ecclesiasticae*, 12 vols. (1588–1607) were in 1600 'in progress'. That L. corresponded with the Papal historian (see Nordman) is a clear inference from one of the many letters L. wrote to Jo. Baptista Baronius, Cent. III, Ad Belgas, No. 51.

10 In context: In (*Opera Omnia*, vol. I) *Justi Lipsi Principiatus*, by Gaugerius Rivius, p. 65, the sentence runs: *CRUCEM quoque statuit, et supplicii varium genus: praemiorum multifariam dedit, et proprio verbo MUNERARIUS fuit. Sed sanguine* (etc.). According to the marginal notes this sentence includes an allusion to L. on *Saturnalia;* but I do not think I have misrepresented the sense.

11 *Pro Manibus J.L. in Anonymum* (see the *Fama Postuma*, no pagination in *Op. Omn.*). The *pietas* and *cura Tonantis* are claimed to be evident in all L. wrote.

12 'Es ist – jedenfalls höchst unwahrscheinlich, daß das Kreuz notwendig, immer und überall, die uns heute geläufige und bei den Kirchenvätern beschriebene Form gehabt habe.' Can discretion go further? More usual are formulations beginning 'contrary to general belief, Roman crucifixions were (thus and thus)'.

13 Lipsius has every right to be heard when he disclaims any *opera* or *schedia* on the Cross bearing his name. There *is* evidence of such versions and drafts, see v.d. Essen and Bouchery, *op. cit.*, note 99, and the items in F. van der Haeghen, *Bibl. Lipsienne*, I, 184 and II, 577, to which they refer. The first is a *De Cruce*, Paris, 1592, which I have so far not been able to see. This may be an *opus*, probably pirated. The second is fairly clearly an example of the *schedia* of which L. speaks. It is *De supplicio Crucis* or *Collectanea varia de Cruce* – the fith of seven items purporting to be *Justi Lipsi Tractatus ad Historiam Romanam cognoscendam apprime utiles* ('Cambridge, 1592'), of which the University Library, Cambridge, has copies. This is a mere three pages of print. After listing a few passages from Roman authors (and from Justinian legislation, see analysis of Book III, Ch. VII, below) it states bluntly: *Idem in Evangelio notamus*.

There follows the uncompromising statement that the bearing of the Cross as it is represented in Christian art is completely wrong: *Ergo pictores ignari prorsus antiquitatis, perperam Christum lignum illud transversum conjunctum oblongo, id est patibulum cruci conjunctum ferre pingitur.* In *De Cruce* 1593 Lipsius will prefer to admit the absolute authority of the Gospel of St John, the Fathers and Christian art for the Christian crucifixion; and to distinguish the Roman custom. Even if we suppose that *De supplicio crucis* faithfully records what L had said in lecture courses, he was, like any of us, entitled to be more cautious and circumspect when he put his name to a substantial monograph.

14 Nisard (*op. cit.*, p. 97) speaks of 'formules de dévotion pateline et dépourvues d'élévation'. This is perhaps excessive; it is probably intended to apply rather to 'formules' of the kind found in Ch. IX than to those of Ch. X.

15 See 'The Gothic Image', here p. 10.

16 Modern commentators have frequently noted that in the apocryphal *Gospel of Peter* (M. R. James, *Apocryphal New Testament*, Oxford, 1924, p. 90f., III, 6) the enemies of Christ 'having taken the Lord pushed him as they ran'. There is no evidence of any knowledge of this Gospel in the West before the late nineteenth century. See also 'The Gothic Image', p.3 (quotation) [and *L. & A.*, p. 274].

17 [Exhaustive treatment of the spike-block in the study of James Marrow, see p. viii.]

18 See 'The Gothic Image', here pp. 6f.

5. Goethe's 'Alexis und Dora' (1796), etc. Translated from 'Der zierlichen Bilder Verknüpfung: Goethes *Alexis und Dora*', etc., *Euphorion* 52 (1958), 341–55. The latter was an outcome of the lecture on 'Fortuna' I delivered in February 1957 in the Kunsthistorisches Institut of the Free University of Berlin, under the chairmanship of Professor Edwin Redslop. My parenthetic remark that Goethe's *Alexis und Dora* was 'eine letzte aber unerreichte dichterische Neugestaltung herkömmlicher Fortuna- und Occasio-Motivik' prompted Richard Alewyn, editor of *Euphorion* at the time, to ask me to work out the idea which was 'completely new'. The essay is now listed as item 1512 in the *Goethe-Bibliographie* begun by Hans Pyritz (2 vols., Heidelberg, 1955–68), II, 172. Claus Bock kindly drew my attention to Horst Rüdiger's very full account of *Occasio* in 'Göttin Gelegenheit: Gestaltwandel einer Allegorie', *Arcadia* I (1966), 121–66, where the essay is quoted and paraphrased, pp. 154f.

1 All references are to *Jubiläumsausgabe*, vol. I, pp. 173–8, based on *Musenalmenach* 1796–9. The *Hamburger Ausgabe* gives the text of *Ausgabe letzter Hand* with the following minor revisions of 1800: lines 6 *für alle*] statt seiner; 15 *du wiegest*] der wieget; 27 die seltne Verknüpfung der zierlichen Bilder; 29 *entdeckt*] gefunden; *schon* lacking; 53 *Flut*] Woge; 75 *Heftiger*] immerfort; 89 *ich stand*] ich ging nicht.

2 Here, for convenience, are the statements of Schiller and Goethe which are translated or paraphrased in the course of the essay:
Letter of Schiller to Goethe, 18 June 1796:

(*a*) 'Gewiß gehört [die Idylle] unter das Schönste, was Sie gemacht haben, so voll Einfalt ist sie, bei einer unergründlichen Tiefe der Empfindung.'

(*b*) 'Es würde schwer sein, einen zweiten Fall zu erdenken, wo die Blume des Dichterischen so rein und so glücklich abgebrochen wird.'

(*c*) 'Daß Sie die Eifersucht so dicht daneben stellen und das Glück so schnell durch die Furcht wieder verschlingen lassen, weiß ich vor meinem Gefühl noch nicht ganz zu rechtfertigen, obgleich ich nichts Befriedigendes dagegen einwenden kann.'

Letter of Goethe to Schiller, 22 June 1796:

(*d*) 'Für die Eifersucht am Ende habe ich zwei Gründe. Einen aus der Natur: weil wirklich jedes unerwartete und unverdiente Liebesglück die Furcht des Verlustes unmittelbar auf der Ferse nach sich führt, und einen aus der Kunst: weil die Idylle durchaus einen pathetischen Gang hat, und also das Leidenschaftliche bis gegen das Ende gesteigert werden mußte, da sie denn durch die Abschiedsverbeugung des Dichters wieder in's Leidliche und Heitere zurückgeführt wird. Soviel zur Rechtfertigung des unerklärlichen Instinctes, durch welchen solche Dinge hervorgebracht werden.'

Quoted from H. G. Gräf, *Goethe über seine Dichtungen*, Section III (*Die lyrischen Dichtungen*), vol. 1 (Frankfurt/Main, 1912), pp. 215–17.

3 On 'Steigerung', see E. M. Wilkinson, '*Tasso – ein gesteigerter Werther* in the light of Goethe's principle of *Steigerung*', *MLR* 44 (1949), 305–28. There is no explicit reference to *Alexis und Dora* in the essay, but the poem is included by implication.

4 Fr. Gundolf, *Goethe*, 13th ed., Berlin, 1930, p. 445.

5 Direct references to lines 25–30 are rare. Jos. Kassewitz, *Darlegung der dichterischen Technik und litterarhistorischen Stellung von Goethe's Elegie 'Alexis und Dora'*, Leipzig, 1893, p. 12 takes the lines (to me incredibly) to be part of Alexis' monologue: 'ihm erscheint die Wandlung, die er in seinem Wesen überrascht gewahr wird. . .als ein Rätsel, durch dessen Lösung er seine Ruhe wieder zurückzuerobern hofft'. This is to ignore (?) the immediately preceding words 'Klage dich, Armer, nicht an', in which the poet apostrophizes Alexis. (Alexis is no simple sailor-boy, but I think it unlikely that he would have thought in his circumstances of the conventions of the charade.) Charlotte von Kalb may have understood the passage in this way too: 'Für die Wesen interessiert man sich nicht, von denen gedichtet wird. Der Jüngling ist ein Dichter und kein Liebhaber, das Mädchen verliebt und keine Geliebte', letter to J. P. Richter, 9 July 1796.

6 *Goethe's Gespräche*, ed. F. v. Biedermann, 5 vols. Leipzig, 1909–11, vol. III, 244f.

7 In this essay I consider only the most generally accepted post-1500 iconography of Fortune: standing on a ball on which she travels overland or sails on the sea. She holds her sail aloft. *Fortuna marina* can easily be confused with *Venus marina* [see now *L. & A.* Ch. III].

8 On Kairos–Occasio see Appendix (p. 89), note on lines 15–18. The close connection between Kairos (later Occasio) and *metanoia* (*poenitentia*) is established in Antiquity. In the oldest representation 'remorse' is a

weeping female figure standing beside the Kairos-group (illustr. in Roscher, see p. 89). See also E. Panofsky, *Studies in Iconology*, 1939 (Harper Torchbook 1962), p. 71f. and notes 4f. Cesare Ripa, *Iconologia*, Padua, 1611, p. 390, glosses *Occasione* with reference to remorse (rue): 'rueful is the man who lets slip opportunity'. R. Wittkower (title p. 89) for other interpretations of the Occasio-image. More useful than further references to images is the following gloss from Giles Corrozet, *Hecatongraphie*, Paris 1543, fol. 82 ('Lymage d'Occasion'); 'Haste toi bien tost d'attrapper/ L'occasion, quand el' s'auance:/Si tu la laisses eschapper/Tu en feras la penitence.'

9 This silence is unrelated to Goethe's suppression of 'Gelegenheit' in *Alexis und Dora*.

10 If 'those who slumber' is to be taken literally, the nearest pictorial example I can quote is an engraving of Johannes Binck (*c.* 1490–1504, Bartsch, *Peintre Graveur*, VIII, 278) where an Occasio (or Fortune?) with spear and bridle stands on the back of a sleeping youth. If the meaning is '. . .caught napping', only the typical Occasio seems to be implied. If Occasio speeds past 'the alert' (as opposed to 'the resolute man of action') the sense, as in the case of Fortune, is that merit and worth are not assured their due. A properly 'seized' Occasio (*or* Fortune) is to be seen in the medallion for Camillo Agrippa reproduced in Doren (see p. 88) fig. 16 (a naked, helmeted warrior seizes a sail-bearing Occasio–Fortuna by the hair; motto: 'velis nolisve'). See also J. de Bie's *La France metallique*, 1636, p. 284 (a warrior grasps Occasio by the hair and is about to sever it with his sword).

11 'Dieses anekdotische Motiv hat nur formal-poetische Bedeutung', H. A. Korff, *Geist d. Goethezeit*, 3 vols. 1923–41, II, p. 332f.

12 Note (by E. von der Hellen) in *Jubiläumsausg.* I, p. 353.

13 Gundolf, *op. cit.* 445f.

14 On the names, see Franz Schallehn, *Jb. d. Goethe-Gesellschaft* 17 (1930), pp. 166–82 *passim*.

15 See note 2, passage (*d*).

16 See *ibid.*, passage (*b*).

II TEXTUAL STUDIES:

HISTORIOGRAPHICAL APPROACHES

6. *Notes on Fate and Fortune*. Reprinted from *Medieval German Studies presented to Frederick Norman*, London 1965, 1–15. This essay is now a tribute to the memory of an old friend (Norman died in December 1968). But I had a number of misgivings in re-submitting it. First, there is the matter of 'repetition' (see Preface, p. ix): even within this volume I come back more than once to *Hildebrandslied, Heliand*, Hartmann's *Armer Heinrich* and *Gregorius* in terms of fortune doctrine. Next, the essay was written some four years before the appearance of a study by Pierre Courcelle who has shown that the authentic text of *De Consolatione Philosophiae* was a Carolingian dis-

covery. Elsewhere (for instance in the essay 'Historical Thought' etc., pp. 130–45) I have taken account of this finding. As for the present essay, one must surely be able to assume that, south of the Alps at any rate, the Christian fortune doctrine of Boethius (senator, friend of Cassiodorus, a notable public figure in the days of Theoderic) was well known in his own lifetime: *De Consolatione* was not created *ex nihilo* in the prison cell. My added Note 10 refers to *this* statement. Finally (see Note 4), at the time of writing I had not re-read Widukind with the guidance I later found in an essay of Helmut Beumann.

1 Under the title 'Augustinus oder Boethius – mittelalterliche Gattungs-probleme' [for the title finally adopted, see *Publications*, p. 226] – in German, because my illustrations are preponderantly from medieval German historiographers and poets. A preliminary indication of the 'Augustine or Boethius' problem in my essay, 'On coming to terms with Curtius' (here pp. 177–90).

   Addendum [1965] *to Note 1*. Since completing this article I have seen Leslie Seiffert's essay, 'The Maiden's Heart', Legend and fairy-tale in Hartmann's *Der arme Heinrich*', *Deutsche Vierteljahrsschrift*, 37 (1963), pp. 384–405. As I find no disagreement between his views and mine, I have not altered what I had already set down. The two genres he recognizes in Hartmann's work (legend and fairy-tale) fall well within the categories of writing with which I deal. I naturally endorse his view that we should not expect to find the theologian's terms (*contritio, satisfactio*) in the work of a layman. In the article for Bithell (above) I used the term 'accommodation' to characterize the kind of mutation to which such terms are subjected in layman's narrative.

2 Boethius' first account of fortune (and Fortune) occurs in a vivid dialogue in Book II of the *De Consolatione*. Philosophy, speaking in the role of Fortune, argues with Fortune's victim, Boethius. The *theoretical* statement on fortune (and on the hierarchy God, Providence, Fate, Fortune, man) comes in Book IV (Prose vi–vii, Loeb ed. pp. 338–61); though the section is difficult and abstruse as it stands, it will have been familiar enough through the good offices of the medieval coaches and crammers.

3 Some ten years ago I suggested to Hilda Swinburne as a neglected *Ackermann* topic, a systematic comparison with Boethius. The result was a Note in *MLR*, 52 (1957), 88–91 ('Echoes of the *De Consolatione Philosophiae* in the *Ackermann aus Böhmen*'). She found in Book II 'arguments which are spread throughout the *Ackermann*'. I shall be going much further than this and treating the *Ackermann* as a fourteenth-century adaptation, modified to match the Ackermann's specific *infortunium*. Death, after the 'Wendepunkt' takes over the role of Philosophia and uses her arguments. The 'adjudication' with reference to the seasons is also present in the *De Consolatione*, and the general lines of the con-cluding prayer are foreshadowed in Philosophy's instruction to Boethius to pray to the *scrutator cunctorum*. (For the phrases of the prayer there are of course nearer models.) [See now *A.o.B.* Part I, pp. 39–43.]

4 [This was an unfortunate example to hazard. On Widukind's use of *fortuna* (it is 'antique'), see *A.o.B.* Part II, pp. 100-4. See also p. 216].

5 i.e. avoidance of these terms to designate the forces controlling the course of the *story*. (I exclude, that is, prologues, author's asides and so on, and, in this short statement, such oddities as the use of 'Trinitas' for God.) On grace, see note 7, below.

6 The Arthurian hero has, strictly speaking, no fate, since fate pre-supposes God's Providence. All that God can have foreseen is that medieval authors would write about Arthur, possibly 'thus'.

7 A. T. Hatto (to whom I am grateful for many helpful critcisms) asked me to include some reference to 'grace' - in Boethius, and in secular narrative literature. I have made some simple insertions, above. Boethius does not, and cannot incorporate 'grace' in his philosophy. As he approaches the end of the *De Consolatione*, however, he prepares the way for his epilogue in an important statement on God's grace and man's need to pray. The epilogue is, correspondingly: 'the rest is prayer', by which we may understand: 'see *inter alia* Boethius, *De fide catholica* etc.'.

As for 'grace' in secular narrative, it can, I think, only appear in various 'accommodations', according to the intentions of the author with his story, as *hilfe*, *triuwe* - or (yet again) *sælde*, *gnâde*; i.e. what is prayed prayed for, or made manifest in answer to prayer.

8 See Fr. Ohly, 'Wolframs Gebet an den Heiligen Geist (etc.)', *ZfdA*, 91 (1961), 1-37.

9 'Das Lied vom alten Hildebrand', *Studi germanici* (No. 5, 1963, 19-44), p. 39.

10 [The statement 'known from about that date' is evidently not correct, see the prefatory note to this essay, above, pp. 215f.]

11 A much quoted passage in *De Civitate Dei*, Book V, ix, where Augustine deals with the problem of God's prescience (and man's free will), and its relation to what had hitherto (in Cicero's *De natura deorum* and *De divinatione*) been called *fatum*.

12 If we forget the *Hildebrandslied* for the moment, the following additional note on Fortune may be helpful. To *men of action* (and their sympathetic advisers) Fortune is a totally unpredictable power governing the outcome of actions, large or small. Her operations bear no discernable relation to the merits of individuals, dynasties or causes (not even crusades). Men act, for whatever motive; Fortune turns the wheel, favours or does not, when and as she pleases. Men may blame Fortune, but theirs is the responsibility. The *systematic philosopher* rationalizes fortune - the irrational aspect of history. For him Fortune is then seen to enjoy a limited freedom as the agent (an *agent provocatrice*) of Providence. Since one of the purposes of Providence with man is to lead him to use his reason and find in the virtues of which he is capable remedies against 'fortune of either kind', it is clearly not man's destiny to be fortune's slave. Even so, says Boethius, one must, in the end, pray; philosophy is not enough. *Poets and moralists* mediate as best they may between men of action, thinkers - and theologians.

13 Der Heliand, theologischer Sinn als tektonische Form (Niederdeutsche Studien, ed. William Foerste, IX), Böhlau, Cologne and Graz, 1962.

14 Here I think that Rathofer, a trained theologian, is wrong. My argument that the Heliand poet is betrayed into unorthodoxy is based indeed largely on his insistence on fate, but finally and particularly on the misinterpretation of the Agony in Gethsemane. Rathofer misses the point that the spiritus promptus, caro autem infirma, which in the New Testament is addressed to the disciples, becomes in the Heliand part of Christ's comment on his own plight, and is rendered explicitly as 'my flesh is weak but my spirit is eager to fulfil the will of the father'. (Min gest is garu an godes uuillean/fus to faranne: min flesk is an sorgun...led is imu suido/uuiti te tholonne, 4781ff.). This is no mere 'Beziehung' established between Christ and these words, as Rathofer says: the poet uses them in a narrative context; to him this is historia. By comparison, the christological speculations of Hrabanus and Bede are feather-weight. But perhaps these points are best reconsidered when the question of dependence on Boethius is looked into more fully.

15 He does in fact mention him, in a last and final footnote to his Exkurs, where the reference is to an article by Hugh Sacker on Heinrich von Veldeke and my essay on Curtius, see note 1. Sacker ('Heinrich von Veldeke's conception of the Æneid', GLL, 10, 1957, 210–18), showed that it was possible for a Christian poet dealing with a pagan subject to refer repeatedly to 'the gods' and yet mean the Christian 'providence'. I endorsed Sacker's view and incorporated it in a statement on Boethius and medieval genres: the statement which has meantime become the formula I am now using.

16 In K. C. King's eminently sensible analysis of Hartmann's Gregorius, 'Zur Frage der Schuld in Hartmanns Gregorius', Euphorion, 57 (1963), 44–66, I note the emphasis he places on Gregorius' misfortunes as being geschiht – something which simply happened. Expressed in Boethian terms: (from the narrator's point of view) an apparently unmotivated disaster decreed by Fate; (to the victim) infortunium – unsælde.

17 Cf. Hebrews 13.2: Et hospitalitatem nolite oblivisci; per hanc enim latuerunt quidam, angelis hospitio recepti.

18 Text edited by F. Maurer, Deutsche Literatur in Entwicklungsreihen, Geistliche Dichtung des MAs., VI (Leipzig, 1934), lines 2820f. gluckes schibe (or sælden schibe) is the rota fortunæ. 'The glorious wheel of fortune (= man's hope of salvation = Christ) rolled through the ear of Mary when the (infinite) love of God propelled it into the womb of the Virgin.' This is, I think, a bold variant on the old conceit of the 'leaps of Christ' [see p. 28], one of which was the leap into the womb of the Virgin.

7. The 'fortune' of Hartmann's Erec. Reprinted from GLL 30 (1977), 94–109, i.e. from the Special Number for A. T. Hatto. The opening sentence provides the only necessary introduction. I merely add with reference to Note 7 (below) that it is unlikely that I shall write about the fortune of Iwein. As for Gottfried's hero Tristan (to whom my references tend to conceal a real concern

for his case), whatever fortune he 'had', he lost it when he drank the love-potion. The love-potion determined the course of his manhood years: this bears no resemblance to the normal heroic career.

1 Here pp. 95–109. [I have deleted 'for Germanisten' from the old title.]
2 *Augustinus oder Boethius* (etc.), see *Publications*, p. 226.
3 For *De Consolatione Philosophiae* see standard editions or the full summary in *A.o.B.* I, pp. 99–153; here pp. 138–41.
4 *A.o.B.* II, pp. 104–18, particularly 108–11.
5 *ibid.*, pp. 111–18. [More details in the present volume, pp. 139–41].
6 *A.o.B.* I, pp. 71–84, and II, pp. 164–8.
7 Remarks in *A.o.B.* (I, p. 87, II, p. 10) suggested I would take *Iwein* as my example, but *Erec* had obviously to be considered first.
8 See references in previous Note.
9 The spell cast by 'Minne' makes Erec and Enite 'hunger' for each other. Cf. *De Consolatione*, Book IV, Metre iii: the story of Ulysses' followers under Circe's spell, and Prose iii which precedes: on the degrees of degradation, down to man 'foedis immundisque libidinis immersus' (*A.o.B.* I, p. 135).
10 I have assumed in quoting this passage that not only Jean Fourquet failed to recognize in line 2935 a reference to loss of 'manliness'. In a textual note in his edition (see Note 26) he remarks: 'expression obscure'.
11 Fate governs the movement of *all* creation, not merely man. It is man's special fate to be subject to the sway of fortune.
12 Analysis of *Anticlaudianus* in *A.o.B.* II, pp. 135–40.
13 For *De Consolatione*, see *A.o.B.* I, pp. 139–41; *Anticlaudianus*, *ibid.* II, pp. 138f.
14 *A.o.B.* I, p. 44 and note 3b, II, pp. 61, 64.
15 Cf. Erec's rejoinder 'ir sprechet niht, ob got wil', 9047 (= 'Not so! – d.v.').
16 Alternatively the lines represent Hartmann's drastic abridgment of Chrétien's rather lavish opening statement on Erec, Chr. lines 82–104.
17 Chrétien compares Erec to 'Assalon, Salemon, Alixandre', and adds: 'de fierté sanbloit lion', 2265–70. (He is, it should be noted, more temperate than Hartmann in his treatment of Erec's 'fall from grace', 2434–68.) On balance I think that the 'fall' as such – rather than the later uxoriousness – of the hero and his prototypes, is the common element.
18 According to *Wörterbuch der deutschen Volkskunde* (*Kröners Taschenausgabe* 127) *s.v.* Johannes der Evangelist and Gertrud, *Erec* offers very early *loci* for the two farewell cups, 'St. Johannes Segen' and 'Gertrudenminne' (here and 4021).
19 *De Consolatione*, Book II, Prose iii, last sentence: 'ultimus tamen vitae dies mors quaedam fortunae est etiam manentis', see *A.o.B.* I, p. 110.
20 Chrétien is more 'correct' in making Enide's beauty the work of nature, or God and nature, 410–14, 421–36, 1672.
21 Here 1 Sam. 2.7f. See *A.o.B.* I and II, indexes *s.v.* 'Hanna'.
22 I have cancelled an analysis of the lament (as an example of Enite's casuistry, an aspect of 'wîbes list').

23 See lines 7767, 7828, 7909, 8150f., 8165, 8195, 8359, 8841, 8850, 9557.
24 *A.o.B.* II, pp. 166f. (with note 37 on *kairos*).
25 *Christian von Troyes sämtliche Werke,* III *Erec und Enide,* ed. Wendelin Foerster, Halle, 1890.
26 *Hartmann d'Aue: Erec, Iwein,* ed. Jean Fourquet. (*Bibl. de philologie germanique* v), Paris, 1944.
27 Vol. I (*Grundlagen der Germanistik* 7), Berlin, 1967. I add here my agreement that Chrétien's Erec is filled with no more than absolute determination to undergo the adventure: 'riens ne me porroit retenir/que je n'aille querre la joie', 5472f. Cf. 'Ci en est la broche tranchiee' (5652)= 'the broach is severed' (let matters take their course).

8. *Historical Thought and Moral Codes* (etc.). Reprinted from *The Epic in Medieval Society: Aesthetic and Moral Values,* ed. Harald Scholler, Tübingen, 1977, pp. 1–17. In revising this text I have reduced references to the occasion for which it was written (a symposium of medievalists at the University of Michigan, Ann Arbor, April 1973), and made minor changes and one major abridgment, see Note 14. Despite my use of passages from *A.o.B., Part II* (not published until 1976) and other repetitions, I include this perhaps extreme instance of an historiographical approach to literature (extreme because I felt we had heard enough about 'Tugendsysteme'). On the other hand I have *excluded* from my selection an essay which frankly exploited a chapter from the same volume, namely 'Mittelalterliche Geschichtsschreibung: das Problem des Königtums', see *Publications,* p. 228. As now printed, it is the record of a lecture delivered in Bremen before the *Hansischer Geschichtsverein* and the *Verein für niederdeutsche Sprachforschung* in May 1975 (revision of a paper read at the Institute of Germanic Studies in London in November, 1972).

1 *Augustinus oder Boethius?* (etc.), see *Publications,* p. 226.
2 An author who invokes fortune commits himself to the Boethian scheme, see previous essay.
3 All the works referred to here are the subject of more or less detailed discussion in *A.o.B.,* II. A reminder in Note 10.
4 Interpretations which seek first to determine the 'economy of ideas' present in a given work, and assume that these will provide a complete gloss on everything said and done by the chief characters.
5 Here the textbook example of Eilhart's *Tristan* may suffice. In a fuller statement one would have to consider whether Hartmann von Aue did indeed always find 'der âventiure meine'.
6 This is the Boethian solution. Augustine endeavoured to dispense with the idea of fortune and to attribute all except the most trivial happenings to God's will.
7 Free-will is common to both schemes, Augustinian and Boethian.
8 I treat the 'historical postulate' in *A.o.B.,* II with particular reference to the OHG *Ludwigslied*: the assertion in the indicative mood of what is a pious hope or a 'confessed' fiction.
9 This does not imply any opposition to Dennis Kratz's interpretation of

Ruodlieb (or of *Waltharius*) in *The Epic in Medieval Society* etc., Tübingen 1977, pp. 126-49.

10 The evidence for this spate of dogmatic assertions will be found in *A.o.B.*, II.

11 'Regino von Prüm und das historische Weltbild der Karolingerzeit' (1952), reprinted in *Geschichtsdenken und Geschichtsbild im Mittelalter* (Wege der Forschung, 21), Darmstadt, 1961, pp. 91-134.

12 This is a literary historian's reading of the evidence, i.e. of the text of Regino's *Chronicle* on the one hand, and Otto's *De Duabus Civitatibus* and *Gesta Frederici* on the other, see *A.o.B.*, II, pp. 104-18 (and above, pp. 110, 114).

13 Quoted from *Quellen zur karolingischen Reichsgeschichte* III, ed. Reinhold Rau, Darmstadt 1966 (= *Ausgewählte Quellen zur deutschen Geschichte des Mittelalters*, vol. VII, Freiherr vom Stein-Gedächtnisausgabe). My translation of the Latin (ibid., pp. 256f.).

14 [This insertion replaces two pages of text superseded by the much fuller account of Otto of Freising in *A.o.B.*, II, see Note 12.]

15 *Sage und Legende in der Kaiserchronik*, Münster, 1940, repr. Darmstadt, 1968, pp. 74-84.

16 A heathen form of the fortune doctrine can be extracted from *De Consolatione Philosophiae* by omitting reference to Providence.

17 [See Preface, p. ix (on 'repetition with variation'); this essay was written in 1972.]

18 ir habet got vil verre/an mir armen geêret/und iuwer heil gemêret,/und nû daz beste vür geleit./nû ist mir mîn tumpheit/also sêre erbolgen,/si enlât mich iu niht volgen, ll. 1480ff.

19 weinde sî des jâhen,/diz wære ein sælic man, ll. 3738f.

20 The notorious lines 'ich enwart nie mit gedanke/ein Beier noch ein Vranke' etc., 1573f.

9. *The Western Image of Byzantium* (etc.). Reprinted from *GLL* 27 (1975), 326-40, the Special Number for C. T. Carr. (Carr died in 1976; I have modified references to him in Notes.) A first draft of this essay was used as a discussion paper at King's College, London, in May 1973. Then followed the Munich lecture referred to in Note 1. By the time I wrote the final English version, here reprinted, I had been generally reassured by the comments of colleagues, including Byzantinists. I should nevertheless welcome a full critical appraisal from the historian's point of view.

1 The subject of a lecture delivered at the invitation of Prof. Karl Bosl in Munich, January 1974; translated and revised for presentation to the late Charles T. Carr.

2 Particularly in the preparation of Part II of *A.o.B.*

3 It was over the discussion of Notker in the edition of Sehrt-Starck for the *Altdeutsche Textbibliothek* (1933-) that C. T. Carr and I first came into closer contact.

4 ed. cit. (vol. I, pp. 3 and 5): tára ze dero mârûn Constantinopoli (source:

Constantinopolim). . .únde ín dâr mít kûollichên êrôn (*magnis honoribus quasi socius regni*) lángo hábeta.

5 They were formulated several years ago for a more polemical context, see Note 2. I have allowed them to stand.

6 Summary and quoted words from *Joinville and Villehardouin, Chronicles of the Crusades*, translated with an Introduction by M. R. B. Shaw, Penguin Classics L 124, 1963, p. 94.

7 The exhibition catalogue and the associated five volumes under the general title *Karl der Grosse, Lebenswerk und Nachleben*, ed. Wolfgang Braunfels, Düsseldorf 1965-8, are works of monumental scholarship. They would not have been required, had Charles the Great not had a timely 'message for Europe', cf. p. 174.

8 On the subject of 'Heilsgeschichte' the medievalist needs to know more than our literary histories relate. I recommend A. Momigliano, 'Pagan and Christian Historiography in the Fourth Century A.D.' in: *The Conflict between Paganism and Christianity in the Fourth Century*, Oxford-Warburg Studies, Oxford 1963, pp. 79-99. My quotation is from p. 2 of Momigliano's introduction.

9 This last idea is less frequent in the West than that the ruler is a second David or Solomon.

10 This scene is dimly reflected, I think, in the Grail ceremony: the grey old man glimpsed by the hero in *Parzival*, Book V, 240, 23f.

11 A simplification, of course, but acceptable in a polemical context.

12 'Augustin ignoriert die für seine Zeit naheliegendste und aktuellste politische Idee, den Mythos von Byzanz als dem "neuen Rom" vollständig.'

13 In his 300-page volume he finds room for only one footnote reference to Augustine! One of my problems in *A.o.B.*, Part II, is to explain why historians, some of them Western, ignore St Augustine completely.

14 'Kultur- und Machtgefälle von Ost nach West', op. cit., p. 289.

15 This observation will surely have its antecedents in medieval imperialist propaganda.

16 'Und doch wurzelte Byzanz in allen Komponenten seines Wesens in der europäischen Tradition und hat für Europa weltgeschichtlich gesehen seine Hauptaufgabe erfüllt', p. 291.

17 *Deutsche Literatur im europäischen Mittelalter*, 2 vols., Munich 1972-3, vol. I, p. 91.

18 I plead lack of time and opportunity during the last few years of my active career to pursue research on any significant scale.

19 'Das Bild der Geschichte in der Enzyklopädie Isidors von Sevilla', *Deutsches Archiv für Erforschung des Mittelalters*, 22 (1966), 1-62.

20 I quote Liudprand's report from Ernest F. Henderson, *Select Historical Documents of the Middle Ages*, Bohn's Antiquarian Library, London, 1925 (reprint N.Y., 1968), pp. 441-77. See also the Latin–German edition of Albert Bauer and Reinhold Rau in *Quellen zur Geschichte der sächsischen Kaiserzeit* (Freiherr vom Stein-Gedächtnisausgabe, vol. VIII), Darmstadt, 1971, pp. 523-89.

21 It is impossible to summarize accurately this exchange of aspersions and innuendoes.

22 See Henderson, p. 452f.

23 Henderson, pp. 456-64. The Byzantinists of our own days see as one of the causes of the downfall of the Eastern Empire the continued interpretation of political and military history in the light of the prophecies of the Book of Daniel. [Some readers will recall Liudprand's endeavours to smuggle out purple cloth for his own use (Henderson pp. 468ff.), i.e. over and above the gift he was to take to Otto (purple was reserved for imperial wear).]

24 I am indebted to Prof. Hans E. Keller, Dr Christopher Thacker and Prof. Wolfgang van Emden for hints, guidance and the loan of texts (including the seventh impression, Leipzig 1923, of the 5th ed. of Ed. Koschwitz, *Karls des Grossen Reise nach Jerusalem und Constantinopel*, etc.). I am of course not qualified to do more than exploit the story as this was told in the now lost British Library manuscript (King's Libr. 16 VIII).

25 [One will rather compare the description of the Magnaura Palace in the same complex of buildings, in Liudprand of Cremona's *Liber Antapodoseos*, Book VI, see the edition quoted in Note 20, pp. 244-495 (pp. 488ff.). The description is translated in a recent comprehensive guide by Walter Hotz: *Byzanz, Konstantinopel, Istanbul* (Handbuch der Kunstdenkmäler), Wissenschaftliche Buchgesellschaft, Darmstadt, 1971, pp. 83f. and p. 80 (map).]

26 '*more Italico longa continuatione peryodorumque circuitibus sermonem producturus*', see *Die Taten Friedrichs (Gesta Frederici)*, ed. Franz-Josef Schmale (*Ausgew. Quellen zur deutschen Geschichte des Mittelalters =* Freiherr vom Stein-Gedächtnisausgabe, vol. XVII), Darmstadt, 1965, pp. 346ff.

27 See Note 17.

28 *Die Reichsidee in deutschen Dichtungen der Salier- und frühen Stauferzeit*, Philologische Studien und Quellen, Heft 16, Erich Schmidt Verlag, Berlin, 1963, p. 27.

10. Economies of History (etc.). Reprinted from *Essays in German Language, Culture and Society*, London, 1969, 59-68. The volume was compiled in honour of Roy Pascal. Many colloquialisms (some of which I no longer seek to isolate by the use of quotation marks) may suggest that I wrote this essay to entertain. It was, rather than that, something I had to get out of my system – which may also be said of essay 12.

III SYLLABUS STUDIES

11. On coming to terms with Curtius. Reprinted from *GLL* 11 (1950), 335-45, the Jethro Bithell Anniversary Number. This is a 'syllabus study' to the extent that it considers a number of frequently prescribed texts, and examines the possibility of modified approaches to them, partly in the light of Curtius's suggestions. It is of course now 'dated' in some of its statements (Hartmann's

Gregorius, for instance, seems to have displaced *Iwein* on the syllabus). I had to make a minor but important correction in Section III where I anticipate the argument of *A.o.B.*, Part I. On the other hand I now find my treatment of 'accommodation' in Section IV in many ways better than my later, more dogmatic and even polemical references to the same phenomenon, see *A.o.B.* II, 209f., where I both look back, and take leave of a subject beyond my competence.

1 Edgar Mertner, 'Topos and Commonplace', *Strena Anglica, Festschrift für Otto Ritter*, Halle, Niemeyer, 1956, pp. 178–224.
2 'The origins of the medieval humility formula', *PMLA*, 69 (1954), pp. 1279–91. Defending his monograph of 1921 against Curtius's summary dismissal, he writes (in English): 'by *formula of humility* I did not mean a *topos* of any kind...I meant rather the whole prayer-complex...within which a special role is played by the mention of the poet's name, so that he may receive his reward of prayer' (p. 1282). . .'From this point of view classical antiquity is not a perfect model but a prefiguratve preliminary stage which has to be overcome and surpassed' (p. 1290).
3 The passages which Curtius quotes from Jerome and Cassiodorus on 'rhetoric in Holy Scripture' are, of course, important, but were written to refute the charge that Holy Scripture was deficient in respect of rhetoric. For better guidance on the way in which the Bible *was* studied, see, of course, Beryl Smalley, *The Study of the Bible in the Middle Ages*, Blackwell, Oxford, second edition, 1952.
4 See, for instance, the introduction by H. F. Stewart and E. K. Rand to the Loeb edition (1926 reprint) of *The Theological Tractates* and *The Consolation of Philosophy*. E. K. Rand, incidentally, earns high praise in the Foreword to the English translation of Curtius (Routledge & Kegan Paul, 1953), p. viii.
5 Particularly in Book II of the *De Consolatione*.
6 The lot of Job should not be referred to as his 'misfortunes'. *Job* was written to deal with the problem of unmerited suffering. Only rarely (and as a solecism) does medieval literature or art associate Job and *infortunium*.
7 'Heinrich von Veldeke's conception of the Aeneid', *GLL*, 10 (1957), pp. 210–18.
8 W. Schwarz, *Gottfried von Strassburg, Tristan und Isolde* (Inaugural lecture, Amsterdam), Groningen, 1955, speaks of 'bewusste Nachahmung und bedingte Profanierung der religiösen Sphäre'. This may be right: I find I can say slightly less with the help of 'accommodation'.
9 Werther's likening of himself to the Prodigal Son, and his use in his plight of the sacred words of the Agony are, coming from him (a 'Genie'), scarcely less than blasphemy. Werfel's use of *erat dolor sicut meus* in the opening lines of his 'Verwundeter Storch' (*War jemals eine Trauer so wie die*) – words traditionally associated with the Man of Sorrows awaiting crucifixion – is reverent, and so clearly intended that we must call it 'accommodation'.
10 [My opinion has meantime changed. I have treated this example of

'accommodation' as a *tour de force*, see *A.o.B.* II, p. 167, *L. & A.*, p. 259.]

11 Here, pp. 5-30 *passim*.

12 *A Reading of George Herbert*, 1952.

13 'Der paradisus der Wiener Genesis', *Euphorion*, 49 (1955), pp. 121-44. I am grateful to L. W. Forster for this reference. With Gruenter's attitude towards the *topos*, compare Schwietering as quoted in note 2, above.

14 [I am aware that this view is not generally accepted.]

12. University German (etc.). Reprinted from *Forum for Modern Language Studies* 5 (1969), 118-25. The inclusion of this essay invites a word about my Reader, *University German*, see Note 1. Whether, as some friends have said, the Reader was ahead of its time, or too difficult for use with undergraduates, or merely withdrawn before it had been given a chance, I hesitate to say. (Some colleagues have persevered with it.) As for the essay itself, I have not seen any response in writing. In revising my text I have left in quotation marks the colloquialisms of staff-room discussion. The background to Reader and essay is over forty years of teaching prose-composition and translation at all levels.

1 An expansion of the Introduction to my *University German, A Reader for Arts Students*, Oxford, Clarendon Press, 1968.

2 In an incidental way the new courses (for combination) show up the inadequacy of the older syllabuses for those students whose final decision is not to teach after all. To know about German literature only is not much of a qualification, and to cite German literature when the real topic is Germany will always seem to be an evasion.

3 As an undergraduate I hoisted up my German by hard work on Arthur Schnitzler's short stories. I could not conceive that anything so enjoyable was of interest to examiners.

4 On this topic I once had a heated discussion with a distinguished Australian 'Germanist' who would clearly defend to the limit *his* thesis that German is the *lingua franca* for the discussion of German literature. German witnesses thought I disagreed because I put pedagogy before 'Wissenschaft'. I do, but that is not why I disagreed.

5 We must of course be allowed to compose, and to make our mistakes, but time can be lost speculating whether what we have written *might* be German, or whether we have conveyed *exactly* the sound of the cracked bell tolling at sundown from the old gaol of Casterbridge.

PUBLICATIONS OF F. P. PICKERING

(* = re-edited in this volume)

BOOKS

1 *Literatur und darstellende Kunst im Mittelalter* (Grundlagen der Germanistik 4), Erich Schmidt Verlag, Berlin, 1966.
2 *Literature and Art in the Middle Ages*, Macmillan, London, 1970. Abbreviated: *L. & A.*
   This is a licensed edition of the above, revised and translated by the author. It also appeared under the imprint of the University of Miami Press, Coral Gables, Fl., 1970 (present distributor: the University of Texas Press).
3 *Augustinus oder Boethius? Geschichtsschreibung und epische Dichtung im Mittelalter – und in der Neuzeit.* 1: *Einführender Teil* (Philologische Studien und Quellen, Heft 39); 11: *Darstellender Teil* (*ibid.* Heft 80), Erich Schmidt Verlag, Berlin, 1967 and 1976 respectively. Abbreviated: *A.o.B.* (1/11).

EDITIONS

1 *Christi Leiden in einer Vision geschaut. . .A critical account of the published and unpublished manuscripts, with an edition based on the text of Ms. Bernkastel-Cues 115*, Manchester University Press, Manchester, 1952.
2 *The Anglo-Norman Text of the Holkham Bible Picture Book* (Anglo-Norman Text Society, vol. xxiii), Blackwell, Oxford 1971.

READER

University German. A Reader for Arts Students, Oxford, Clarendon Press, 1968.

CONTRIBUTIONS TO REFERENCE WORKS

1 The chapters 'Medieval German Literature' and 'Danish Studies' respectively in *The Year's Work in Modern Language Studies*, vols 7–9 (1937–9) and 7–8 (1937–8).
2 The articles (about 150) on medieval German authors, anonymous works, genres, in *Cassell's Encyclopaedia of World Literature*, first and second editions, London, 1953 and 1973.

3 Peter Jørgensen, *German Grammar*, 3 vols, Heineman, London 1959–66.
This is a revised edition of Jørgensen's *Tysk Grammatik*, 3 vols, Copenhagen, 1953–64. It was 'translated by G[ertrude] Kolisko in consultation with the author and F. P. Pickering'. The consultation included in Pickering's case reviews of *Tysk Grammatik*, vols 1 (*MLR* 50, 1955, p. 93) and 2 (*ibid.* 55, 1960, p. 290), translation of part of vol. 2, and a general oversight.

4 The article 'Christi Leiden in einer Vision geschaut' in *Deutsche Literatur des Mittelalters: Verfasserlexikon*, second edition edited by Kurt Ruh, Walther de Gruyter, Berlin and New York, 1977– , vol. 1, cols 1218–21.

CONTRIBUTIONS TO LEARNED JOURNALS (ARTICLES)

1 'A German Mystic Miscellany of the late fifteenth century in the John Rylands Library', *Bulletin of the John Rylands Library* 22 (1938), 455–92.

2 'Notes on late medieval German tales in praise of *docta ignorantia*', *ibid.* 24 (1940), 121–37.

*3 'Das gotische Christusbild. Zu den Quellen mittelalterlicher Passionsdarstellungen', *Euphorion* 47 (1953), 16–37.

4 'Christlicher Erzählstoff bei Otfrid und im *Heliand*', *ZfdA* 85 (1955), 262–91.

5 'Zu den Bildern der altdeutschen *Genesis*. Die Ikonographie der *trinitas creator*', *ZfdPh* 75 (1956), 23–34.

*6 'On coming to terms with Curtius', *GLL* 11 (1958), No. 4 (Jethro Bithell Anniversary Number), 335–45.

*7 'Der zierlichen Bilder Verknüpfung. Goethes *Alexis und Dora* – 1796', *Euphorion* 52 (1958), 341–55.

*8 'Justus Lipsius' *De Cruce Libri tres (1593)* or The Historian's Dilemma', *Festgabe für L. L. Hammerich*, Naturmetodens Sproginstitut, Copenhagen, 1962, 199–214.

9 'Erwägungen zum Studium des deutschen Mittelalters', *Die Wissenschaft von deutscher Sprache und Dichtung: Methoden, Probleme, Aufgaben* (Festschrift für Friedrich Maurer zum 65. Geburtstag), Ernst Klett Verlag, Stuttgart, 1963, 383–98.

10 'Zu den Bildern der altdeutschen *Genesis*. Die Ikonographie der *trinitas creator* (II)', *ZfdPh* 83 (1964), 99–114.

*11 'Notes on Fate and Fortune (for Germanisten)', *Medieval German Studies presented to Frederick Norman*, University of London, Institute of Germanic Studies, London, 1965, 1–15.

12 'Wieder "Apokryphes im *Heliand*"', *ZfdA* 95 (1966), 79f.

*13 'Economies of History. What is Fiction?', *Essays in German Language, Culture and Society* [dedicated to Roy Pascal], University of London, Institute of Germanic Studies, London, 1969, 59–68.

*14 'University German and the Syllabus of Studies', *Forum for Modern Language Studies* 5 (1969), 118–25.

*15 'Irrwege der mittelalterlichen Geschichtsschreibung: Rupert von Deutz, Joachim von Fiore', *ZfdA* 100 (1971), 270–96.

*16 'The Western Image of Byzantium in the Middle Ages', *GLL* 28 (1975), No. 3 (Special Number for C. T. Carr), 326–40.

17 'Mittelalterliche Geschichtsschreibung: das Problem des Königtums', *Niederdeutsches Jahrbuch* 98/99 (1975–6), 63–77.

*18 '*Trinitas Creator:* Word and Image', *Reading Medieval Studies* 2 (1976), 77–90.

*19 'Historical Thought and Moral Codes in Medieval Epic', *The Epic in Medieval Society. Aesthetic and Moral Values*, ed. Harald Scholler, Max Niemeyer Verlag, Tübingen, 1977, 1–17.

*20 'The "fortune" of Hartmann's Erec', *GLL* 30 (1977), No. 2 (Special Number for A. T. Hatto), 94–109.

CONTRIBUTIONS TO LEARNED JOURNALS (REVIEWS)

Approaching 150 review-articles, reviews and short notices are to be found in the principal journals. All are signed except 'Hölderlin Collected', *TLS* 29 July 1955 (a review of the early volumes of the 'Stuttgart' Hölderlin edition of Friedrich Beissner).

CONTRIBUTIONS TO ARCHIVES

Descriptions of the medieval German and Dutch manuscripts in the John Rylands Library, Manchester, prepared for the 'Handschriftenarchiv' of the Preussische (*now* Deutsche) Akademie der Wissenschaften, Berlin.

MISCELLANEOUS ITEMS

Die Sprache der Heidelberger Handschrift (H) von Gottfried von Strassburgs Tristan, Ohlau, Eschenhagen, 1934. (Diss. Breslau). *Hauptschwierigkeiten der englischen Sprache*, English Society E.V., Münster, 1953, 15 pages.

www.ingramcontent.com/pod-product-compliance
Ingram Content Group UK Ltd.
Pitfield, Milton Keynes, MK11 3LW, UK
UKHW042153280225
455719UK00001B/326